1996

MANAGEMENT OF
PUBLIC SECTOR AND
NONPROFIT ORGANIZATIONS

Leslie E. Grayson
The Colgate Darden Graduate School
of Business Administration
University of Virginia

Curtis J. Tompkins
West Virginia University

Reston Publishing Company, Inc.
A Prentice-Hall Company
Reston, Virginia

TO OUR WIVES, OLIVIA AND KATHY

ISBN 0-8359-4240-6

©1984 by Reston Publishing Company, Inc.
A Prentice-Hall Company
Reston, Virginia 22090

10 9 8 7 6 5 4 3 2 1

Printed in the United States of America

Designed and typeset by Publications Development
Company of Texas, Crockett, Texas. Production
Editor: Nancy Marcus Land.

CONTENTS

iii

PREFACE

Business schools and schools of administration prepare potential managers for the world of practical affairs; that world includes an increasingly large segment of public sector and nonprofit organizations. Most management books and programs address the objectives of private, profit-oriented organizations rather than nonprofit organizations such as hospitals, churches and libraries. Although there are principles universal to all areas of management, certain concepts and techniques have specific application to public and nonprofit organizations.

Our book surveys major concepts of management as applied to public sector and nonprofit organizations using a case study approach. Performance measurements, planning, control, budgeting, organizational image, managerial environment, marketing concepts, pricing, and "accountability" are different when dealing with nonprofit organizations.

The book consists of seven chapters. Chapter 1 includes two introductory cases and one dealing with the issue of trusteeship. Chapter 2 on Systems Analysis contains case studies describing a city sanitation department and a community hospital. In Chapter 3 the measurement of productivity and performance is illustrated in two case studies. Chapter 4 focuses on strategic planning. Four case studies in Chapter 5 demonstrate accounting and control. Chapter 6 presents two different types of budgeting situations. The final chapter deals with the relationship between organizational performance and marketing-related decisions and activities.

The case studies included vary in their complexity. The length and content of the book make it adaptable for use both in full semester courses and in shorter survey courses on management of nonprofit organizations.

ACKNOWLEDGMENTS

In 1972, with encouragement from Dean Charles C. Abbott of The Colgate Darden Graduate School of Business Administration, University of Virginia, we started the course which bears the title of this book; in 1974, Curtis Tompkins took sole responsibility for the course and taught it until 1977, when he moved to West Virginia University. Our intellectual indebtedness is twofold: first, to the many students who elected the course, who helped us improve and shape it, and some of whose individual contributions are represented here; the second is to the retired Dean, Charles C. Abbott. Long interested in nonprofit organizations, Dean Abbott actively encouraged and supported us and continued to show interest in our efforts after he was no longer directing the school. We received support for the preparation of this volume from The Darden School, University of Virginia.

Olivia Grayson acted as research assistant to Tompkins, reading and evaluating hundreds of articles, cases, and notes with diligence and imagination. She also edited the introductory manual, the three notes and the three cases that Grayson authored in this volume. Lonnie Beagle, Kathryn Wiencek, Noanie Busch, and Nancy Beer typed numerous drafts, corresponded with authors and publishers, and administered the project involving two author-editors who were, occasionally, out of step with one another. Throughout this, they proved to be efficient, as well as keeping their equanimity.

ONE

INTRODUCTION

One challenge in compiling a book of cases and readings is balance. Since our aim is to reach as wide an audience as possible, we included material that can be read by the nonmathematically oriented reader and also by the full-time and part-time practitioners of the public sector and nonprofit organizations. If, in the process, we sacrifice some "rigor" or "elegance," our choice is intentional. We have attempted to cover the important analytical concepts and tools. Finally, we include management policies and procedures that are applicable to most nonprofit areas, striking a balance between governmental agencies, educational institutions, health care delivery, cultural programs, and social services. The material in this book was chosen to fill a gap which we believe exists in the available sources.

The cases simulate the learning experience that we and our students experienced in the classroom. The cases allow the readers to test their ability to handle the concepts and tools discussed.

The book consists of seven chapters. The first of the three cases in Chapter 1 introduces the management of "nonprofit" private and public enterprises, respectively. The case studies describe the start-up and demise of a small professional theatre company and the financial and marketing problems of a public transit service. The chapter concludes on the issue of trusteeship. Accountability for nonprofit institutions has long been demanded but it has been a long time arriving. The criticisms that have been leveled against the nonprofit organizations have been harsh. The public no longer accepts unquestioningly the efficiency or utility of many of these organizations, the goods they produce, or the services they deliver. The self-perpetuating boards—for decades features of public sector and nonprofit organizations—have come under scrutiny.

Trustees of nonprofit organizations represent privileged positions among "establishment" Americans as do the organizations they represent. Also, trustees represent a heterogeneous group of leaders; vision and concern on the one hand and excessive privacy and complacency on the other. Trustees seem to have been particularly inept at performing the planning function. Frequently they are preoccupied with daily operational problems that might best have been delegated to administrators. Because the public sector operates with public funds and nonprofit organizations with tax-exempt funds, the monies that the trustees control is, in the final analysis, to be committed to the service of the public good.

The case study, "Martha Jefferson Hospital," describes one situation—we think a typical one—of how trustees performed during a sizeable expansion program in a medium-sized community hospital.

Chapter 2, Systems Analysis, considers nonprofit organizations as parts of larger entities such as the "health care delivery system," "the higher education system," or "the welfare system." The chapter starts with an *Introductory Note to Systems Analysis*. This section explains what systems analysis is, how it may be applied and in what ways managers can make the best use of quantitative methods within the context of systems analysis.

In recent years, the literature has abounded with examples of applications of the "systems approach," "systems analysis," "operations research," "management science," and "industrial engineering" to management problems in nonprofit and public sector organizations. With the increased availability and affordability of electronic, digital computers and the improvement of data and information bases, more and more quantitative analysis is being conducted in these organizations. Behavioral as well as financial aspects are included in these activities.

Yet, it should be recognized that this is still an emerging and growing area of management. This is an area deserving much more attention in terms of management development and continuing education. Most major business schools are producing graduates who are well qualified in statistical analysis and popular quantitative methods, but who still lack a complete understanding of systems analysis.

There are two particular challenges related to systems analysis. One is the all-too-frequent lack of complete, accurate, dependable, timely data and information pertinent to a management problem or opportunity in a nonprofit organization. The other is the occasional difficulty of *implementing* the methods described and illustrated in this chapter. The former is often the result of benign neglect, lack of foresight, or severely constrained resources. The latter may sometimes be attributed to lack of managerial competence, organizational resistance, or limited experience. All of these constraints can be alleviated eventually, but it takes persistence and dedication to develop the systems analysis/management science area in most nonprofit institutions. The long-term payoff is worth the relatively short-term sacrifices required in developing this aspect of management capability.

The case of the "Morgantown Sanitation Department" provides an illustration of an application of systems analysis. The "Richmond Memorial Hospital" case concludes the chapter. It deals with alternative forecasting methods and their interpretation.

Chapter 3 eases the reader into the murky waters of productivity. In the *Economic Report of the President,* January 1981, the President pointed out the clear relationship between growth, inflation and lagging productivity in the U.S. economy. The suggestion was clear; if we, Americans, don't come to grips with our productivity problems, we stand little chance of either overcoming inflation or continuing to enjoy economic growth. Causes of the productivity "crisis" include lagging capital investment, the negative influence of government regulations, worker alienation and insufficient labor and management attention. The increasing shift from agriculture and industry—traditionally high productivity areas—to service industries (many in the nonprofit or public sector and traditionally showing low productivity) is an important contributor to the sorry state of productivity growth in the United States.

Proposition 13 passed in 1978 in California and other states have passed or introduced similar legislation. The message that is being conveyed is that people demand more (or at least not reduced) public services without increased taxation or, preferably, with lower rates of taxation. These objectives can only be achieved through increases in productivity. Proposition 13-type attempts also strongly communicate the public's desire to ensure that waste will not occur through mismanagement, but rather that the public's resources be managed with increasing efficiency and economy.

There are several ways of measuring productivity comparisons, all valid if applied correctly. The traditional method is the historical one. Equally valid are cross-section comparisons where a public or nonprofit sector or industry is compared with another sector or industry (frequently private and profit-oriented) of the economy. Also available are cross-country comparisons. The main problem with the cross-section comparisons is the quality of the service being performed. For instance, in the private sector there is frequently, though not always, workable competition to assure quality. Such competition is lacking in most (not all) public sector and nonprofit services.

Performance measurement in, say, higher education and medical care has long been one of the societal "untouchables." Educators and doctors claimed that the service they provide is "quality" and, therefore, not subject to productivity measures. While there is an element of validity in this, it turns out that the delivery of most nonprofit services are measurable. One reason for the apparent low productivity in the nonprofit sector is the *ad hoc* nature of management and the short, if any, planning horizon.

Whether measuring productivity is difficult or not, it has to be done—not only to monitor performance—but also to satisfy the general notion of accountability. The issue of how well the public's resources are used for the public's benefit is a real one. Increased productivity does require a strong public commitment to this end. As reported in the August 10, 1981 issue of *Fortune,* this is particularly true of the largest public agencies such as in education, welfare, and health where even small improvements in productivity appear difficult but would result in large savings.

The two case studies describe measures of effectiveness and productivity in a fire department and in the social service division of a medical center.

Chapter 4 focuses on strategic planning. There is an apt cliche that says: "a plan is worthless unless it degenerates into work." In many senses this is true, but in a subtle, yet significant way, planning may produce benefits to the organization even before it "degenerates into work." The process of planning can influence the motivation, behavior, attitudes, perception, and performance of people in an organization to the extent they have been involved in that process, distinct from the formal implementation of the plan. This is often an important factor in organizations that depend on volunteers. Involvement in the planning process can foster commitment and lead to better results. The process of planning is important to organizational performance.

The plan (that is, output from the planning process) is important to management control in any organization, and to the direction of that organization. From the planning system, the organization receives goals, objectives, measures of performance, and priorities. The control system (which includes evaluation of actual versus planned performance) depends on the planning system for measurable objectives and measures of performance. Generally speaking, to the extent the planning system is weak, the control system will likewise be weak.

The translation of plans into positive actions is the key to long-term organizational success. Converting a strategic plan into operational plans and activities is dependent on good communication, management and worker competence, performance accountability, and management follow-through.

In a sense, the subject of planning is included in every chapter of this book. While planning is not a panacea, it is recognized by most managers as an indispensible component of a successful management system. Some managers see themselves only as "operators," people who "make things happen." A good manager, one who is helping his or her organization improve and grow, is one who is aware and sensitive to the futurity of his/her present decisions and actions and who is almost constantly thinking about "what things we should make happen."

"Adaptive Forward Planning" is the lead essay of Chapter 4. This selection presents the key concepts essential to successful strategic and operational planning in nonprofit organizations. The second piece, "Common Cause," describes a strategic choice by a "citizens lobby." The chapter closes with a case on athletics at "The College of William and Mary," by Derek Newton.

How much does it cost to produce a bushel of wheat or a ton of steel? To deliver a letter from New York to Washington? Or, to perform a kidney transplant? Even more interesting are the questions which either relate to the future, i.e., how much will it (wheat to transplants) cost two years hence or to a different level of activity, i.e., if wheat production would decrease X% or if the number of transplants performed increased y%.[1]

Chapter 5 has as its lead piece a note by Richard Brownlee on "Cost Analysis for Nonprofit Organizations." Accountants have frequently been thought of as historians and in a sense they are; they record and report financial data. They are more than historians though. They provide financial information about firms and industries in a form that makes interpretation possible. Under ideal circumstances, accounting data is used in the process of economic decision-making. Balance sheets and profit and loss statements are the universal language of business.

Cost analyses are used by firms—profit and nonprofit, private and public alike—for a variety of purposes. These include planning, pricing, the establishment of profit centers and the measuring of performance

---

[1] For reference, W. Rotch, B. R. Allen, C. R. Smith, *Management Accounting and Control Systems,* Richmond, Va., Robert F. Dame, Inc., 1982, especially Part I; and A. R. Coleman, E. R. Brownlee, and C. R. Smith, *Financial Accounting for Management,* Robert F. Dame, Inc., Richmond, Va., 1981, Chapter 1.

both in terms of processes and labor force. Cost analysis is part of management accounting, as distinct from financial accounting. The latter provides data to investors, financial intermediaries, regulatory agencies, the press and the public. Financial accounts are standardized to conform with the standards set by, say, the Securities and Exchange Commission. Not so with management accounting where the use is essentially internal with the eye on operations as well as financial statements. Management needs reports on cost control and productivity measures. Management accounting reports frequently vary in content and in presentation to satisfy the informational needs of management. While the discipline of accounting developed based on profit-oriented business organizations, the concepts and techniques can be adapted to the public sector and to nonprofit firms.

The first case study in Chapter 5 written by William Rotch concerns the appropriate method of distributing the costs of services which are shared among five nonprofit organizations. Three cases follow as illustrations of "proper" cost analysis. "Children's Rehabilitation Center," discusses cost systems in hospitals and develops a superior—to the existing—cost information system for the Center. The second case demonstrates how cost accounting can be used for analysis and decision-making in financing public construction projects and the third case demonstrates the usefulness of accounting data for determining a state's future debt requirements.

"Budgeting" (Chapter 6) follows logically from Planning and Cost Analysis. Budgeting has been the subject of many books and articles in recent years. Yet, it is something that many public sector and nonprofit organizations do not do well. The process of budgeting could be improved in many nonprofit organizations. The role of the budgeting process could be better defined and articulated in many organizations.

Management attitudes and behavior in budget-based organizations frequently differ from management attitudes and behavior in other types of organizations. Most nonprofit organizations are budget-based organizations. Incentives for cost containment and cost reduction are often limited in budget-based nonprofit organizations which are not able to carry resources forward from one fiscal year to the next. In such organizations, the budget becomes a major control device, with less than totally positive behavioral ramifications. A "spend it or lose it" philosophy is not uncommon among managers of budget-based organizations. Managerial success (as judged by the manager and his peers) may be partially measured by percentage (or absolute dollar) increases in the annual budget for his area of responsibility. (Example: "We had a great year in 1980: our budget was increased by 15 percent over last year!")

This chapter presents two different types of budgeting situations; a state government and a health center. In these selections, the student should seek ideas about how the other subjects covered in this book are related to budgeting and *vice versa*. Budgeting should be treated as an integral part of the management process; good budgeting should have positive impact on an organization.

The final chapter, Chapter 7, deals with the relationship between organizational performance and marketing-related decisions and activities. Users of goods and services are households, firms, and government entities. Assuming that the consumers have the ability to buy (income), they have to be persuaded to do two things. One is to spend (rather than save) and second is to buy a specific product or service. The combination of the two represents the willingness to buy.

The discipline of marketing and advertising—to increase the willingness to buy—developed essentially around private, profit-oriented firms. With the advent of television, a most persuasive channel of communication has been found to augment the traditional sales force and other advertising media. With modification, some of the marketing and advertising concepts may be applied to the public and nonprofit sectors. The modifications involve the market structure of the public sector, namely, that there are activities where the public agency has monopoly power, as in the case of police forces; the provision of law and order is exclusively in the public domain. Other activities include limited competition between public and private enterprises, for instance, the parcel post delivery of the U.S. Postal Service and the United Parcel Service. The extent of allowable competition is regulated at the federal, state, and local levels. Finally, some public or nonprofit activities take place in a generally competitive market structure. Higher education, some health-care activities, almost all cultural activities and philanthropic organizations compete for the consumers' disposable income.

Whether it is raising funds, attracting students, persuading people to become organ donors or use contraceptives, to become tourists in New York City or Austria—all of these require marketing and advertising. In contrast to private goods and services, it is frequently difficult to define the market for the goods and services provided by the public or nonprofit sectors; yet, obviously, it has to be done. The traditional bag of tricks of product managers—product life cycle, marketing mix, position and segmentation—as well as distribution channels are applicable to all economic activities. Obviously, concepts and techniques developed in the private, profit sector have to be adapted to the public and nonprofit sector for optimum effectiveness and economy.

"Marketing" (Chapter 7) consists of three cases. Of these two deal with the arts: The "Tuesday Evening Concert Series" and the "University Arts Progam." The third case involves the launching of a volunteer gallery in Central Virginia.

Case 1

The Heritage Repertory Theatre*

Late in 1976, David W. Weiss, Producing Director of the Heritage Repertory Theatre, paced the floor and shook his head as he addressed the members of his staff assembled in his office. "I agree with what is obviously the unanimous concensus of the entire staff: we should reopen the Heritage Theatre in 1977. But we simply cannot. We must face the hard facts. Financially we have failed. Therefore, I feel we have no choice but to announce that we will not reopen for the 1977 season."

Exhibit I is a letter, written by the Heritage staff as an introduction to the Theatre for prospective donors. This letter presents a summary of the purpose, history, structure, and flavor of the Repertory Company as it entered its most anxiously awaited "Bicentennial Season" of 1976.

Unfortunately, the 1976 season was the Heritage's last. Exhibit II shows a $4,695 deficit at the end of the 1975 season. Exhibit III indicates that there was a $5,791.72 budget overrun during the 1975 season. Preliminary estimates at the end of the 1976 season indicated that a deficit of around $20,000 had occurred during that season. The proposed budget for 1977 predicted a deficit of $29,750.

Attendance in 1976 was a major disappointment to Mr. Weiss. Exhibit II shows the attendance history of the Repertory Theatre. Budgeting

*This case was written by Marc Puntereri, Roz Rivin, Marjorie Wait and Curtis J. Tompkins, April, 1977. Revised by Curtis J. Tompkins, April, 1979. Copyright © 1979, C. J. Tompkins.

for the Heritage Repertory Theatre was done annually, based on a specified seating capacity. During the first three years of its existence, the budgeted use of capacity proved to be overly optimistic:

Percentage Utilization of Seating Capacity		
Season	Budgeted	Actual
1974	60%	33%
1975	60	55
1976	75	45

Mr. Weiss believed the Repertory Theatre could be financially self-sufficient at an 85 percent average capacity utilization. However, he expressed concern that financial self-sufficiency might be achieved through the sacrifice of performance toward the Theatre's objectives, which were stated as follows:

1. To provide an educational adjunct to the University's drama teaching program with an example of superior theatre practice and as a training opportunity for our students as well as students and young professionals from other parts of the nation.
2. To establish a theatre company that will serve to maintain and, eventually, develop America's dramatic heritage.
3. To develop subsidiary studies of American theatre and techniques.
4. To establish and encourage related studies in other disciplines with the presentation of plays from various periods and locales utilized as a study resource.

These objectives supported the goal that the Heritage Company would be a professional theatre company serving a cultural need of the community, the University and visitors to the area.

DEVELOPMENT OF THE HERITAGE THEATRE

From an idea that was initially discussed during the mid-sixties to assemble a theatre company that would encourage visitors to prolong their stay in Charlottesville, the Heritage Repertory Theatre eventually emerged. As 1970 approached and talk of a Bicentennial celebration increased, the concept of establishing a company dedicated to American plays developed.

When the original idea of a professional summer theatre in Charlottesville arose, it was Mr. Weiss more than any one person who developed the idea to fruition. The goals of having a series of American plays to encourage visitors to the Charlottesville area to remain there; to give local residents an attractive professional theatre group; and to provide an educational, developmental program for aspiring theatrical performers and producers were very clear in his mind from the very beginning. As a Professor of Drama at the University, the complex goals of education and professional performance were not contradictory to him, but rather synergistic for a successful summer theatre. He knew he would draw on the talents of his drama department through the summer to add to the professional atmosphere while providing educational leadership.

Through the first season, however, it became painfully obvious that, in fact, the development and administration of the Heritage Theatre required too much from those people thoroughly committed to the academic world, thus requiring outside, professional-administrative help. The Foundation for the Extension and Development of the American Professional Theatre, an organization that gave the Heritage much early advisory help, also found a man to assist in the general management of the organization, Mark Page. (Exhibit IV shows the evolution of the organizational structure; Exhibit V gives job definition for management positions; Exhibit VI shows a list of personnel necessary for the operation of the Theatre group).

Mr. Page's main responsibility, apart from business matters such as bookkeeping and other fiscal responsibilities, was audience development. In Mr. Weiss' opinion, Mr. Page was very effective in this role as an audience-developer. Yet the fundamental goals of professionalism and education never became clear to him; he could not understand the feasibility of having both. Throughout his stay with the Heritage, he would ask Mr. Weiss "just what are we?", never clearly visualizing what the Heritage should be.

Mr. Page's fiscal accountability unfortunately suffered due to his necessary effort in theatre development and marketing. A painful example occurred when Mr. Page failed to meet a printing deadline for certain brochures, resulting in having to use a different printer at an additional cost of $5,000, a significant unneeded expense for an organization the size of the Heritage, and an expense concealed from Mr. Weiss.

This example points out as well the breakdown of communications that was to occur throughout the Heritage's term. It was not until the Spring of 1976 that formal, regularly scheduled weekly meetings were instituted to alleviate confusion and wasted time; an idea that should have been implemented much earlier and one that is necessary for success.

As the demands on Mr. Page grew, it was necessary to add a Business Manager to free Mr. Page's time for continuing development. This occurred after the second season, but came rather abruptly, as the Business Manager's position was not "budgeted for" in a strict sense. The work of one man, the General Manager, soon became the work of five, adding, as well, a new secretary, receptionist, and assistant for promotion. The effect on the payroll was even greater: Mr. Page was initially employed through a grant from the Virginia Commission on the Arts and Humanities, a source that could not give aid to Steve Reed, the newly appointed Business Manager.

Once again, the lines of authority and job responsibilities were not clear-cut to the managers. When Mr. Weiss left for Europe in the Fall of 1975, very few decisions that he implicitly and explicitly assumed were being made in his absence were actually made. Upon his return, Mr. Weiss himself had to resume his role as chief decision maker.

It must be remembered that Mr. Weiss had academic responsibilities throughout this time, and thus wished to remove himself as much as possible from the day-to-day operations. It was rather impossible to do, however, as decision making as well as fund raising continuously fell on his shoulders. When Mark Page left in 1976, the absorption of the General Manager's duties by Steve Reed was too great for Mr. Reed, resulting in Mr. Weiss' involvement to a greater degree than was comfortable.

To compound this, the level of artistic acceptability, as determined by the Artistic Director, was not the same as hoped for by Mr. Weiss, leading to some consternation by the Producing Director. "Quality control" of a theatrical performance is much less tangible than the quality assurance for products of other organizations. It requires great closeness of tastes and ideals between policy makers and artistic direction, that must be formed from the very beginning.

The Advisory Board

After looking at the structure of other theatrical companies throughout the country, Mr. Weiss and his management personnel decided in 1976 to establish an Advisory Board of locally "influential" members. The role and function of the board was not explicitly defined, although it was hoped that the board would strengthen the relationship between the theatre and the community, particularly the business community, as well as aiding Mr. Weiss in the solicitation of funding. It was Mr. Weiss' objective to make up the board with interested individuals who could provide guidance and practical assistance in the company's financial affairs. (Heretofore, Mr. Weiss was the prime, if not sole, mover in obtaining funding.)

The Board's interest at the first meeting was encouraging: they asked discerning questions such as the true status of the company's financial condition, if the Theatre was trying to be too much too soon, and what the formal policies were. Unfortunately, the Board's interest did not become any more active as they casually accepted budgets and offered limited fund-raising abilities.

Heritage Associates

The Heritage Associates, an auxiliary group made up of interested community members, has had great success in aiding community relations and audience development through several social functions ranging from coffees to house tours. It was clear that, as a group, they had no decision-making authority, but were to render suggestions and opinions, as well as solicit contributions, if they liked. Headed by a steering committee, the Associates grew from six people in 1975 to over eighty in 1976.

The individual Associates had mixed feelings about what their roles were to be: some actually wanted to be fund raisers while others were hesitant to join for they expressly didn't want to solicit.

Marketing and Promotion: Consultant's Recommendations

Prior to their planning and preparation for the 1976 season, the Heritage Repertory Company had the benefit of consultants from FEDAPT (Foundation for the Extension and Development of the American Professional Theatre). These consultants worked with the Heritage Company first to ascertain existing problem areas and then to offer possible alternatives.

Although FEDAPT (Mr. Fred Vogel in particular) expressed some concern about expanding the 1976 season, the goal was set at achieving a total of $4,000 subscribers to attend a summer season that doubled the number of performances produced in 1975.

On June 5, 1975, Nance Mousesian (the first consultant) held a session in which a College Representative Program was discussed in detail. Such a program would be aimed at having students supply subscription information to fellow students. Other promotional strategies outlined were group sales, a student scholarship program and ticket stub and industrial promotion.

Harvey Sabinson's visit on June 11 and 12, 1975, was directed towards discussing how to tap the tourist trade. He suggested that key locations needed more than having brochures mailed to them. Personal contact must be established with the proprietors of Monticello and the Skyline Drive Lodges. The people who are in direct contact with the thousands of travelers must be better informed about the Heritage Theatre.

A suggestion was also made to hold an informal press party for the area press, including not only personnel from the Charlottesville paper, radio and TV stations, but also those within a fifty-mile radius. "This would help Mark and his staff to develop personal relationships and give the media a feeling of involvement," (memo from Harvey Savinson).

Further ideas included tie-ins with Amtrak, AAA, and bus tours. In order to widen the audience currently being reached, it was proposed that the Mayor of Charlottesville invite the mayors of surrounding communities to be her guest at a premiere production.

In working on plans for the 1976 renewal campaign, Nance Mousesian spent August 13-15, 1975 going over some tentative plans with Mark Page. A need for a full-time press agent, in addition to an intern to handle the task of brochure distribution, was identified and the concept of switching from a Sunday evening to a Sunday matinee was explored.

Due to the saturation point of Charlottesville, a 1976 expanded season was deemed to necessitate more promotion to outlying areas. A newspaper supplement to the Washington Post and an expanded press operation to include the Washington area was mentioned. Also discussed was an "instant charge" phone line.

Part of this consulting trip included observation time at two other theatres. The Harvard Summer School Repertory Theatre was found to be producing four shows a season and had dropped the rotating repertory style because of the expense. This gave them the flexibility of hiring equity members for four week actor/teacher contracts, and not sacrificing the casting of a play to make maximum (though not necessarily qualitative) use of these people. At Boston University, it was discovered that Mouzan Law felt very strongly about using professional directors. Since the cast was designed to be a mixture of equity and non-equity actors, students did have the opportunity to participate in this realm. However, he felt more learning was possible when all students were directed by a "pro" rather than a few students having the chance to direct.

On January 9-10, 1976, David Frank, Managing Director of the Loretto-Hilton Repertory Theater, visited Charlottesville on a final consulting trip. The outcome of this trip was that the Heritage was left with some very strong suggestions to consider. Mr. Frank noted that the structure of the theatre was informal; without any clear chain of command and with no specific decisions made about long-term goals or a commitment from the University for continued access to Culbreth Theatre. A recommendation was made for the Heritage administrative staff to engage in some specific inward examination, and to consider all the feasible alternatives. Discussion of the operational functions, brought out the idea that a $50,000 deficit should not be projected unless some realistic sources were better identified to cope with the loss.

The University and the Theatre Company

The relationship of the Heritage Company to the University of Virginia might be viewed as both fortunate and unfortunate. The physical facilities, supporting students and faculty, and various donations were provided by the University. Indeed, the whole idea for the Heritage Repertory Theatre hatched from within the University's drama department.

But this strong connection led to problems. First the image of the company was confusing: to many people it was a summer adjunct to the University's Virginia Players, or some other such University activity. Ties with the University also slowed down the process of involving the community. Citizens seemed to have had trouble feeling that Heritage Repertory Theatre was "theirs" when it was so clearly connected with the University of Virginia. On the other hand, students, faculty and staff of the University formed a fairly large and supportive constituency for the Heritage Company.

EXHIBIT I

Heritage Repertory Theatre

May 1, 1976

AN INTRODUCTION TO THE HERITAGE REPERTORY THEATRE

This company was founded in 1974 as a project of the Department of Drama of the University of Virginia and is housed in the Culbreth Theatre on the Grounds of the University. Though related to the academic program of the department and utilizing some of the personnel of the drama department, the primary objective for the company was and remains the establishment of a continuing professional theatre that will serve the needs of the community, the University and visitors to the Charlottesville-Albemarle area. Within this context our objectives are:

1. To provide an educational adjunct to the University's drama teaching program with an example of superior theatre practice and as a training opportunity for our students as well as students and young professionals from other parts of the nation;
2. To establish a theatre company that will serve to maintain and, eventually, develop America's dramatic heritage;
3. To develop subsidiary studies of American theatre and techniques;
4. To establish and encourage related studies in other disciplines with the presentation of plays from various periods and locales utilized as a study resource.

A Brief History

The idea for a company of this kind was discussed by David Weiss, then chairman of the Department of Drama, and a number of local business representatives interested in the development of cultural opportunities for this area during the mid-sixties. There was common agreement that a theatre company was a desirable adjunct to the cultural opportunities of the area and that a company dedicated to the production of American plays was especially appropriate to the home territory of Thomas Jefferson. However, despite some very active interest nothing developed at that time simply because of the lack of a suitable home for the company.

As national interest in the celebration of the nation's Bicentennial began to gain interest in this decade, the idea came to the surface again. Gradually a plan developed for establishing a company dedicated to the American theatre with the intention to provide a home for the theatre in the building under construction as the new home of the department. In 1973, as the building came closer to completion, Prof. Weiss presented the idea to the faculty indicating that there was more than a little merit in starting the company in the summer of 1974, thereby developing an audience and experience before 1976. This was immediately agreed upon.

The work of organization, fund raising and operation in that first season fell almost entirely on the faculty of the department and a few interested students. A company was established utilizing some local students and a considerable number of students and recent graduates from throughout the Eastern United States. Despite a rather youthful cast the quality of the performances was generally good and four plays were presented in daily rotating repertory for eight weeks. The plays were: *The Contrast, The Streets of New York, Spoon River Anthology* and *The Patriots,* Sidney Kingsley's prize winning play about Mr. Jefferson. That first season would not have been possible without two grants totaling $50,000 coupled with the underwriting of $25,000 worth of ticket sales by the Virginia National Bank.

Though 1974 was not as successful as one might have hoped, audience response was significant enough to encourage continuing the company. Perhaps the most important lesson learned in that initial season was that faculty members simply could not give enough time during the school year to the work of development and promotion of the company. We had already received some encouragement from the Foundation for the Extension and Development of the American Professional Theatre for our project and now they assisted us in formulating a more practical program. In addition to advising us on our whole program, this organization assisted us in locating an experienced theatre manager who came to Charlottesville early in 1975 and began a general development campaign for the company's forthcoming season.

In the 1975 season we expanded our run by two weeks. Through the efforts of our new general manager, Mark Page, we expanded our audience, more than doubling attendance over the previous year. Of particular interest is the fact that twice as many area citizens subscribed to the theatre in that second year. We also took steps toward a more professional quality in our work by bringing a guest director in to do two of our productions, Ed Stern, Artistic Director of the very successful Indiana Repertory Theatre. The plays presented in this season were: *Fashion, Under the Gaslight, Ah, Wilderness!* and *The Crucible.*

It became apparent in this second year of operation that a full time staff working year-round was essential to our continuing success. With that in mind, a Business Manager, Steve Reed, was added to the company, Mr. Page and Mr. Reed took over the mechanics of operation and added staff as needed as the 1976 season approached.

Given the importance of this area in the Bicentennial year, it was decided that the season should be expanded with the hope that many of the visitors to the area would find our offerings of interest. It was also agreed that it would be appropriate to offer a work about Jefferson and his contemporaries. Though we had earlier considered offering *The Patriots* again, it was decided that something more encompassing would be desirable. We then commissioned the development of a work that would draw upon the writings of the period for its material and *That Man Jefferson* is the result.

The 1976 season will be twice as long as the previous one. In addition to the original work, *That Man Jefferson,* we are offering *The Little Foxes, The Philadelphia Story, Beggar on Horseback* and a new musical based on an early 19th century play, *She Would Be a Soldier.* A further step forward came with the decision to add four experienced professionals to the company and an agreement with Actor's Equity was reached to make this possible. Three of these professionals will teach in our summer academic program and one will direct one play. We also engaged the services of William Martin, a director from New York, who has co-authored *That Man Jefferson* with David Cupp, a member of the Drama Department's staff. Mr. Martin also is the director of the production and *She Would Be a Soldier.*

With the addition of these seasoned professionals we believe the company has begun to reach the status that will make it the company it should be and can be. Moreover, the simple fact that we are doing two new works indicates that we are attempting to meet our objectives. That support for us in the community continues is shown by the fact that we have already acquired more subscribers than we had through all of the 1975 season.

Structure of the Company

At present the governance of policy for the company is in the hands of three members of the departmental faculty: Producing Director, David W. Weiss, Professor of Drama; Artistic Director, George Black, Department Chairman; Associate Director, E. Roger Boyle, Associate Professor of Drama. Most of the policies of the company are established by these men. They are advised by an Advisory Board made up of interested members of the community. Management of the promotion and business affairs for the company are under the direction of General Manager Steve Reed. (Mr. Page recently left the company to assume the managership of the John Drew Playhouse in East Hampton, Long Island.)

Though faculty members are involved with the management and operation of the company, there is a clear separation of the department and the Heritage in actual operation. In fact, one of our tasks has been to make clear to the public that this company is not simply an extension of the school year play producing organization. We believe this distinction is finally becoming clear to the public.

The University of Virginia provides the facilities of the Culbreth Theatre, rehearsal rooms and shops to the company without charge. The administration of the University clearly recognizes the value of our presence to the community as well as the institution. However, the University is unable to offer any financial support from state funds for our day-to-day operation. The only additional service provided by the University is the bookkeeping and auditing service normally offered to a departmental activity.

It is the intention of the present management to establish a full board of directors in the near future. With that step the intention is to establish a separate corporation thereby emphasizing the separate professional character of the company. Even though this is likely to happen, there is no intention to separate entirely from the University or the department; the educational relationship should be maintained and developed.

The Future

The 1976 season is an ambitious one, fraught with some peril. Cost of operation has increased considerably due to the length of our season coupled with the additional expense of Equity level salaries. Naturally the management hopes that both of these developments will prove advantageous to the health of the company and that we will simply be encouraged to continue, to grow and to more fully meet our objectives.

Unfortunately anticipated income at realistic projections will not meet our needs. We are therefore seeking grant aids in the amount of $60,000 to meet the costs of this season and guarantee our costs for operating through the winter as we prepare for the 1977 season. We believe that in another season of continued growth we can establish the Heritage Repertory Theatre as an active addition to the cultural life of this area and, perhaps, to the nation.

We are grateful for past support from the following foundations and organizations which have made this company possible:

THE UNIVERSITY OF VIRGINIA ENDOWMENT FUND
THE VIRGINIA NATIONAL BANK
THE BOAR'S HEAD INN
THE VIRGINIA COMMISSION ON THE ARTS AND HUMANITIES
OPPORTUNITY RESOURCES
THE FOUNDATION FOR THE EXTENSION AND DEVELOPMENT OF THE AMERICAN
     PROFESSIONAL THEATRE
ACTOR'S EQUITY ASSOCIATION
THE CHARLOTTESVILLE-ALBEMARLE CHAMBER OF COMMERCE

Many individuals and business concerns in this vicinity have also assisted us with cash donations and in-kind services for which we are indeed grateful.

EXHIBIT II

INCOME HISTORY AT A GLANCE

	Earned Income	Unearned Income	Total Income	% Earned Income to Total Budget	Income Over (Under) Expenses
1974	$ 27,467	$50,000	$ 77,467	37%	$4,785
1975	61,584	35,916	97,500	60%	($4,695)
1976 (Budgeted)	106,000	59,000*	165,000	64%	

*To date, actual unearned income for 1976: $-0-

Note: Unearned Income does not include in-kind contributions from the University of Virginia, the Boar's Head Inn, or Virginia National Bank.

ATTENDANCE HISTORY AT A GLANCE

	No. of Performances	Total Audience	Average per Performance	% of Capacity
1974	43	8,463	196	33%
1975	52	17,079	328	55%
1976 (to date)	64	17,254	270	45%

EXHIBIT III
SEASONAL FINANCIAL STATEMENT

Expenses (Production)	Budgeted	Spent	Variance	
Scripts	$143.75	$143.00	+	0.75
Royalties	700.00	700.00		----
Scenery & Properties	2,500.00	3,697.22	−	1,197.22
Costumes	1,800.00	1,783.89	+	16.11
Sound & Lights	200.00	360.07	−	160.07
Subtotals	$5,343.75	$6,684.18		−$1,340.43

Expenses (Non-Production)	Budgeted	Spent	Variance	
Advertising & Promotion	$3,500.00	$4,881.06	−	$1,381.06
Newspaper Display	2,000.00	1,902.18	+	97.82
Brochures	2,000.00	4,849.00	−	2,849.00
Postage	700.00	1,434.67	−	734.67
Tickets	435.00	553.83	−	118.83
Programs	2,000.00	----	+	2,000.00
Office Expenses	600.00	1,239.57	−	639.57
Travel—Production	500.00	179.29	+	320.71
Travel—Non-Production	1,000.00	528.91	+	471.09
Audition Expenses	----	826.87	−	826.87
Make-up	----	29.97	−	29.97
Miscellaneous	----	760.94	−	760.94
Subtotals	$12,735.00	$17,186.29		−$4,451.29
Totals	$18,078.75	$23,870.47		−$5,791.72

21

EXHIBIT IV
Organizational Evolution

1974

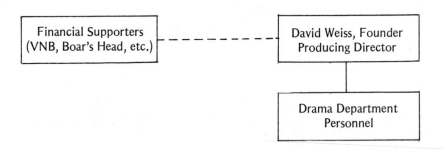

1974-1975

1975-1976

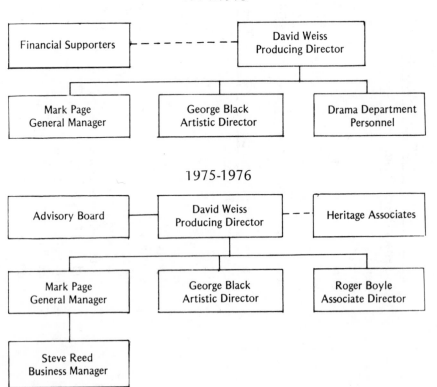

EXHIBIT V

ADMINISTRATIVE ORGANIZATION

Producing Director (Weiss)

General supervision of all policy, budgetary and developmental matters
for the company
Final approval of all personnel appointments and separations
Coordinator of artistic and business matters at the policy level
Coordinator of relations between the company and the University

Artistic Director (Black)

Arbiter of the total artistic aspect of the company, delegating decision
making aspects as deemed practical or necessary
Responsibility for casting and appointment of all design and directing
personnel with the additional responsibility of regular review of
the activities of those personnel
Responsibility for continuing review of all visual aspects of company
activities whether to do with performance or promotional materials;
this would include coordination of graphics used in publicity and advertising, lobby displays, programs and exterior advertising materials
Responsibility for review of all media advertising as deemed necessary
Approval of all public appearances of members of the company for
promotional purposes
Approval of news and feature stories prepared for release by publicity staff

Associate Director (Boyle)

Advisor and consultant to other directors on policy and artistic
matters as deemed necessary
Responsibility for dramaturgical needs of the company; this will include the review and selection of possible plays for production by
the company to be considered and voted upon by the directors
jointly
Coordinator of activities between the company and the Virginia
Players

General Manager (Page)

Responsibility for the overall supervision of all non-performance activities of the company including:

Advertising and promotion
Community relations development

      Financial development and fund raising

      General coordination of the budget on an immediate as well as
long-range scale

      Responsible to the Artistic Director on all matters indicated above;
responsible to the Producing Director for all matters concerning
basic policy of the company, employment of new personnel relative to his areas of responsibility and the development of the
company in the normal growth process

Business Manager (Reed)

      Responsibility for all financial control and recording

      Responsibility for box office and all front-of-the-house operations
and personnel

      Has initial and final approval of all expenditures (NB: no bulk ex-
penditure in excess of $500 may be made without the approval of
the Business Manager *and* the Producing Director)

      Responsibility for payroll and all final contractual arrangements with
individuals or companies

      Responsible for all financial relationships between the company and
the University or the Virginia Players

EXHIBIT VI

PERSONNEL REQUIREMENTS

Producer	Technical Apprentices (4)	Assistant Wardrobe Mistress
Associate Producer	Acting Interns (5)	Advertising Manager
General Manager	Technical Interns (4)	Business Manager**
Artistic Director	Master Carpenter	House Manager/Public
Associate Director	Assistant Carpenter	Relations Director
Scene Designer	Master Propertyman	Box Office Manager**
Costume Designer	Assistant Propertyman	Assistant Box Office Manager
Lighting Designer*	Master Electrician*	Secretary (part-time)
Technical Director	Assistant Electrician and Sound	Ushers (6)
Assistant Technical Director	Production Stage Manager	Preseason Wardrobe Staff (4)
Actors, Core Company (10)	Stage Manager	Preseason Scenery
Acting Apprentices (5)	Wardrobe Mistress	Construction Staff (4)

Total Personnel on Payroll or Stipend: 68

    (* and ** means that these positions might be combined)

It is possible that a child or two and a pianist might have to be added on a part-time
basis. This will depend considerably on the basic casting and the awarding of Intern-
ships and Apprenticeships.

Case 2

Charlottesville Transit Service*

In September, 1975, the city of Charlottesville (population 40,000) began operating a public bus system, replacing the transit service provided by a private operator since 1964. Prior to 1964, there had been no transit system in Charlottesville.

The financial performance of the privately operated system had deteriorated during the 1969-1974 period, as shown in Exhibit I. To offset rising expenses, the private operator reduced the service level (i.e., bus-miles) which, in turn, decreased the number of passengers, causing revenues to decline. The city began subsidizing the private operator's deficit in 1973 in order to insure the existence of an urban transit system. The subsidy increased in 1974, rising to $126,000; $150,000 was requested for 1975.

The city began to study the feasibility of a public transit system in 1972. During 1973 and 1974, an outside consulting firm worked with city staff and the Transportation Task Force (twenty local citizens); a publicly-owned transit system was recommended. The proposed public system would meet eligibility requirements for federal and state capital grants and would allow the city to control the level of service. In Charlottesville, transit service was viewed mainly as a public service; it was projected that city subsidies would continue to be necessary to finance the gap between revenues and expenses.

*This case was prepared by Katharine L. Bradshaw, Barbara A. Frantz and Curtis J. Tompkins, April, 1977. Revised by Curtis J. Tompkins, April, 1979. Copyright © C. J. Tompkins, 1979.

25

EXHIBIT I

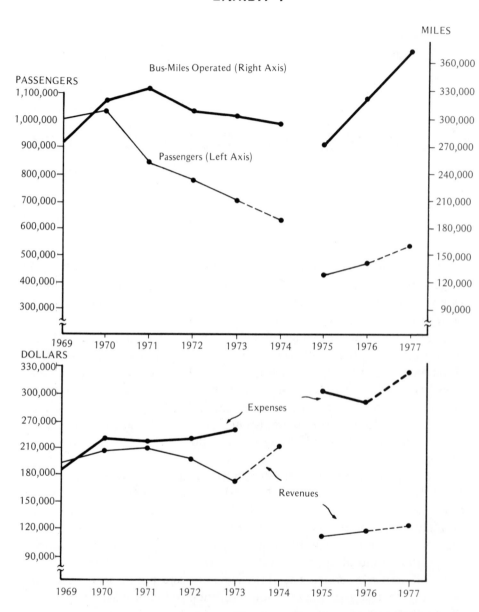

Note 1: Slashed lines represent projected figures. Revenues and bus-miles for 1976 were not plotted separately, but are shown only as the midpoint between 1975 and 1977. Revenues for 1975 represent ten months actual data on an annualized basis.

Note 2: Although accurate figures for the 1974-75 transition period do not exist, the *Virginia State-wide Transit Statistics Report,* for which all transit systems must report annual statistics on ridership, revenues, and miles, reported that in the 1974-76 period, there was a 129% increase in ridership in Charlottesville.

GOALS OF THE PUBLIC SYSTEM

The goals of the public transit service in 1975 were:

1. To maintain the existing level of service,
2. To operate on a more cost-effective basis, and
3. To improve the quality of service sufficiently to attract some of the 8638 potential users estimated by the outside consulting firm's research.

Goals through 1980 included:

1. To add routes in the northern part of the city,
2. To decrease headways on existing routes,
3. To coordinate with the University Transit System as much as possible,
4. To experiment with demand-responsive service on a limited basis,
5. To develop a system of routes responsive to the needs of potential riders, and
6. To develop self-supporting contract services for large employers and group trips.[1]

BACKGROUND ON URBAN TRANSIT SYSTEMS

Charlottesville's problems with urban mass transportation were not unique. Between 1965 and 1973, Urban Mass Transportation Act (UMTA) grants had helped to finance public conversion of private bus systems in 49 cities. For the most part, the systems had failed the test of the market-place; consumer demand did not generate sufficient revenues and deficits were projected to continue.

A study of the product life cycle of urban mass transportation in the early 1970s suggests that urban bus systems were in the declining stage of maturity. Bus systems experienced their heyday during World War II, when consumer expenditures on durables were restricted: nineteen billion riders a year supported mass transit operations. By 1974, that figure had reached its lowest point *since 1900:* 5.6 billion riders (these figures

[1] *Application for a Mass Transportation Improvement Grant,* City of Charlottesville, June, 1975.

refer to patronage on all forms of urban mass transportation).[2] George Hilton provides further statistics in support of the hypothesis that bus systems have passed their prime.[3]

> Buses carried 8% of the work force to their jobs in 1960, but only 5.5% in 1970. The transit industry first reported a net deficit in 1963. By 1965, the net deficit reached $11 million. By 1972, the deficit was $413 million, frequently doubling annually in the interim. . . . All-bus systems as a whole were profitable until 1968.

A major factor influencing the declining use of mass transit was the rising popularity of the private auto. The family car offers several advantages over mass transit:[4]

Comfort	Freedom from schedules and routing
Privacy	Provides a direct trip
Limited walking	Space for packages
Minimum waiting	Protection from inclement weather
Guaranteed seat	Extra passengers at no extra cost
	Faster and cheaper (except in crowded traffic jams)—for short trips, the perceived marginal cost of a car may be zero.

These advantages contrast sharply with the situation of a bus rider, as described by Wilfred Owens:[5]

> He must walk, wait, stand, and be exposed to the elements. The ride is apt to be costly, slow, and uncomfortable because of antiquated equipment, poor ventilation, and service that is congested in rush hours, infrequent during any other time of day, inoperative at night, and non-existent in suburbia.

The rejuvenation of mass transportation's life cycle can occur only if the advantages of mass transportation can offset the advantages of private cars. This situation was not encouraged during the sixties when public transportation funds were largely directed toward improvement of highway systems. Now, however, population growth in urban areas and in-

---

[2] Wilfred Owens, *Transportation for Cities: The Role of Federal Policy*, The Brookings Institution, Washington, D.C., 1976.

[3] George W. Hilton, *Federal Transit Subsidies: The Urban Mass Transportation Assistance Program*, American Enterprise Institute for Public Policy Research, Washington, D.C., 1974, page 97.

[4] W. Owens, op. cit., pages 5-6.

[5] W. Owens, op. cit., p. 6.

creasing concern with energy availability have caused increased interest in mass transportation. This increased attention is most evident in large urban areas, where limited parking and traffic jams have made cars less convenient and less efficient. The problems of congestion, air and noise pollution have increased public support of mass transportation development and discouragement of car usage (higher inner-city parking prices, restricted parking, bus-only highway lanes).

In Charlottesville, however, no crisis situation exists to encourage a major shift in lifestyle back to bus riding. The city is small (10 square miles); almost any area served by bus can be reached by car in less than ten minutes with minimal impact on the amount of gasoline in the car's gas tank. The worst traffic jams are minor: one might wait five or ten minutes at one or two traffic lights during the evening rush hour, but for the most part, traffic flows at the designated speed limit. The major encouragement is limited parking in the University area, but most people affected by this have access to the University Transit Service. Therefore, people in Charlottesville who have a choice between car and bus usually opt for car. Improving bus service does not eliminate some of its inherent disadvantages over the car. Increased bus ridership results when the advantages of car riding diminish.

BACKGROUND ON UMTA

General objectives of the UMTA grant program were:[6]

1. To reinvigorate public transportation in order to provide service that will attract new riders regardless of their social or economic group or the purpose of their journey. The aim is to increase transit use differentially with respect to automobiles.
2. To provide greater mobility for substantial groups of people who are totally dependent on public transportation by providing better general service and developing special services. (Target groups include the young, aged, poor, handicapped, unemployed, and secondary workers.)
3. To promote transit as a positive force in influencing and supporting desired development patterns in urban areas and in improving environmental conditions.

[6]Capital Grants for Urban Mass Transit: Information for Applicants, quoted in G. Hilton, op. cit., p. 78.

The objectives did *not* include profitability of transit systems; increased ridership was cited as a measure of a system's success in reaching the above objectives. In small urban areas (under 250,000 population) like Charlottesville, the second objective, mobility for the disadvantaged, was the most important goal according to UMTA, since congestion and uncontrolled growth are not major factors. Smaller systems were expected to:

1. Maintain and increase use of the city transit system.
2. Undertake corrective measures if the systems are inferior to industry standards in average cost per vehicle-mile, vehicle-hour, passenger-mile.[7]

CTS IN 1976-1977

The Charlottesville Transit Service's primary goal was safe, convenient, and comfortable transportation for its "captive" riders, those people without cars. According to on-bus surveys of riders, 60 percent of the riders were members of households without cars, 70 percent did not drive, 87 percent needed the bus to make the trip, 75 percent had monthly incomes of $750 or less, 50 percent rode the bus daily, and less than 10 percent were students.[8] Average bus ridership on CTS's 16- to 20-passenger minibuses was four persons per bus at the time of this April 1976 survey. Further statistics from this survey appear in Exhibit II; these statistics show that 62 percent of the riders were employed and 56 percent were in the 25-64 age range.

In Charlottesville's population of 40,000, 16 percent were members of minority races; 12 percent were sixty years or older. The majority of these senior citizens (70 percent) lived in or near the center city. Average autos per household in the city were 1.21.

The Charlottesville Transit Service was administered by an administrative assistant and by Charlottesville's Public Service Chief, who allocated approximately 10 percent of his time and attention to CTS. In 1976, 48 percent of CTS expenditures were covered by revenues; the city subsidized the remaining 52 percent. These expenditures consisted primarily of salaries (62 percent).

[7]G. Hilton, op. cit., pages 79-80.
[8]*Evaluation of Transit System Coordination and Future Services in the Charlottesville Urbanized Area*, draft, April, 1976.

In 1976-77, CTS operated six routes six days a week, on hourly headways; one of these routes was served by two buses traveling in opposite directions. Each route was independent of the other routes, so that a bus traveled in a loop between its service area and downtown, thus minimizing the amount of transfers and walking required. A computer analysis of alternative systems (loop and trunk-line feeder) was performed by University of Virginia Traffic Engineering professors using the Urban Transportation Planning System computer program. The loop system would also minimize transfers, but would reduce trip time and waiting time, using 14 percent more bus miles. The trunk-line feeder system would minimize total travel time, thus attracting short-trip riders; but it would require more transfers and 27 percent higher operating costs. These professors also projected that ridership demand in the city would increase to 2500 riders per day in 1985 (based on populatiion growth and increased usage).

The feasibility of coordinating the University Transit Service (UTS) and Charlottesville Transit Service and of expanding service into Albemarle County had also been studied. Financial consideration inhibited the implementation of these alternatives. Shared bus stops with UTS did exist on some routes. Exhibit III shows that CTS accounted for only about 5 percent of the public transportation business in Charlottesville in 1976.

CTS's marketing goals during its introductory period had been to increase awareness of the bus system; media advertisements, a bright logo painted on the buses, and new uniforms for drivers called attention to the system. A telephone survey of 100 non-bus-riding Charlottesville residents (in which bus riders were purposely screened out) in April 1977, revealed the success of these marketing efforts: 100 percent of the sample felt that Charlottesville should have a bus system, 50 percent would pay higher taxes to support bus service (42 percent would not), only 8 percent did not know the location of the bus stop nearest their home. However, 49 percent admitted they did not know the fare (39 percent knew or guessed correctly that the fare was 25 cents) and 85 percent were thinking of other people's needs when they voiced support of city bus service. In this non-bus-riding sample, 30 percent of the respondents were 60 years or older; 6 percent were members of households without cars.

Exhibit II

Ridership Statistics
(From the April, 1976 Survey of Bus Riders)

Trip Purpose

Work	47.6%
Shopping	22.5%
Medical	4.4%
School	5.0%
Personal business	12.1%
Social/recreation	1.7%
Other	6.7%

Auto Ownership

No cars	58.1%
One car	31.2%
Two or more	10.8%

Frequency of Transit Usage

Daily	49.8%
Weekly	32.7%
Infrequent	17.5%

Frequency of Taxi Usage

Daily	4.1%
Weekly	20.9%
Infrequent	75.0%

Approval Rate of Service

Dependable	85.7%
Safe	90.7%
Convenient	86.7%
Comfortable	88.2%

Age Distribution of Riders

Age	%
0-14	1.6
15-19	7.8
20-24	17.2
25-44	28.9
45-64	26.6
65+	17.9

Valid Sample: 945

Occupation of Riders

Status	%
Employed	62.0
Housewife	11.7
Student	9.3
Retired	13.0
Unemployed	3.9

Valid Sample: 966

Income Distribution of Riders

Monthly Income ($)	%
0-249	20.1
250-499	36.3
500-749	21.8
750-999	9.2
1000-1249	4.8
1250+	7.8

Valid Sample: 642

EXHIBIT III

Public Transportation in Charlottesville in 1976.

100% = 32,000 riders

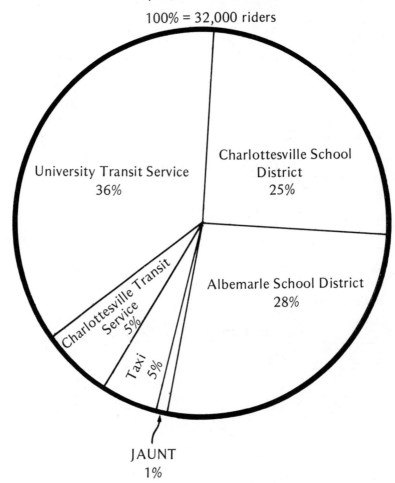

Case 3

Martha Jefferson Hospital*

As early as 1965 Gene Carpenter, the administrator of Martha Jefferson Hospital, was concerned with the increased utilization rates of all hospital departments and service facilities. Even with the twenty-four bed addition in October 1964, he knew that there would have to be further expansion to accommodate growing population within Martha Jefferson Hospital's (MJH) primary service area (Exhibit 1). Future pressures for new beds therefore meant that MJH would have to expand existing core facilities.

In 1968 the Board of Trustees adopted an expansion program which would increase both bed complement and respective capacity for core facilities—general storage, surgery, laundry, etc. Between 1968 and 1973, when the project was launched, the scope of services and facilities changed. The Board, having conferred with architects, engineers, and consultants, decided to embark upon a three-phase, long range expansion program. Phase I was to begin in April 1973. With the expansion in scope, the cost of construction had risen from estimates of $5,139,000 in 1968 to $14,500,000 in 1973. Approximately $12,500,000 in financing had been arranged. The shortfall of $2,000,000 was to be raised through a community fund drive. There was some question as to whether

---

*This case was prepared by Douglas S. Holladay and Curtis J. Tompkins. Copyright © 1981 by C. J. Tompkins.

EXHIBIT 1

such a drive could be successful in view of a similar $2,000,000 drive in 1969.

ENVIRONMENT

Martha Jefferson Hospital was one of two general hospitals located within the Charlottesville service area. MJH was founded in 1904 to extend care and ancillary services to patients in Charlottesville-Albemarle and surrounding counties. It had grown from 25 beds in 1904 to 136 beds in 1975 while serving an area with a population of 161,500.

MJH differed from its nearby neighbor, the University of Virginia Hospital, in several respects. Martha Jefferson did not have emergency room facilities which operated on a full-service basis. 85 percent of the surgical procedures performed at MJH were elective in nature. Patient stays were relatively short, and patients could only be admitted by one of 67 active doctors or 33 courtesy staff doctors, who were privileged to use MJH. There was also a community misconception about MJH. Many people felt that it was a profit making rather than a nonprofit community hospital.

The University of Virginia was a much larger facility with 560 short-term acute beds. Its primary mission was to act as a teaching institution and referral medical center for the entire state. It supported both research efforts and a large medical school. Its patients were those from the immediate area and from the entire state. Unlike MJH it was equipped with extensive emergency room and outpatient facilities.

On the other hand, Martha Jefferson enjoyed a community reputation of being a "warm, family hospital, and a friendly place with a very close home atmosphere." Patients had characterized nurses and employees as "exhibiting a personal interest that makes one feel like a person, not a number." A survey done in April 1975 by Ketchum, Inc. to determine fund-raising potential, confirmed the hospital's community image in a poll of 59 community leaders as follows: good—56, average—3, and poor—0.

Ketchum, Inc. was regarded as the leading fund-raising firm for non-profit institutions in the country. Since its incorporation in 1919 the firm had served more than 6,000 clients. In 1975 Ketchum's 110 project directors had organized and coordinated campaigns totalling $60,000,000. Its success rate had been high. An example was a $100,000,000 campaign at Johns Hopkins which was currently 80 percent completed and ahead of schedule.

Nursing staff and employees categorized their environment as one relatively free from pressure and tension. Even with overcrowded conditions and departments strained to provide supportive functions, personnel rarely felt that demands could not be met. Since most surgical procedures were elective, a sense of urgency and intensity was not felt to the degree that it might be in a more critical care facility; working conditions were therefore perceived to be more pleasant.

ORGANIZATION

During 1975 there were 425 employees involved in administering a number of services, including clinical laboratories, four operating rooms, four coronary beds, x-ray facilities, laundry, maintenance, kitchen and

EXHIBIT 2

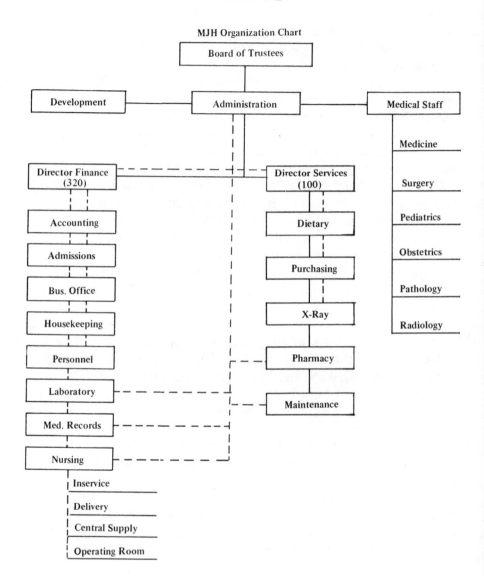

MJH Organization Chart

( ) Parenthesis indicate personnel under director
--- Indicates functional control
— Indicates administrative control

cafeteria, and outpatient care. The organizational structure is depicted in Exhibit 2. A profile of key employees is included in Exhibit 3.

Gene Carpenter, the Administrator, had come from a West Virginia community hospital where his experience had been in management control. He brought with him a managing style which was personal and informal in nature. He took pride in knowing many of his 425 employees by their first names. In administering MJH he felt that patient service was of primary importance. If problems arose, he wanted to be informed immediately and would usually contribute ideas for solutions. He enjoyed making daily policy decisions, and his "can do" attitude appeared to permeate to the lowest employee level.

The administrator had recently reorganized the departments so that for administrative purposes each would report to either the Director of Finance or the Director of Services. Prior to this arrangement all departments had reported directly to the administrator in functional and administrative capacities. Mr. Carpenter believed that his close communication with all departments was essential to successful execution. However, with the expansion program he was no longer available to resolve the countless day-to-day policy decisions as he once had. The shift of administrative responsibility to his two directors had proven to be a sound decision in Mr. Carpenter's view. Both men were highly motivated and very interested in their different departments.

Don Sandridge, the Director of Finance, had joined MJH in 1965 without prior nonprofit experience. In his ten years at MJH, he had been energetic, enthusiastic, and interested in learning how each department functioned. As a result he had been promoted to assume greater managing responsibility. In many cases he found that he was still involved in the day-to-day detail of subordinates' work. This situation was partially due to the increased work load that was experienced at MJH as it neared capacity. Yet he considered this involvement in detail important because it allowed him an opportunity to examine bottlenecks and improve efficiency.

Mr. Sandridge viewed his new role as that of a buffer between the departments he administered and the Administrator. He believed that he and the Director of Services were there to identify problems, reduce situations to facts, sift out personnel emotions, and resolve many policy decisions before they reached the Administrator.

Board of Trustees

The Board was composed of an equal number of medical staff members and lay members. (Exhibit 4) According to the Bylaws of MJH the

EXHIBIT 3

Departmental/Divisional Heads

Age	Title	Education	Experience	Joined MJH	Present Position Since
46	Administrator	2 yrs. college	11 yrs. in accounting/Managing W. Va. community hospital	July 1961	1962
34	Finance Director	2 yrs. college	Accounting—Pepsico Operations—Trailways	Aug. 1965	Oct. 1970
50	Service Dir.	B.S.	Purchasing	May 1968	May 1968
59	Development Director	B.S.	28 yrs. Foreign Service Management/Administration	July 1974	July 1974
*54	Nursing	B.S.	Inservice, Supervisor	Oct. 1969	Oct. 1969
53	Maintenance	H.S.	Plumbing Contractor	Jan. 1955	Jan. 1955
*56	Personnel	1 yr. college	Personnel—large local firm	Jan. 1975	Jan. 1975
38	Pharmacy	B.S.	Chief Pharmacist—Retail	Oct. 1967	Oct. 1967
*37	Medical Records	H.S.	20 yrs. Medical Records U. Va. Hospital	Mar. 1974	Mar. 1974
*35	X-Ray	H.S.	15 yrs. X-Ray Technician	June 1974	June 1974
44	Dietary	H.S.	Military Service	Jan. 1974	Jan. 1974
28	Housekeeping	H.S.	Employed by Servicemaster Corporation	July 1974	July 1974
41	Laboratory	B.S.	Laboratory Technician	Feb. 1963	Feb. 1963

*Women

EXHIBIT 4

Age	Education	Title	Experience	Joined Board	Number Years Served
*58	B.A.	Community Leader	Director—Local Bank Civic Affairs	1971	11
*68	B.A.	Community Leader	Past President of City Civic League	1971	5
**56	B.S.	Regional Insurance Manager	Insurance, Board—United Givers Fund	1971	5
52	B.A.	Trust Officer	Sales/Banking	1974	2
55	B.S.	Manager—Local Textile Firm	Textiles	1974	2
***50	B.A.	President—Local Insurance Co.	Insurance, Director Local Bank, Chairman 1969 Hospital Fund Drive	1970	12
***48	M.D.	Ob/Gyn		1970	5
61	M.D.	Internist	Director—Local Bank Director—Prep School	1973	3
74	M.D.	Urologist		1971	5
60	M.D.	Surgeon		1972	4
***73	M.D.	Surgeon		1970	24
50	M.D.	Opthamologist		1973	3

*Women
**Present President of the Board
***Past President of the Board

minimum number had to be twelve, and it could not exceed twenty. Medical staff members had to be active voting members of the hospital. Elected terms were for a period of three years. After serving two successive terms, a member could not be re-elected to the Board for a period of one year. Elections were staggered so that only four members were elected each year.

The Trustees chose a president, vice president, secretary, and treasurer. The top two positions were terms of two years. Each office was held alternately by a lay and medical staff member. The secretary and treasurer served for one year terms.

The president, as stated in the bylaws, was the chief executive officer and head of the corporation. He was to sign, on behalf of the corporation, all sealed instruments required to be executed by the corporation.

The vice president was to perform the duties of the president in the absence or disability of the president.

The secretary was to retain custory of the corporate seal and keep minutes of Board meetings. It was possible for a secretary to be elected who was not a Board member. If this nonBoard member were elected, he would be without voting power in Board meetings. The Administrator held this position as a nonvoting member and had retained this office for the last 13 years.

The Board was further subdivided into seven committees: executive, medical affairs, finance, building and grounds, special, and inspection with the executive committee generally acknowledged as the most powerful. The executive committee was comprised of five members; namely, the president, the vice president, the treasurer, a medical member, and a medical or lay member. This committee had the power to act for the Board in all matters not committed to the authority of other committees, and excepting power to buy or sell real estate or mortgage or create a lien on property.

Administrator

The Administrator was selected by the Board. He was given necessary authority and was held responsible for the administration of the hospital in all activities and departments. He acted as the authorized representative of the Board in all matters in which the Board had not formally designated the responsibility to some other committee. Specifically, he had supervision and control over records, accounts, buildings, internal affairs, and he enforced complicance of all regulations. He made policy decisions with regard to all regulations such that they were not inconsistent with the directions of the Board. He had the authority to engage or discharge any employee. With regard to finances, he was responsible for causing proper accounts of operations to be kept on a daily basis, and he ensured all funds were collected and expended to the best possible advantage. Finally, he was required to attend all Board meetings.

PLANNING AND CONTROL

MJH enjoyed a unique position relative to many other hospitals. The American Hospital Association recommended an average occupancy of medical/surgical beds not to exceed 80 percent. This percentage would allow for sufficient beds for emergencies, epidemics, and seasonal factors which could quickly drive usage to 100 percent. The medical/surgical bed occupancy rate at MJH was 87.2 percent. This percentage was based upon weekly averages. Few surgical procedures were done on weekends. On week days nearly every bed was filled.

To seek admission for tests, observation, and nonsurgical treatment, beds had to be reserved two to three weeks in advance. For elective surgery, reservations had to be made four to six weeks in advance. There were seasonal differences which contributed to variations in monthly occupancy rates. Since low points in the seasonal pattern were still above national averages, the Administrator saw no need to forecast daily patient census. (Exhibit 5)

Since Martha Jefferson was a nonprofit community hospital, it received no subsidies from any outside source; therefore, revenues were required to cover expenses. (Comparative balance sheet and operating statements are given in Exhibits 6, 7, and 8). Although there was no annual budget for the forthcoming year, needs were determined on a monthly basis by comparing existing to previous monthly operations of past years. (Exhibit 9) Departments were not set up as profit centers; rather, revenues and expenses were allocated to various services on the following basis: the prior year's service as a proportion of the total revenue or expense was applied toward the current year's average daily patient rate. (It should be kept in mind that this was an average daily rate. The range of each patient's charges could vary considerably. The daily rate was calculated by dividing total revenues by total patient day utilization.)

EXHIBIT 5

History of Patient Load

Year	Number of Beds*	Admissions**	Percent Occupancy	Average Patient Stay*	Procedures
1975	136	7,423	87.2	5.83	6,078
1974	136	7,225	86.5	5.94	6,017
1973	136	6,994	87.8	6.23	6,147
1972	136	6,784	85.8	6.28	6,460
1971	136	6,507	83.0	6.33	5,837
1970	136	6,463	85.6	6.57	5,554
1969	136	6,283	87.0	6.87	
1968	136	6,150	87.5	7.06	
1967	136	5,927	86.0	7.20	
1966	136	5,827	81.6	6.95	
1965	136	5,777	82.4	7.08	
1964	112	5,336	85.4	6.54	
1963	112	5,140	88.2	7.01	

*20 infant beds not counted as part of bed complement.
**Admissions do not include births.

EXHIBIT 6

Comparative Balance Sheets of General Fund

	1973	1974	1975 (Unaudited)
ASSETS			
Cash on hand and in bank	$ 32,017	$ 103,322	$ 62,949
Cash—savings accounts and certificates of deposit	343,563	247,569	20,121
Accounts receivable (net uncollectible accounts)	572,854	828,729	1,232,979
Accrued Interest		3,639	3,709
Settlements from Blue Cross	64,763	100,176	66,312
Inventory of drugs and supplies	95,623	124,698	142,778
Prepaid expenses	9,666	12,211	63,944
Deferred pension expense	14,853		
	$1,133,339	$1,420,344	$1,592,792
LIABILITIES			
Accounts payable	87,714	82,362	107,352
Accrued expense	46,763	78,311	157,710
Due Blue Cross	50,054		
Due plant fund (less capital expenditures)		36,942	27,863
	$ 184,441	$ 197,616	$ 292,925
RESERVE FOR SPECIAL FUNDS			
Total reserves	42,562	35,726	30,188
GENERAL FUND BALANCE	906,336	1,187,002	1,269,679
Total	$1,133,339	$1,420,344	$1,592,792

EXHIBIT 7

Comparative Statement of Operations

Revenues from Services to Patients	1973*	1974	1975 (Unaudited)
Adult patients	$1,834,307	$2,047,420	$2,494,241
Nursery	76,950	89,543	134,383
Operating rooms	321,167	417,660	560,023
Delivery rooms	48,389	47,921	67,125
Anesthesiology	47,390	57,104	59,024
Radiology	49,924	197,494	235,201
Laboratory	483,148	543,294	599,539
Blood bank	13,419	21,629	21,637
Electrocardiograms	41,533	52,069	64,667
Physical therapy	22,483	35,954	42,839
Recovery	35,620	57,217	96,045
Emergency service	23,985	30,068	29,215
Medical/surgical	113,264	129,499	143,291
Pharmacy	231,966	286,849	345,235
Inhalation therapy	14,920	17,897	27,928
Cardiac unit	52,863	66,241	93,784
Dietary			64,918
Total	$3,411,328	$4,097,859	$5,079,095
Deduction from Revenue			
Total	110,217	57,330	269,470
Total Revenue	$3,301,111	$4,040,529	$4,809,625

*Fiscal year: October 1—September 30.

EXPANSION

The scope of services and facilities at MJH changed between 1968, when the Board adopted a resolution to expand existing facilities, and 1973, when construction was launched. Many factors identified in 1965 had become increasingly critical issues. Patient volume had increased 28 percent while the number of beds had remained the same. Additional staffing accommodated increased volume, thereby solving a short-term crisis; however, increasingly obsolete equipment severely limited patient services in many areas. Plant facilities needed refurbishing. Such modernization could not be carried out without some loss in patient care.

In 1965 the director of the medical center of the University of Vir-

EXHIBIT 8

Comparative Statement of Operations

Operating Expenses	1973	1974	1975 (Unaudited)
Administrative	$ 457,480	$ 519,741	$ 689,794
Dietary	334,438	420,928	471,234
Housekeeping	120,919	128,981	153,166
Laundry	67,435	68,877	88,987
Operation of plant	50,705	66,211	106,553
Repairs and maintenance	78,337	85,467	122,656
Hospital security	8,788	11,177	12,887
Depreciation	78,119	82,400	84,000
Nursing service	1,043,913	1,095,759	1,246,817
Central supply	65,229	72,728	84,505
Nursing education	7,205	1,108	6,504
Medical-surgical	48,301	41,273	69,030
Cardiac unit	62,576	67,042	72,680
Pharmacy	160,330	158,782	202,700
Medical records	52,318	60,043	73,538
Operating/recovery rooms	275,643	328,384	380,119
Delivery rooms	74,008	75,134	49,817
Anesthesiology	38,320	40,228	89,769
Radiology		90,123	148,487
Laboratory	251,194	342,421	431,946
Electrocardiogram	22,746	25,274	29,788
Emergency room	32,613	37,464	42,394
Blood bank	19,351	30,611	34,250
Inhalation therapy	15,958	18,288	25,831
Physical therapy	15,435	21,487	26,826
Total	$3,381,361	$3,889,931	$4,744,278
Reduction in Expense			
Purchase discounts	6,306	6,508	7,361
Other income	61,285	82,758	9,969
*Net Income (Loss)	$ (12,659)	$ 239,864	$ 82,677

*Net income in 1972—$107,004

ginia Hospital stated that there were no immediate plans for its expansion of beds. He did foresee some expansion in the next ten years.

There were increasing industry demands. Health care was experiencing a trend toward patients choosing more specialists to perform proced-

EXHIBIT 9

Comparative Monthly Revenues and Expenses
1974-1975

Month	Revenue From Services Fiscal '75	Revenue From Services Fiscal '74	Increase (Decrease)
October	$416,935	$303,693	$113,242
November	353,903	303,361	50,542
December	346,984	278,479	68,505
January	382,104	281,569	100,535
February	348,445	286,631	61,814
March	392,102	326,497	65,605
April	533,774	325,791	207,983
May	417,241	377,660	39,581
June	423,614	384,917	38,697
July	433,445	518,098	(84,653)
August	413,712	375,971	37,741
September	389,803	332,755	57,048

Month	Expenses From Operations Fiscal '75	Expenses From Operations Fiscal '74	Increase (Decrease)
October	$374,555	$300,897	$ 73,658
November	371,215	298,600	72,615
December	382,963	308,970	73,993
January	363,834	333,484	30,350
February	348,463	284,730	63,733

March	407,848	321,723	86,125
April	403,573	331,038	72,535
May	389,752	335,118	54,634
June	397,233	326,041	71,192
July	415,843	374,130	41,713
August	420,420	356,345	64,075
September	468-576	325,349	143,227

EXHIBIT 10

Projected Service Area Population

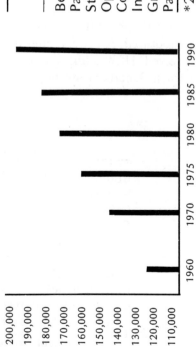

Projections based on Tayloe Murphy Institute Figures, Gilliam & Serow, August, 1975.

EXHIBIT 11

Physical Expansion

	Base Year 1973/74	1976/77	1984/85	1995/96
Beds	136	232	355	445
Patients	7,225	11,000	16,500	21,200
Staff	425	603*	923	1,150
Operating rooms	4	6	8	10
Coronary beds	4	4	10	10
Intensive care beds	—	4	10	10
Gross space (sq. ft.)	63,550	249,190	279,190	309,190
Parking deck				500 spaces

*2.6 employees per bed is national average

ures. There was a greater public sense of urgency in correcting physical disability. People no longer wanted to live with an ailment and therefore actively sought elective surgery. Although of slight impact upon MJH, Medicare/Medicaid policies would increase patient volume.

Population increases within the primary service area were a very real concern. (Exhibit 10) For fiscal year 1974, 60 percent of total admissions were from Charlottesville-Albemarle with most of the balance coming from the seven surrounding counties. To meet growing demands, MJH had to build new core facilities to support expanded bed capacity.

In early 1973 the Board authorized phase I of the expansion program which called for a 96-bed addition with core facilities for a 445-bed hospital to be completed by October 1976. The two additional bed expansions of 123 beds and 90 beds were to be added in 1984 and 1995 respectively. The costs of furnishings for the additional capacity had not been included in the $14,517,000 estimate.

Physical developments are shown in Exhibit 11.

FINANCING

It was apparent that substantial outside funding for the project would be required. A Federal Hill-Burton Grant of $1,000,000 was sought and received. HEW additionally guaranteed an $8,000,000 commercial loan with a 3 percent subsidy toward the negotiated interest rate of 7.86

Expansion Project Costs

Building work	$ 9,589,000
Site work	228,000
Off-site work	75,000
Change orders	10,000
Fixed equipment	418,000
Architect and engineer fees	823,000
Movable equipment	2,100,000
Contingencies	309,000
Construction interest	750,000
Anatomical laboratory addition	215,000
Total Project Costs	$14,517,000

percent. (Exhibit 12 reveals the sources of available funds.) When the major funding of the project was resolved, the Board signed a contract for $9,892,000 with English Construction Company in April 1973.

Although a substantial portion of the funding had been obtained, there were covenants with regard to the draw procedures for federal monies which would cause cash problems in the fall of 1975 when equipment receipts fell due.

HEW recognized $12,500,000 as the funding base. There were certain parts of the project where federal money could not be applied. With this base no more than 66.27 percent of the construction bill, as it was presented, could be paid out of the $8,000,000. At each step of the building process MJH had to contribute its share of the construction costs. This factor created a severe cash strain on the hospital cash resources. The situation was further aggravated by thirty-day delays in some instances where government agencies required construction receipts to validate loan withdrawals. Exhibit 13 is the finance director's projected cash resources and uses as of July 1975. This statement was presented to the Board at that time. The finance director's projections had not included certain architect and contingency fees nor $130,000 in additional construction costs. The difference created by adding these additions to Exhibit 13 and comparing that total to $14,517,000 was the result of refinements which were made after the $14,517,000 estimation.

EXHIBIT 12

Expansion Project
Source of Available Funds

Mortgage—Virginia National Bank	$ 8,000,000.00
Hill-Burton Grant	1,000,000.00
Fund Campaigns Paid Pledges—1969	1,544,011.89
Current Fund Drive—Initiated 1974	102,720.26
Mildred R. Pickett Estate	1,024,406.26
Interest Earned	412,070.30
MJH Endowment Transfer	178,750.00
MJH Plant Fund Transfer	57,682.00
Miscellaneous	151,022.54
Total Available Funds	$12,470,663.25

Total Projected Costs	$14,517,744.87	
Total Available Funds	12,470,663.25	
Project Deficit	$ 2,047,081.62	

EXHIBIT 13

	Cash Uses				
Date Needed	Construction	Equipment	Interest	Total	Loan Proceeds
7-21-75	$ 7,275,243	$ 372,198	$150,000	$ 7,797,441	$4,821,304
8-20-75	300,000		19,500	319,500	198,810
9-20-75	300,000	342,263	20,750	663,013	425,628
10-20-75	300,000		22,465	322,465	198,010
11-20-75	250,000	331,123	23,270	604,393	385,110
12-20-75	250,000	42,275	24,830	317,105	193,691
1-20-76	250,000	49,323	25,614	324,937	198,361
2-20-76	200,000		26,418	226,418	132,540
3-20-76	110,000	750,000	26,955	886,955	569,922
4-20-76	125,000		29,263	154,263	82,838
5-20-76	125,000		29,598	154,598	82,838
6-20-76	125,000		29,934	154,934	82,838
7-20-76	125,000	250,000	30,269	405,269	248,513
8-20-76	120,000		31,276	151,276	79,524
9-20-76	120,000		31,598	151,598	79,524
10-20-76	115,000		31,920	146,920	76,210
11-20-76	115,000		32,228	147,220	76,210
12-20-76	100,000		32,400	132,400	67,329
1-20-77	100,000		32,400	132,400	—
	$10,405,243	$2,137,182	$650,688	$13,193,113	$8,000,000

*First draw on loan proceeds Dec. 1, 1974.

On November 1, 1976 the first monthly repayment of the HEW 22-year loan would fall due in the amount of $62,227. Since MJH was a nonprofit concern, additional revenue could be achieved by raising daily room rates. Room rates at MJH in 1975 were $68 per day, relatively low as compared with health field averages. The finance director had felt that MJH could raise its rates to as much as $90 per day. This range would have been more than adequate considering the current method of financing, using an 80 percent occupancy rate applied to a base of 232 beds.

The Funding Gap

The basic problem facing the Board was how to close the funding gap in the expansion program. Alternatives were to borrow money or to

Projected Sources and Uses for Expansion

	Cash Sources				
Hospital Funds	Endowment Interest	Pickett Fund	Hill-Burton Grant	Total	Balance (Deficit)
$2,470,237			$ 505,900	$ 7,797,441	$301,673
120,690				319,500	180,983
237,385				663,013	(56,402)
(193,045)	$ 24,000	$293,500		322,465	137,443
(5,717)			225,000	604,303	143,160
123,414				317,105	19,746
87,576	24,000	15,000		324,937	(67,830)
93,878				226,418	(151,708)
317,033				886,955	(468,741)
(236,675)	24,000	15,000	269,100	154,263	(232,066)
71,760				154,598	(303,826)
72,096				154,934	(375,922)
117,756	24,000	15,000		405,269	(493,678)
71,752				151,276	(565,430)
72,074				151,598	(637,504)
(76,665)	24,000	123,375		146,920	(560,839)
71,018				147,220	(631,857)
65,071				132,400	(696,928)
94,400	24,000	14,000		132,400	(791,328)
$3,573,238	$144,000	$475,875	$1,000,000	$13,193,113	

launch a fund drive. Neither solution appeared adequate in view of the economic climate in 1975. Interest rates were rising. The economy appeared to be slipping into a recession. Also, in 1969 MJH had a fund drive in which $1,500,000 was raised; whereas the goal had been $2,000,000.

Community Fund Drive

In early January 1975, the Board decided to pursue a recommendation of having a professional consultant study the feasibility of a campaign effort. In that same month the administrator met with a representative of Ketchum, Inc. to determine the courses of action MJH should pursue. The following recommendations were made as a result of that meeting: (1) build a prospect list, (2) determine who utilizes the hospital—business, etc., (3) create a cultivation program to educate prospects about MJH needs, and (4) hire two Ketchum personnel—staff and publicity—to implement the proposals.

A decision was also made to employ a survey director to conduct confidential interviews from March 24-April 5, 1975, with selected Board and medical staff members, local businessmen, and other prominent community leaders. The results of the survey are shown in Exhibit 14. Ketchum's distillation of the survey as written in May 1975 was that "in original discussions we were taking into consideration a capital fund-raising effort." Ketchum's report went on to say, "It became apparent in the survey that if you were to campaign now, probably the most you could raise would be $750,000 or maybe $1,000,000 against a hoped-for objective of $2,000,000." Although the timing was not right for a campaign, Ketchum still suggested that the above recommendations be implemented so as to start a hospital development program.

As a result of the May Board meeting, Ketchum, Inc. was retained to set up a hospital development program and make it a going concern. The decision as to how the $2,000,000 shortfall was to be obtained was deferred to a later date.

During the five and a half week period which ended on August 12, the Ketchum Project Director and his publicity assistant set forth the following objectives for the Development Office for 1975-76:

1. To begin to build toward a complete management information system.
2. To lay groundwork for all areas of fund-raising.

EXHIBIT 14

Campaign Survey Results—April 1975

Receptiveness of Constituency to Campaign	Yes	− 29	No	− 21	Perhaps −	9
Prospect of Attaining $2,000,000 Goal	Yes	− 21	No	− 23	Perhaps −	15
Volunteer Potential (willing to work)	Yes	− 33	No	− 23	Perhaps −	3
Volunteer Potential (willing to lead)	Yes	− 1	No	− 54	Perhaps −	4
Attitude Toward Giving	Yes	− 43	No	− 9	Perhaps −	7
Campaign Timing	Good −	3	Bad	− 26	Perhaps −	30
Community Economic Outlook	Good −	31	Bad	− 26	Level −	3

3. To maintain, expand, and refine the record keeping system, prospect lists and other techniques as they relate to development.
4. To implement cultivation activities for area-wide support of selected prospects.
5. To institute a year-end giving program.
6. To develop and implement a fund-raising program for support of present needs—including timetables for fall 1975.
7. To develop and initiate a deferred giving program.
8. To initiate a public relations program.

While their program dealt extensively with the mechanics of implementing various collection and recording processes, their major thrust was a Ketchum outline of how MJH should organize and run a community campaign. This plan was supplemented with the publicity assistant's current "case for support." This brochure gave an up-to-date accounting of MJH's service to the community and explained the hospital's need for $2,000,000. A brief explanation of the plan used prior to the campaign is given in Appendix I.

On August 4, 1975 the Ketchum Project Director presented his program to nine members of the Board (the president was absent but had been briefed) and selected guests in the monthly Board meeting. Although the Project Director's report covered the eight objectives mentioned above, the emphasis of his presentation was how MJH should run its pre-campaign activities. He had made it clear that after the cultivation period if response from prospects were not favorable, then the solicitation phase should be postponed. Although some members voiced skepticism about the success of such a campaign effort, the meeting adjourned with little debate.

Clear definition as to which course the Board should pursue was not decided at the August meeting. However, planning for the fall months had to be initiated. In late August the Director of Development met with three officers of the Board who comprised the executive committee and obtained their consent to implement the planning for the precampaign activities.

The Director of Development had joined MJH in July of 1974. Prior to this time he had had a distinguished career with the State Department. His first exposure to the systematic approach required to raise $2,000,000 was in July of 1975 when Ketchum's Project Director came to MJH. Since Ketchum would not be involved with MJH after August 12 except as an infrequent advisor, the Development Director was expected to organize and coordinate the precampaign and campaign activities. (Exhibit 15 outlines the events between September 1 and De-

EXHIBIT 15

Pre-Campaign Plan

	Sept. 1-6	Sept. 7-13	Sept. 14-20	Sept. 21-27	Sept. 28-Oct. 4	Oct. 5-11
Development and Planning Committee	3—Select 10 Candidates for Prospect Review		15—Select Members Cultivation & Public Relations Committees		3—Approve Memorial Brochure	
Prospect Review Committee		10—Orientation Choose Campaign Executive Comm. 12—Categorize Prospects	15—Categorize Prospects 18—Begin Evaluation Top 200 Prospects	22—Evaluate Prospects 25—Evaluate Prospects	29—Evaluate Prospects/ Campaign Executive Comm. 3—Select Key Prospects	7—List top 150 Prospects in Descending Order Match with Cultivation Comm.
Cultivation Committee					30—Orientation Act on Internal Hospital Program	7—Meet with Medical Staff 8—Women's Aux. 9—MJH Employees 10—MJH Employees
Campaign Executive Committee					1—Orientation Elect Chairman 3—Meet with Prospect Review Comm.	7—Solicit Each Other 8—Cultivate Top 12 Prospects

Pre-Campaign Plan

	Oct. 12-18	Oct. 19-25	Oct. 16-Nov. 1	Nov. 2-8	Nov. 9-15	Nov. 16-Dec. 6
Development & Planning Committee	13—Approve Public Relations Plan				13—Recommend Go/No Go for Campaign	
Prospect Review Committee	13—Discuss Plans for Major Gifts' Division Cultivation		27—Evaluate Major Gifts Prospects			
Cultivation Committee	Four Cultivation Meetings to be Scheduled with Prospects	Four Cultivation Meetings to be Scheduled with Prospects	Four Cultivation Meetings to be Scheduled with Prospects	Four Cultivation Meetings to be Scheduled with Prospects	Four Cultivation Meetings to be Scheduled with Prospects	1—Organize Industrial Prospects
Campaign Executive Committee	Cultivate Prospects 13-24	Cultivate Prospects 25-36	Cultivate Prospects 37-47			17—Choose Campaign Chairman 24—Organize Campaign Structure 1—Pacesetter Campaign

EXHIBIT 16

Board Membership on Precampaign Committees

Medical Staff	Executive Campaign Committee	Prospect Review Committee	Cultivation Committee	Development Committee
1	X	X	X	X
2		X	X	
3			X	
4			X	
5			X	
6			X	
Lay Members	Executive Campaign Committee	Prospect Review Committee	Cultivation Committee	Development Committee
1*	X	X	X	X
2**	X	X	X	
3	X	X	X	X
4	X	X	X	
5	X	X	X	
6			X	

*President
**Campaign Chairperson

Executive Committee 11 members
Prospect Review Committee 20 members
Cultivation Committee 25 members
Development Committee 9 members
Total members available for all committees 33

cember 6 as planned by the Development Director. Exhibit 16 shows the extent to which each Board member was involved.)

Initially the Director of Development found that although his schedule was tight, most committee members attended their meetings. However, by mid-October enthusiasm had begun to wane. Prospects who had been selected during prospect review meetings needed to be cultivated. The immediate cultivation priorities lay with the top prospects in the pacesetter division. Ketchum recommended 33; MJH had 47. These top prospects were to be cultivated by the campaign executive committee. The reason was that this committee represented the inner core of the campaign process. Their stature in the hospital and community best lent itself to the cultivation of the most prestigious prospects.

The Development Director was finding that those who had volunteered to cultivate top prospects were having to reschedule conferences to later dates. Some prospects were not being seen. Attendance at various meetings was beginning to become a problem. Very quickly the Director found that the only leverage was peer pressure. More lasting solutions had to be found. Deadlines were extended. Because of the tight schedule the prospect review committee went out of existence before it made any detailed evaluations on major prospect divisions. The development and planning committee tended to merge with the cultivation committee as some members dropped out of each.

Report meetings to evaluate pacesetter cultivation findings were rescheduled since initial conferences were postponed. Several cultivation committee members had overextended themselves in their volunteering to call on prospects. The reason other assignments were not made was that given the size of the cultivation committee, it was critical that the "right" member or members call on the "right" prospect. In the committee's judgment there was often no one else there capable of making the call.

Cultivation of pacesetters began to extend through November into December. However, the medical staff campaign was launched as scheduled on November 13. At first there was less than full endorsement. However, results of pledges as of December 6 revealed that the medical staff was firmly behind the campaign. There was every indication that they would exceed their assigned goal. Those who had not contributed indicated that they would do so by the end of the year.

During the first week of December the campaign executive committee elected a campaign chairperson. In the selection process, the nominee was in attendance at the campaign executive committee meeting. Her nomination was confirmed at the same meeting. As a member of the Board she was an influential member of the community who drew on her experience as past president of the Civic League. After having assumed her position, she evaluated what had been done by the Development Director, his secretary, and various committees. As a result she was not sure that the Ketchum approach was the best for the Charlottesville-Albemarle community.

APPENDIX I
COMMITTEE RESPONSIBILITY FOR
PRECAMPAIGN ACTIVITY

The plan prior to a campaign does not deal in any respect with solicitation of prospects. It is rather the product of coordination of the following committees: Development and Planning, Prospect Review, Cultivation, Campaign Executive, and Public Relations.

Development and Planning

This committee's function was twofold. First, it nominated those members who were to serve on other committees. Its other responsibility was to monitor and approve recommendations as made by other committees. It was further responsible for insuring existing schedules were maintained.

Prospect Review Committee

No major campaign can be conducted successfully without evaluation of potential subscribers. Evaluation is the process whereby well informed local citizens estimate the fair share which prospective donors could be expected to give. They also suggest who in their estimation is the best qualified person or persons to approach a prospect. One of the most serious dangers in a campaign is the tendency for persons to subscribe to a degree consistent with their giving to the United Way or earlier programs with substantially lower goals. In reviewing a prospect, consideration should be given to what he can give over four tax years. Because of the nature of responsibility of the Prospect Review Committee, its operations should be held in strict confidence. The review of prospects should be conducted with reference tables of standards as set forth in Exhibit 1 of the Appendix. Past experience indicates that three good prospects are necessary for one gift. The standards represented are averages which Ketchum, Inc. has found to be necessary to meet established campaign goals. The committee should decide upon a suggested amount for each prospect.

It is recommended that membership be not less than seven and not in excess of fifteen. Experience has shown that the best type of people suited for this task ought to come from the following segments: bankers, attorneys, realtors, insurance underwriters, accountants, and other civic leaders. It is important that membership include as many outside the hospital family as possible (i.e., lay members of the board).

Cultivation Committee

The Cultivation Committee is composed of segments of the hospital family, including Board, Medical Staff, and Administration, as well as

EXHIBIT 1

Standards for Giving
Goal — $2,000,000

No. Pledges	Amount	Cumulative Total	Prospects Needed	Actual MJH Prospects
1	300,000	300,000	3	2
1	150,000	450,000	3	1
1	100,000	550,000	3	0
1	75,000	625,000	3	8
2	50,000	725,000	6	12
4	25,000	825,000	12	24
5	20,000	925,000	15	
7	15,000	1,030,000	21	
10	10,000	1,130,000	30	
15	7,500	1,242,500	45	
20	5,000	1,342,500	60	
25	4,000	1,442,500	75	
35	3,000	1,547,500	105	
50	2,000	1,647,500	150	

Annual Giving would make up the balance of $352,500.

carefully selected individuals throughout the community who have no current official affiliation with the hospital. These persons would be executives of corporations and past major donors. Their responsibility is to inform prospects chosen by the prospect review committee of the needs of the hospital. They also recruit future members of their ever expanding committee as the object is to eventually meet with every prospect. No member of the committee solicits. The primary mission is to inform the community of the hospital's needs.

The Campaign Executive Committee

This committee is made up of several Board, as well as several influential, development committee members who are in charge of cultivating the top thirty-three prospects of the campaign. These persons are felt to be the most influential members of the effort. This committee also selects the campaign general chairman.

The campaign chairman should have all of the following character-istics:

1. He must be one of the most influential leaders of the community and recognized as such by the existing power and social structure.
2. He should be the president of a large corporation.
3. He should hold several directorships of other prestigious insti-tutions.
4. He must contribute a lead gift—one in excess of $100,000.
5. He must understand organizational structures and be able to delegate responsibility.

Public Relations Committee

This committee must inform the community of where the hospital has been and where it is going. The importance of a well-conceived public relations program to keep the name of the hospital before the pub-lic is one of the cornerstones of both work-up and campaign execution.

Based upon the coordinated efforts of the committees, the Develop-ment and Planning Committee is in the best position to make a recom-mendation to the Board of Trustees with regard to the implementation or postponement of a community fund drive. Were a campaign to be implemented, its organization would be structured such that there would be two divisions: pacesetters capable of donating $5,000 and up and major gifts ranging from $2,000-$5,000.

TWO

SYSTEMS ANALYSIS

*Introduction to Systems Analysis**

Management science is to the manager what bacteriology and blood chemistry are to the physician. Peter Drucker had this to say:

> There is no more reason for a manager to be a management scientist than there is for a physician to be a blood chemist or a bacteriologist. But a manager needs to know what to expect of the management sciences and how to use them as managerial tools, just as the physician needs to know what to expect of blood chemistry and bacteriology and how to use them as diagnostic tools. Few managers, so far, have acquired the skill of making the management sciences contribute to their managerial work. Few, so far, are putting these new tools to effective work.[1]

In using the management sciences the manager might take an approach similar to that taken by a physician who uses the physical sciences. Both should engage in *descriptive* and *diagnostic* activities before *prescribing* therapeutic or preventive actions. In so doing both would be (or at least should be) engaging in *systematic or systems analysis.*

The purpose of this note is to introduce the concept of systematic analysis, or systems analysis as it is often called. We will explore the place

---

*Written by Curtis J. Tompkins. Copyright ©1981 by C. J. Tompkins.
[1] Drucker, Peter F., *Management,* Harper & Row, 1973.

of quantitative methods in the overall scheme of things; most importantly we will propose that the manager can make best use of management science/quantitative methods within the context of systems analysis.

AN ANALOGY

The patient sat on the side of the examining table as the doctor concluded his preliminary examination. "Mr. Huffman," said the doctor, "the pain in your lower right abdomen is probably appendicitis. Before we operate, though, I want to have some tests performed to make sure this isn't a kidney problem. Also, I want to let a bit more time pass and take another white cell count to see if there is any significant change. Your recent anxieties about your company's financial difficulties and the Board meeting tomorrow could have induced the symptoms you have been experiencing for the past several hours."

Mr. Gene Huffman, President of Worldway Adhesives, Inc., had experienced severe abdominal pain since about 8 o'clock on the previous night. He had thought at first it was indigestion caused by the hot Mexican food he had eaten for dinner; then he was afraid he had food poisoning. Checking into the emergency room at Community Hospital, Mr. Huffman described his symptoms to the young resident physician who ran some blood and urine tests. The resident informed Mr. Huffman that the tests did not indicate food poisoning, but that a high white blood cell count did indicate the possibility of appendicitis.

As he had lain on the table in the examining room, Mr. Huffman's pain subsided somewhat. He looked at his watch and saw that it was nearly midnight. "I feel better now, Doc," he said to the resident. "I really don't think its my appendix. I've been under a lot of pressure recently, and I wonder if I might not have an ulcer. I'll just drink plenty of milk and stay away from spicy food."

But by 3:00 a.m. the pain had returned and intensified to an almost unbearable level. At 8:30 a.m., Mr. Huffman's wife delivered him to their family physician, Dr. Lindsay. By 9:30 a.m., Dr. Lindsay had considered the following possible problems in conjunction with Mr. Huffman's symptoms:

1. Appendicitis
2. Stomach Ulcer
3. Kidney Infection
4. Food Poisoning
5. Indigestion
6. Intestinal Blockage
7. Psychosomatic Causes

The doctor had talked extensively with Mr. Huffman about Huffman's corporate difficulties, the upcoming "showdown meeting" with his Board of Directors, his dietary practices, his lack of sleep and proper exercise, his habit of chain-smoking cigarettes, and many other topics.

Description, Diagnosis, Prescription

The analysis of a business problem bears similarity to the analysis performed by a medical doctor on a person who complains of some physical discomfort. In each case, the analyst needs to first gain an adequate *description* of the situation. This descriptive phase should be conducted with an awareness of the "systems" and "subsystems" involved. The medical doctor thinks in terms of physiological systems and the interrelationships among those systems. The "digestive system," the "renal (kidney) system," and the "nervous system" were all considered by Dr. Lindsay in Mr. Huffman's case.

In analyzing a business problem we might speak about the production system, the distribution system, the marketing system, the accounting system, the management control system, and so on. For example, the plant manager of a small textile fiber company was concerned about his production scheduling system. He hired a consultant to solve the "scheduling problem." The consultant, in turn, discovered that the scheduling procedures used at the plant were essentially adequate, but that there were numerous problems with the management information system, the management control system, the sales/production interface, and several other aspects of the business that were causing problems in timely shipment to customers, inventory of raw materials and production bottlenecks that generated the plant manager's concern.

Diagnosis of a case should be done on the basis of as good a description as possible. It would have been a mistake (and probably the basis of a malpractice suit!) for Dr. Lindsay to make a diagnosis regarding appendicitis in Mr. Huffman's case without having taken a white blood cell count. On the other hand, it might prove to be an even riskier managerial mistake to spend time and money to gather too much information. The patient might die from a ruptured appendix if extensive tests were undertaken before deciding to operate. This is a continual challenge to the manager: How much information is enough?

Generally, we assume that the "level of uncertainty" is reduced as more information becomes available as illustrated in Figure 1.

After descriptive and diagnostic steps have been taken, one might wish to *prescribe* actions for the future. In so doing, numerous questions

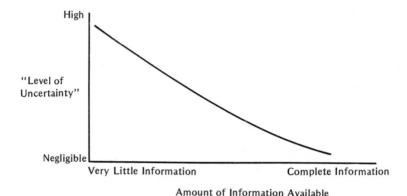

Figure 1 General Relationship Between the Level of
Uncertainty and the Amount of Available Information

should be considered, one of the most obvious of which is: Will the patterns and circumstances experienced in the past continue into the future? If we prescribe on the basis of diagnosis dealing with historical description, will the environment change enough to invalidate our prescription? In many prescriptive situations, the manager should *anticipate* what future circumstances will be.

SYSTEMS AND SUBSYSTEMS

Three management analysts viewed a business corporation as follows:

Analyst 1: As is the case with most companies, this company (system) is composed of the following subsystems:
a. Marketing Subsystem
b. Finance and Accounting Subsystems
c. Production Subsystem
d. Engineering Subsystem

Analyst 2: It's best to forget departmental distinctions and think about the company as being composed of the following subsystems:
a. Management Systems
(1) Planning Subsystem
(2) Control Subsystem
(3) Information Subsystem
b. Client/Customer Systems

c. Supplier/Vendor Systems
d. Stockholder Systems
e. Employee Systems

Analyst 3: I prefer to view the company as a multidimensional matrix that incorporates both of the previous viewpoints. The way one looks at subsystems depends on what one is trying to do. For example:

Dimension 1 (Traditional)

a. Production
b. Marketing
c. Finance

d. Accounting
e. Engineering
f. Personnel

Dimension 2 (Management Subsystems)

a. Planning
   1. Policy Formulation
   2. Operational Planning
b. Control
c. Evaluation
d. Information

Dimension 3 (Constituent–Oriented)

a. Stockholders
b. Directors
c. Management
d. Employees
e. Customers

f. Suppliers
g. Bankers
h. Competitors
i. General Public

There are usually several ways of analyzing a system. It is sometimes helpful to analyze a system more than one way, thereby gaining insight into the total system.

Mayor John Lindsay of New York City was concerned about the complaints his office had been receiving about the emergency ambulance services in his city in 1966 and 1967; he asked one of his staff members to develop proposals for improving the emergency ambulance services provided by the city. In looking at previous work done on the management of the ambulance system, the staff members found that the following components of the system had been identified:

1. Doctors
2. Nurses
3. Drivers

4. Mechanics
5. Dispatchers
6. Police

7. Hospitals
8. Attendants
9. Ambulances

The staff member in turn viewed the emergency ambulance system as being composed of three major subsystems:

1. The Communication Subsystem
2. The Transportation Subsystem
3. The Medical Treatment Subsystem

With this as the basis of a rather extensive analysis, the staff member eventually recommended major changes in the organization and operation of the ambulance service.[2]

THE CLASSICAL STEPS OF ANALYSIS

In one of the most cited references on systems analysis,[3] E. S. Quade points out that there is no single methodology for systems analysis for "systems analysis is still largely a form of art." An art can be taught in part, but not by means of fixed rules which need only to be followed with exactness. Realizing that each systems analysis must be tailored to the specific situation being analyzed, we might borrow Graeme Taylor's conceptual framework for systematic analysis[4] as follows:

Analytic Step
1. Define Problem(s)
   a. Issue(s)
   b. Scope
   c. Viewpoint
2. State Objectives and Measures of Effectiveness
3. Generate Alternatives
4. Construct Model(s)
   a. Assumptions Stated
   b. Description of Relationships
   c. Constraints
5. Gather Data
6. Compute (For example, Cost/Benefit and Cost/Effectiveness Calculations, Return on Investment and Payback, Market Share, Earnings, etc.)

[2] Savas, E.S., "Simulation and Cost-Effectiveness Analysis of New York's Emergency Ambulance Service," *Management Science*, Vol. 15, No. 12, August 1969, pp. B-608-627.
[3] Quade, E.S., *Systems Analysis Techniques for Planning-Programming-Budgeting*, RAND Corporation Report, March 1966, p. 3322.
[4] Hinrichs, H. and Graeme M. Taylor, *Systematic Analysis*, Goodyear Publishing, 1973.

7. Test results
8. Consider "Non-quantifiable Factors"
9. Reformulate Problem
10. Return to step 1 and continue cycle until satisfied; then go to step 11.
11. Interpret and Communicate Conclusions

E. S. Quade[5] presents a slightly different version of the iterative systems and analytic approach as follows:

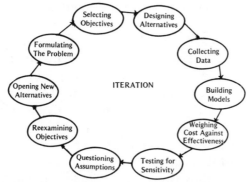

In practice there is no clearcut distinction of the steps in the actual analysis; the important thing to understand, however, is that there is a general scheme of analysis which can be followed and which does lead from the problem formulation through the communication of conclusions. All too often there is a tendency to jump right into steps 3 and 6 without adequate attention to steps 1 and 2. The "discipline" involved in systems analysis is certainly an important aspect of the approach. At the same time, it should be a creative process.

PROBLEMS, SYMPTOMS, CAUSES

Deciding what the problem really is can be one of the most challenging aspects of a systems analysis, especially when the system being analyzed is fairly complex. It is usually helpful to distinguish, to the extent possible, between "symptoms" and problems and between problems and causes of those problems. Further, the manager searches for "leading indicators" to forewarn him (or her) that a problem may

[5] Quade, op. cit.

emerge in the future. The American Cancer Society has publicized the "Seven Warning Signs of Cancer" and has implicitly warned that it would be fallacious to treat one of these seven symptoms without realizing that the underlying problem might be cancer.

A small company, founded in 1972, experienced an operating deficit during each of the first ten quarters of operation. The president of the company complained quarterly to the Directors that the company had always been undercapitalized, and he requested injections of new capital each quarter to make up the operating deficit. Of course, the Directors complained to the president about the continuing operating deficit. During the first year, the Directors readily accepted the quarterly operating deficits as a "fact of life" during a start up operation. During the second year, the Directors indicated increasing disappointment with the president's performance; whereas the Directors initially had viewed the operating deficit as a problem to be expected, they eventually began to interpret the deficit as a *symptom* of an underlying problem. Now, directors quickly tire of having to treat symptoms; in fact, they generally dislike having to deal with the same problem more than once. Furthermore, in the case of the small company, it became more difficult to raise new capital as the enthusiasm of stockholders, potential stockholders and bankers was diluted by the continuing operating deficit. At the end of the second year, the directors decided to hire a new president; an objective was established for the new president: to achieve an operating *surplus* by the end of the second quarter of his tenure as president.

Again, distinguishing among symptoms, problems and causes can be difficult. Yet, it is vital to the development of action plans for the manager to carefully make the distinction. A bad cough may be only a momentary minor problem or it may be a symptom of some other problem. The possible *causes* of the cough or of the underlying problem could be air pollution, excessive smoking, or an allergy.

A good manager is not in the business of treating symptoms. He *is* in the business of preventing problems or satisfactorily solving problems when they occur. Understanding the cause-effect relationships in a business system can make the difference between excellent and mediocre management.

Whose Point of View?

How one defines the problem in a systems analysis often depends on the point of view taken. A few years ago, the Bureau of National Capital Airports addressed the question of how the three major airports in the Washington-Baltimore area could be coordinated better. In viewing changes in the operations of the Washington National, Dulles International, and Friendship (Baltimore) Airports, one needed to recognize several categories of "constituents" including:

1. Congressmen
2. FAA
3. Local Governments in the Area
4. Businessmen
5. Tourists
6. General Public
7. Local Transportation Authorities (including the one responsible for the planned Metro subway system).

To allocate more flights to Dulles in order to relieve the heavy traffic into National Airport was not favorably viewed by certain influential constituencies of the Bureau of National Capital Airports. To expand the capacity of Washington National Airport was not favorably viewed by certain other constituencies. What was a problem to one was not viewed as a problem by another.

GOALS, OBJECTIVES AND MEASURES OF PERFORMANCE

An *objective* should be specific, measurable, and realistically attainable. It should be stated in terms of a time scale; that is, when it is to be achieved. In most managerial situations, an objective should also be challenging. These are five criteria a good statement of an objective should satisfy. Unfortunately, in practice one can find numerous examples of so-called objectives which do not satisfy these five criteria.

The manager of a District in the U.S. Postal Service asked the 12 managers of Sectional Center Facilities (SCF) reporting to him to develop statements of operating objectives for the next fiscal year. He was concerned when all 12 managers responded with objectives typified by the following examples:

"To increase our customers' satisfaction during the year."
"To reduce sick leave as much as possible."

In the New York Emergency Ambulance System the objectives and output measures initially formulated by the staff analyst were as follows:

For the Communication Subsystem:

Objective: To allocate scarce emergency care resources on the basis of degree of need, and as rapidly as possible.

Output Measures: Time from receipt of call to dispatch of aid.
                    Number of nonemergency calls mistakenly treated as emergencies.

Assumptions: That the seriousness of an "emergency" can, to some extent, be determined other than by the physical presence of a trained medical person.

For the Transportation Subsystem:

Objective: Place the victim under professional medical care as safely and as rapidly as possible.
                    To administer necessary emergency aid at the scene.

Output Measures: Response time (i.e., from dispatch to arrival on the scene).
                    Round trip time (i.e., from dispatch to delivery at medical facility).
                    Lives saved by emergency first-aid.
                    Reduction in accidents caused by ambulances themselves.

Assumptions: That saving lives is related to the speed with which the victim gets professional medical care.

For the Medical Treatment Subsystem:

Objective: To render timely and appropriate medical treatment to all victims.

Output Measures: Extent to which patients must wait for "appropriate" treatment.
                    Extent to which patients must be transferred to other facilities to obtain treatment.
                    Ideally, effectiveness of medical treatment rendered in reducing suffering and saving lives.

Assumptions: That "appropriate" treatment is a function of manpower, procedures, and facilities, and can be defined for any malady.

That delay in treatment is in some way related
to the patient's chance for survival.

The foregoing "objectives" are actually goals of the ambulance system.
The confusion between what is a goal and what is an objective is widespread in practice and in literature. Often it doesn't really make much
difference what one calls the statement as long as it satisfies the five
criteria we mentioned earlier, i.e., an objective is:

1. Measurable   4. Challenging
2. Specific   5. On a Time Scale
3. Attainable

From a management point of view if one cannot measure accomplishment, it is difficult to manage a system effectively. The question of
measurement in management is an interesting one. In practice widespread examples can be found of misleading, inappropriate, or inadequate measures being employed by managers. Current profitability and
cost measures may be inadequate; especially in service organizations,
one needs to have other types of measures of performance.
Categories of measures include the following:

1. Profit-Related   5. Efficiency
2. Input (e.g. expenditures)   6. Productivity
3. Output (e.g. services or   7. Benefits
       products produced)   8. Net Worth-Related
4. Effectiveness (relative to 9. Customer Satisfaction
       objectives)   10. Market Share

To focus on a subset of these categories of measures while ignoring
the remainder could be myopic. Of course the usual difficulty is that
data are not readily available or easily attainable to allow employment
of some of these categories of measures. To use this as an alibi for not attempting measurement of performance should, as a general principle, be
unacceptable to the manager. Realistically, what one frequently must
do is to seek "indicators" in lieu of "exact measures." For example, it
may be very difficult to measure customer satisfaction with precision,
and one may in fact not want to "measure" customer satisfaction anyway. Surrogate indicators of customer satisfaction may include profitability, sales or market share: one may desire to perform a survey of a
sample of customers to gain better insight into the level of satisfaction.

Quantitative Analysis

Within the context of systems analysis, quantitative analysis usually plays a role primarily in constructing models, gathering data, and computing (i.e., steps 4, 5, and 6 in the systems analysis cycle presented on page 68). Yet the purview of management science is the full scope of the systems analytic approach. While we will focus on particular quantitative methods in this chapter, this does *not* mean that management science in practice is highly restricted or myopic. It certainly does not have to be.

The "artistic side" of management science resides mostly in problem definition, generation of alternatives, and construction of models. Indeed, the manager's role in problem definition and generation of alternatives should be equal to that of the management scientist in most cases. Knowledge of the problem environment and understanding the potential and the limitations of a system are assets the manager should bring to the systems analysis effort.

The subjective judgment and intuition of the manager, continually improved and sharpened through experience, are always important in the world of practical affairs. The manager who understands systems analysis and management science will have some powerful supplements to his judgment and intuition; the synergism between judgment/intuition and management science/systems analysis can produce increasingly higher levels of sophisticated decision-making ability.

REFERENCES

1. Blumstein, A. and R. C. Larson, "A Systems Approach to the Study of Crime and Criminal Justice," in *Operations Research for Public Systems,* P.M. Morse and L.W. Bacon, eds., Chapter 7, MIT Press, 1968.
2. Chacko, G.K., ed., *The Recognition of Systems in Health Services,* Operations Research Society of America, 1969.
3. Churchman, C.W., *The Systems Approach,* Dell Publishing, 1968.
4. Cleland, D. and W. King, *Systems Analysis and Project Management,* McGraw-Hill, 1971.
5. deNeufville, R. and J.H. Stafford, *Systems Analysis for Engineers and Managers,* McGraw Hill, 1971.
6. *Emergency Ambulance Service (A) & (B),* ICH 13C25 and 13C26, Intercollegiate Case Clearing House, Soldiers Field, Boston.
7. Forrester, J.W., *Industrial Dynamics,* MIT Press, Cambridge, 1961.

8. Hoos, I.R., *Systems Analysis in Public Policy*, University of California Pr., Berkeley, 1972.

9. *Note on Systems Approach*, 9-670-028, Intercollegiate Case Clearing House, Soldiers Field, Boston, 1970.

10. *Note on Systems Concepts*, 9-669-013, Intercollegiate Case Clearing House, Soldiers Field, Boston, 1969.

11. Sheldon, A., F. Baker, and C.P. McLaughlin, eds., *Systems and Medical Care*, MIT Pr., 1970.

12. Tilles, S., "The Manager's Job—A Systems Approach," *Harvard Business Review*, January-February 1963.

13. Van Court, Hare, Jr., *Systems Analysis: A Diagnostic Approach*, Harcourt Brace and World, 1967.

14. White, H.J., and S. Tauber, *Systems Analysis*, W.B. Saunders Company, 1969.

Case 4

Morgantown Sanitation Department*

Morgantown's sanitation department had been incurring deficits of around $30,000 a year during the past two years of operations. A proposal from the Finance Committee of City Council would increase the sanitation fees by 30 percent to recoup the financial losses of the sanitation department.

After passing a first ordinance reading, a public hearing was scheduled concerning the sanitation rate increase. At the hearing, many of the community's older citizens appeared and urged the council to vote against the proposal. They stressed that their budgets could not withstand such an increase in sanitation fees. The number of citizens attending council and their impressive arguments led the city council to reject the Finance Committee ordinance on its second reading.

Subsequent to council action, the Mayor began to take a look at the options available to the city to put the sanitation department back on a sound financial basis. It was apparent that the costs of the sanitation department must be reduced. He asked the sanitation department director, Chris Bond, to meet with him to discuss reduction options.

The Mayor invited Kelly McClain, an industrial engineering senior at West Virginia University, to attend the meeting since his intentions

*Case written by Jack Byrd, Jr. and Curtis J. Tompkins, Department of Industrial Engineering, West Virginia University. Copyright © Jack Byrd, Jr. and Curtis J. Tompkins, 1978.

were to assign her to the problem of the Sanitation Department for a while to help determine what costs could be reduced.

MEETING WITH THE SANITATION
DEPARTMENT DIRECTOR

The Mayor began the meeting by introducing McClain and explaining her function as student intern in the Mayor's office. He then asked Chris Bond to describe any problems related to cost reduction.

Bond responded by detailing how his labor costs had increased over the past years as sanitation workers gained large wage settlements. He indicated that the costs of garbage collection itself constituted approximately 75 percent of the total costs of the sanitation department. "If we could reduce our labor costs we should be able to alleviate our budget deficits."

The Mayor then asked, "What suggestions do you have, Chris, for reducing labor costs?"

"Mayor, there are two things that we could do to reduce our costs right away. First, we could have council pass an ordinance which would require citizens to place their cans next to the curb on collection days. We could save some time by not having to go to the rear of the building to collect the garbage. We could also reduce our costs considerably by having collections only one day a week instead of two as we now have."

"Chris, you realize that both of those suggestions are going to run into a lot of criticism from city council."

"Yes, I know, Mayor, but I'm at a loss as to what else I can do."

"That's why I've asked Kelly to work with you on this problem. Kelly, would you take two weeks to review the operations of the sanitation department and let me know what we should do on this problem?"

"Fine, Mayor, but could I ask about the ground rules first? I know that the sanitation workers have a union. Do you want me to consider options which may violate the current union contract?"

"You're free to consider any options that you want to. We are going to bargain a lot harder this year and we're going to need all the information we can get."

INITIAL INVESTIGATIONS

McClain began her study by reviewing the records kept by the sanitation department. The record keeping at the disposal sites was fairly detailed and consisted of the time that each truck came to the site and the tonnage of waste disposed. From this data McClain obtained information on the present workload of each of the trucks.

McClain also reviewed the data that was available from the sanitation department's billing records. From this data, she found that information on the number of families along each route could be determined. In addition, data could be obtained on the number of dwellings to be collected from on each street.

Data was also available on the present routes in use, the number of trucks assigned to each area, and the number of workers on each truck. In general, neighborhood blocks formed the basis of the routes with one truck being assigned to each of the city's seven wards.

McClain reviewed the union contract to identify the restrictions placed on work practices, and found that they pertained to the number of helpers per truck (five plus a driver), and the realignment of routes. The contract specified that a minimum number of helpers should be assigned to each truck. In addition the contract restricted the number of route realignments to one a year. In general sanitation workers opposed route realignments since it took them time to learn the new routes and their jobs took longer.

McClain also spent two days travelling with sanitation trucks to see the collection operations first hand. While there was initial union opposition to such observation, Bond met with the union leaders and gained their approval. At first the laborers who McClain observed grudgingly accepted her observations and questions. As the observation period continued they began to use the opportunity to air their gripes and make suggestions on how service could be improved. They also liked the publicity that arose from an article in the Morgantown newspaper: "Female Observer Rides With Garbage Trucks." During her observations, McClain took some time studies to gain a rough idea of the times required to do different operations.

After gathering the initial data and insights into the problem, McClain began an analysis of the problem. One of the first phases of this analysis consisted of an analysis of the distribution of workload between the different trucks. McClain discovered that seven trucks were employed. The routes were determined according to the ward boundaries. Since each ward had the same population, the Sanitation Department felt that routes determined by ward boundaries would be adequate.

Using the data collected from the disposal sites McClain summarized the workloads being experienced by each truck. Table 1 shows the average times that each truck finished its assignment as a function of the

Table 1   Average Completion Times
(Times in hours and minutes)

Truck	Monday	Tuesday	Wednesday	Thursday	Friday	Weekly Average Per Truck
1	1:29*	1:43	2:01	1:15	1:32	1:36
2	2:52	3:10	3:20	2:57	2:45	3:01
3	2:01	1:46	2:22	2:07	2:16	2:06
4	1:26	1:43	2:06	2:04	2:12	1:54
5	2:21	2:33	2:42	2:16	2:32	2:29
6	1:45	2:16	2:07	2:08	2:10	2:05
7	1:32	1:42	1:07	1:21	1:44	1:29
Daily Average	1:55	2:08	2:15	2:01	2:10	
Idle Time	1:35	1:22	1:15	1:29	1:20	

*One hour, twenty-nine minutes

day of the week. As shown in the table, there was considerable variation in the route assignments.

Truck 2, the busiest, completed its collections nearly an hour and a half after Truck 7. The total idle time for the trucks was also found to be approximately seven hours.

Viewing these initial findings McClain concluded that substantial savings could be obtained if the routes were realigned. In order to test alternative routes, however, she concluded that some measure of workload was necessary. Thus if one area of the city were added to a different truck, there should be a way of measuring the impact of this on the workload.

McClain went to one of the professors in Sanitary Engineering to see if she could find previous studies which measured workloads for solid waste collection. She found that the national average was seven pounds of waste per capita for residential, commercial, and general municipal solid waste. However, there was such a variation in this amount that it was impractical for use in route determination. The professor suggested that she sample some of the routes and develop a prediction model for the amount of waste generated. He gave her some reports of studies in which waste amounts were predicted.

Upon study of the previous reports McClain found that the procedures used in these other areas would be of little use. Most of the studies contained prediction models which related waste amounts to the number of families, number of stops, family incomes, and persons per household. In order to use such models, information would be necessary on each of the model parameters for each area of the city. Collecting such data seemed to be impossible and too costly. The only alternative to workload predictions seemed to be actual data collection on the amount of waste generated. McClain wondered if samples could be taken in similar sections of the city.

With a tentative method for finding workloads, McClain next turned to the problem of how to evaluate alternative cost reduction ideas. Different route realignments could be found by taking the workloads for each neighborhood unit and assigning these to different routes according to some prescribed process. However, the actual collection of solid waste was only one part of the total collection effort. From her experience observing the actual trucks, McClain formulated an equation for the total time to cover a route.

$$T = T_{CD} + T_E + T_{TS} + T_{TB} + T_{TDS} + T_B$$

Where T = total time to cover a route, T_{CD} = time to collect and return cans once empty, T_E = time to empty the cans into the truck, T_{TS} = time to travel between stops, T_{TB} = time to travel from one block to the next, T_{TDS} = time to travel to the disposal site and return, and T_B = time at the beginning of the day to start up.

This equation would allow the evaluation of different alternatives. In developing route realignments the value of T could be used to evaluate the uniformity among routes as well as the amount of idle time for a route. In evaluating the consequences of curb pickup only (i.e. families must place their garbage next to the street), the value of T_{CD} could be adjusted to reflect the different time to collect and return the cans. The consequences of once-a-week collections as opposed to twice-a-week collections could be found by adjusting the values to T_E since more cans must be emptied. Once-a-week collections would also result in more frequent trips to the disposal site.

Data would have to be collected on the different elements of the cost formula. This aspect of the analysis left McClain with doubts as to the amount of effort the Mayor and the sanitation department were willing to put into such a study. She decided at this point to ask to meet with the Mayor and Chris Bond again.

SECOND MEETING WITH THE SANITATION DEPARTMENT
DIRECTOR AND THE MAYOR

At the second meeting, Kelly McClain began by describing her activities investigating the problem assigned to her. She then showed the Mayor and Chris Bond her findings on the completion times currently being experienced by the trucks. While the Mayor seemed to be surprised by the results, Chris Bond indicated little dismay at the findings.

"I've felt that this has been the case but I didn't have the facts to back up my beliefs. You see, I've had to generate those route assignments by hand and it takes so long to figure one out that I'm generally stuck with it. I know that I could make improvements in the assignments but I just don't have the time."

"I understand your problem, Chris," said the Mayor. "How much savings do you think we could get if Kelly could develop a quicker procedure for route assignments?"

McClain interjected at this point. "According to my calculations there is at least seven hours of idle time. When you consider lunch breaks that means that one truck could probably be eliminated for one day."

"Wait, Kelly, you're forgetting something," responded Chris Bond. "If you eliminated one truck, you would be pushing all the trucks to the limit as far as the workday is concerned. What happens if we experience increases in solid waste collections? We're going to start paying for a lot of overtime. Also don't forget that we have to hire people for a five-day week. We just don't have the flexibility to hire like you suggest."

"I agree with you, Chris," said the Mayor. "But doesn't this analysis give us some indication of where we can achieve some savings?"

"Yes, it does. Just let me say that if Kelly could just find a quicker way for evaluating route assignments that would be of great help to me. I think that I might be able to reduce the overall route times by 10 percent. That would give us even more idle time and we might be able to reassign some of our men to those special collection problems where in the past we have used overtime. Although there is some idle time now, we really need a truck for a full day for these jobs. I would also like to know if we could perhaps eliminate extra helpers on some of our routes. I know that we're going to face some union pressure to keep them on but I think normal attrition will permit us to reduce our work force without any layoffs."

When Bond was finished, McClain took the opportunity to explain her proposed solution to the problem. She presented her equation for determining the total time to cover a route and illustrated how the different alternatives could be tested. Chris Bond's suggestion on reducing extra helpers on some routes could be reflected in the calculation of the times to pick up the cans, empty them into the truck, and return them once empty. The Mayor and Chris Bond seemed to agree with the approach, but the Director brought up the important question.

"Kelly, I'm certain you realize that the data for your equation doesn't exist. How are you going to get the data?"

McClain responded, "The data collection problem is the main reason I wanted to meet with you and the Mayor. I've outlined on this form (Exhibit 1) the data that we will need for each block. I know that this is a large amount of data to ask for, but I don't think we will get the information we need without this amount of data. With twice a week collections, we should be able to get eight samples on each block in a month. I believe that should be accurate enough data for our purposes. I would think that the truck driver could collect the data if the union would permit this."

"Chris, what do you think?" asked the Mayor.

"As you know, Mayor, the union contract places the driver in a supervisory role, and for this we have agreed to extra compensation for the driver. It seems to me that data collection is an appropriate task to ask of our drivers. We have a prior precedent for this if you remember the time we asked them to collect data on the number of cans our trucks were holding with the new compaction device we were thinking about buying. In fact, that's what initiated the extra compensation feature in the last contract. I'm sure they won't like it, but I don't think they have any options."

"Chris, what about the amount of data and the length of time it will take to collect it?" asked the mayor.

"I'll have to defer to Kelly's judgment on that. I will say this, it does give us valuable information that we have wanted for years," replied Bond.

"Well, Kelly, everything looks okay," the Mayor responded. "Is that all the data you will need?"

"We also have to find travel times from one block to another and from each block to the disposal site. But I think we can collect those from the city map using an assumption about the travel speed of the trucks. My guess is that the time from one block to another will be fairly constant for most of the route alternatives."

"What about personnel requirements?" asked the Mayor.

"We're going to need clerical support to summarize the data and prepare it for computer processing. I can do the computer programming. I imagine that we will need one clerk for a month. The computer costs

EXHIBIT 1

Route _____   No. of Helpers _____   Day _____

Block	No. of Cans Collected	No. of Stops Made	No. of Households	Time for Total Block Collection

will probably be $500 to both process the data and develop the route reallignment model."

"Before I give the go ahead on this project," said the Mayor, "I'm going to have to know what the potential savings are. Chris, do you think we'll be able to cut your costs enough to warrant the project?"

"Mayor, I don't know how to answer that question," responded Bond. "Route reallignment will help us be more equitable in work assignments, but the cost savings in terms of reduced manpower may be small. I see the value of the project to be mostly that it gives us better ways to manage our resources. When the labor contract expires, it should give us a powerful bargaining tool in issues such as the minimum crew size. In addition, we may be able to convince City Council on the desirability of once-a-week collections. While I can't give you a numerical value, I'd say the potential savings far outweigh the costs."

"All right, Kelly, you're free to pursue the project. Keep us abreast of what happens. Chris, I'm giving you the responsibility to see that the data is collected. Kelly, I'll assign one of our clerks from the general office pool to work with you."

DATA COLLECTION AND MODEL DEVELOPMENT

After initial negative reactions from the union, data collection procedures were established. Because of suspicions that some of the data might be biased, Chris Bond gave his top supervisor, who was a former driver, the job of seeing that the data was reasonable.

McClain spent a week writing programs to summarize the data and researching models which could be used in identifying optimal routes.

The dimensions of the problem and its peculiarities seemed to limit the use of any of the conventional network procedures. Frustrated and concerned about the future of the project, McClain visited her industrial engineering professor. He suggested that she follow an heuristic approach; that is, she should try to develop some procedure which would give good answers in a reasonable period of time even though they may not be optimal. Before getting more specific, he suggested that she read an article entitled "Models and Managers: The Concept of a Decision Calculus" by John D.C. Little.[1]

[1] Little, John D. C., "Models and Managers: The Concept of a Decision Calculus," *Management Science*, Volume 16, April 1970, pp. B-466 to B-485.

Upon reading the article, McClain gained a different perspective on the type of model she needed. The key aspects of the decision calculus concept as Kelly perceived it were that the model should update a "manager's intuition" not replace it and the model should be "an extension of his ability to think about and analyze his operation."[2] Thus, instead of developing a model which would attempt to optimize route assignments, McClain felt that she should build a model which would take route assignments generated by the Sanitation Department director and from this model the total time required could be calculated. With the director's wealth of experience in route assignments, it seemed unlikely that a model could be built which would generate better assignments than the director when all of the real-life complications were taken into account. Even if such a model could be developed, it would probably be very costly and time consuming to build. Using Little's concept, McClain developed a flowchart of the logic to be used in the model (Exhibit 2).

McClain returned to talk with her professor and show him her tentative model. His general reaction was that the model seemed to be appropriate. He cautioned her to work closely with the sanitation department director to insure that the model would possess the language and structure to be readily usable.

Taking this advice, McClain next scheduled a meeting with Chris Bond to explain her procedure. While Bond was unfamiliar with model development, he was able to understand the flowchart which McClain showed him since the process closely resembled the actual collection procedure. He was hesitant about using the time-sharing terminal but seemed willing to try to use it as the procedure required.

With the data summarization programs developed, McClain began to write the program for the model. The data collection effort continued without undue problems, and McClain trained the clerk to use the programs to summarize the data. At the end of the fourth week, complete data summaries were developed and converted into input for the route assignment model.

VALIDATION OF THE MODEL
AND INITIAL RESULTS

In order to validate the model, McClain used the current conditions as a test. The test was run for a sample of days and trucks as shown in Table 2.

[2] *Ibid*, p. B-469.

EXHIBIT 2
Route Assignment Evaluation Model Logic

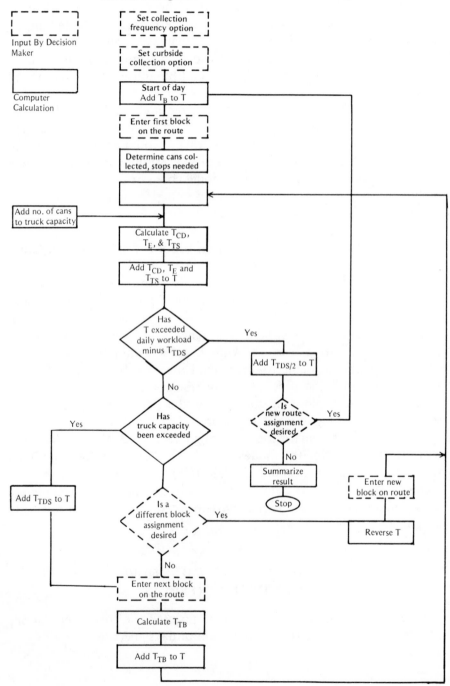

Table 2   Validation of the Model
(Time in hours and minutes)

Test Conditions	Model Prediction for Completion Time	Observed Completion Time	Difference
Truck 1 Monday	1:42*	1:29	0:13
Truck 3 Wednesday	1:58	2:22	−0:24
Truck 6 Friday	1:42	2:10	−0:28
Truck 4 Tuesday	2:01	1:43	0:18
Truck 2 Thursday	2:54	2:57	0:03

*One hour, forty-two minutes

The results of the model were encouraging since none was more than a half-hour in error from the observed conditions. It was also noted that both positive and negative conditions were observed. Thus, it didn't appear that the model had any biases to either under- or over-estimate the total route times.

With the model displaying a reasonable amount of accuracy, McClain scheduled a meeting with Chris Bond to show him the procedure. In order to test his understanding of the model, McClain worked with him on generating a route for which there was currently significant idle time. As blocks were assigned to the route, they were checked off on a master sheet and the route was recorded as it was being developed. This initial test, conducted on the Monday-Truck 1 route gave estimated completion time of 3:02. Although a better improvement in idle time could have been obtained, Bond and McClain decided that half an hour should be left as a safety margin to avoid extensive overtime which might have developed if tighter assignments were made. This initial assignment procedure took approximately 25 minutes with extensive questions and delays as Bond began to understand the process.

Subsequent assignments were made for truck number 1 for the remaining days of the week. The Friday assignment took only 10 minutes as Bond became more proficient in the process. Also as the process continued, Bond began to see how substantial time savings could be achieved by going beyond the ward boundaries. The model seemed to meet Bond's needs and expectations, and he readily accepted the process as a means for investigating cost reduction programs.

APPLICATION OF THE MODEL

With the initial operational success of the model, Bond with McClain's assistance, began to test some of the alternatives for cost reduction. While his initial route realignment effort alleviated the need for a truck on one day a week, he felt that even greater reductions could be made if he were to reapply the same process. With greater insights into the re-alignment process, Bond developed a new set of route assignments which deviated from conventional ward boundaries. This new alignment of routes allowed for the completion of the total collection without the use of three trucks for one day. From past experience, Bond felt that these trucks would be capable of handling all of the special collections during the year.

With an average wage of $4 per hour, the savings on special collections were estimated to be $2 per hour. During the past years, there had been an average of 1256 hours of special collections. Since the volume of special collections did not seem to be on the increase, Bond estimated the savings to be:

Annual Savings = $2/hour $\times$ 1256 hours/year = $2512/year

While the projected savings were encouraging they did not contribute significantly to the department's overall budget deficit. With the annual increase in collection quantitites from the newer areas of the city, the realignment would probably delay the need for a new truck for another two years; however, the current budget deficit remained a problem.

In order to achieve greater savings, Bond asked McClain if there was a way to test the effect of reduced helpers on each truck. Since this option had been developed into the model, McClain altered the formulas for calculating T_{CD} and T_E to reflect the decrease of one helper per hour. Bond proceeded to realign the routes with the new manpower level.

The new assignment which was generated gave a very tight time schedule for each truck to complete its route prior to the 3:30 p.m. quitting time. The incidence of overtime was considered very likely under this plan. In order to evaluate the savings from this plan, the savings from the reduction of seven helpers was calculated to be:

Annual Savings = 7 helpers $\times$ $6400/helper = $44,800

However, from this savings had to be subtracted the annual increase in overtime necessitated by the tighter schedules. To determine this, McClain took the current completion times of each truck and found the distribution of completion times above and below the mean as shown in Figure 1.

McClain then found a mathematical relationship for the variation and using probability theory developed a formula for the expected overtime costs. From this relationship, the overtime costs were estimated. Thus the total estimated savings would be $44,800 — $5,200 = $39,600.

While the elimination of extra helpers on each route would meet the sanitation department's budget deficit, this alternative would undoubtedly meet union resistance. The city had unwisely agreed upon a fixed number of helpers in the previous union agreement. To implement such a policy would require a new agreement when the contract expired in three months. On the plus side of this issue, however, was the increased overtime for the employees who were retained. With a fairly high turnover each year in employees, it was felt that the reduction of helpers could be accommodated through attrition rather than by firings. With the acceptability of this alternative in mind, Bond asked McClain to help him evaluate the savings if collections were made strictly from curbside locations.

To test this alternative, the value of T_{CD} was reduced. The amount of reduction was estimated to be 60 percent as identified from the time studies which McClain had taken during her initial observation period. Route assignments were again made under these changed conditions. The result of this process was a reduction in the need for one truck with

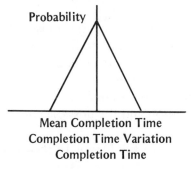

Probability

Mean Completion Time
Completion Time Variation
Completion Time

Figure 1   Distribution of Completion Times

little need for overtime on the other routes. The estimated savings for this alternative were:

One driver (supervisor)	$ 7,500
Four helpers @ $6,400	25,600
Fuel, maintenance of truck	5,000
Miscellaneous expenses	2,000
Total Savings	$ 40,100

It was assumed that the truck would not be sold but used as a back-up vehicle for other trucks as they undergo maintenance. The savings from the alternative would help alleviate the budget deficit but the operational changes to bring about curbside deliveries faced strong opposition in city council.

The alternative of once-a-week collections was the next cost reduction program to be investigated. It was assumed that the number of cans to be collected would double and the value of T_E would double. The value of T_{CD} was also adjusted to reflect the increased number of cans to be collected. The route assignment process was reapplied with only single collections required each week.

The result of this program was the reduction of trucks needed to four. The estimated savings were:

Three drivers (supervisor)	$ 22,500
Twelve helpers @ $6400	76,800
Fuel, maintenance of trucks	15,000
Miscellaneous expenses	6,000
Salvage (two trucks)	10,000
Total Savings	$130,300

While this alternative contained the most attractive cost savings, it was considered the most difficult to implement politically. Similar suggestions had been made in surrounding communities and had been soundly rejected by their citizens.

With this final alternative evaluated, McClain prepared a report for the Mayor on each option and the possible consequences of that option as shown in Table 3.

The report was given to the Mayor to read and a third meeting was scheduled.

Table 3   Evaluation of Different Alternatives

Alternative	Dollar Savings
1. Better Alignment of Routes	$ 2,512/year
2. Reduce Helpers on Each Truck	39,600
3. Curbside Collection	40,100
4. Once-a-Week Collection	$130,300

THIRD MEETING WITH THE SANITATION DEPARTMENT DIRECTOR AND THE MAYOR

The Mayor began the meeting by complimenting Kelly McClain and Chris Bond on the degree of cooperation which they displayed in this project. He then continued: "Of course you realize that we are going to have some strong opposition to each of these proposals. While the first alternative faces the least amount of opposition, it doesn't give us the amount of savings that we really need. If we decide upon any of the other alternatives, we must have the strong backing of city council. Any reduction in the current labor force will probably precipitate a strike or at least the threat of one. Chris, what do you think is our best option?

"I'm hesitant to make a commitment. The first alternative doesn't help us much, and I'm certain that City Council won't go along with the fourth alternative. However, we can use the fourth alternative in our bargaining sessions with the union. As for the second and third alternatives, they are nearly equal in cost savings. I know that council representatives of wards with larger percentages of elderly persons will object strenuously that we are placing their citizens under an extreme burden. On the other hand, the union will probably give us more trouble on the second alternative. I really don't know which one is best."

"Kelly, do you have any thoughts on which alternative is best?" asked the Mayor.

"One aspect of the analysis that I think we have to consider is the future growth in collection requirements and how they will be solved. The alternative of curbside collection seems to give the greatest flexibility for the future. Our analysis showed that the reduction of one helper pushed us to the limit as far as work scheduling was concerned. With small increases in collection quantitites, we'll have to start hiring additional helpers and I'm afraid that we will be in the same situation again as we are now. We still have some slack in work assignments for the curbside alternative, and we should be able to get by for several more years without undue extra labor costs."

"You have a good idea there, Kelly," responded the Mayor. "Frankly, I don't know what Council will do. I'll tell you my strategy. I think that I'll talk with the Sanitation Workers Union leader next, and brief him on the alternatives before us. I'm going to keep the last alternative alive as a bargaining tool. As it stands now, only the second alternative requires a change in the union contract, but if we don't give them advance notice on this, I'm sure that we'll have all kinds of secrecy charges thrown at us. Once I get some sounding on the strength of their objections, I'll have the subject brought to Council's attention and try to get action on the adoption of one of the alternatives."

MEETING BETWEEN THE MAYOR AND THE SANITATION WORKERS UNION LEADER

The meeting began on a somber note since the Mayor had given David Fowler, the union leader, a copy of the report which Kelly had written. David Fowler, being an astute judge of public sentiment, realized that his union would be on shaky ground if it staged a blustery attack on all of the recommendations without concrete proposals for remedying the department's budget crisis. Morgantown's citizens had shown an increasing discontent with the growing cost of municipal government.

Since each of the proposals involved increased work load assignments, David Fowler felt that he could gain union support if he could obtain an added incentive for the increased tonnage collected. With this in mind, he proposed that each worker receive an incentive of 50 cents per ton collected above the current average of eight tons per day. The mayor agreed to the concept in principle, but indicated that he would have to talk to his advisors before agreeing on an exact incentive rate. With this general understanding, Fowler indicated that he would not oppose the first three recommendations. He was quite emphatic that the adoption of the fourth alternative would lead to a long and bitter strike.

ANALYSIS OF INCENTIVE PROPOSALS

The Mayor briefed McClain on the union's proposals and asked her to reevaluate the cost savings. Since the estimated tons collected on each route was a part of the computer output, the determination of the incentive proposal costs was easy to perform. In order to provide an estimate of the costs for different incentive proposals, the cost per ton incentive was varied as shown below:

Alternative No. 2

Increased Tonnage =9.5 tons per day — 8.0 tons per day per truck
$\qquad$ incentive = 1.5 tons per day
Incentive Costs $\qquad$ =1.5 tons/day X 200 days/year X 4 workers/truck
$\qquad$ X 7 trucks X C_1 ($/ton) = 8400 C_1

where C_1 = the incentive payment for extra tons collected ($/ton) per worker.

Alternative No. 3

Increased Tonnage =9.2 tons/day — 8.0 tons/day = 1.2 tons/day
Incentive Costs $\qquad$ =1.2 tons/day X 200 days/year X 5 workers/truck
$\qquad$ X 6 trucks X C_1 = 7200 C_1

Alternative No. 4

Increased Tonnage =9.0 tons/day — 8.0 tons/day = 1.0 tons/day
Incentive Costs $\qquad$ =1.0 tons/day X 200 days/vear X 5 workers/truck
$\qquad$ X 4 trucks X C_1 (tons/day) = 4000 C_1

With this formulation, McClain then determined the extra labor costs for different incentive payment rates as shown in Table 4.

McClain then determined that if the 50 cents per ton/day rate were accepted, that this would have reduced the original anticipated savings to:

Reduce Helper Savings $\qquad$ = $39,600 — $4,200 = $35,400
Curbside Collection Savings = $40,100 — $3,600 = $36,500

Table 4   Increased Costs Due to Incentive Payments

Alternative	Incentive Payment Rates ($/tons above 8.0)				
	.30	.35	.40	.45	.50
Reduce Helpers on Each Truck	2520	2940	3360	3870	4200
Curbside Collection	2160	2520	2880	3240	3600
Once-a-Week Collection	1200	1400	1600	1800	2000

McClain then reported her findings to the Mayor.

The Mayor was pleased with the results and decided to accept the union rate in the hopes that this would foster a spirit of good will and improve the overall chances of the acceptance of one of the cost reduction plans. With these results, the Mayor then prepared the presentation to the City Council.

CITY COUNCIL ACTION

At the City Council meeting, the Mayor briefed the Council on the intent of the study, introduced Kelly McClain and explained her role in the study, and then gave a synopsis of the alternatives of the cost reduction plans. As expected, the Council focused their attention on the second and third alternatives. The 14 council persons appeared to be split into three groups. A minority of three were opposed to any of the alternatives and felt that improper accounting methods were the cause of the "spurious" deficit. Six members of council were in favor of the curbside collection alternative, while the remaining five were in favor of the alternative of reducing one helper on each truck.

Those favoring the curbside collection alternative favored it because of its long-range impacts. Those favoring the reduction of workers supported it because it would not cause undue hardships for the elderly citizens in their wards.

Although only the curbside collection alternative required action from Council, the Mayor wanted a consensus from Council so that he would be in a better position to deal with the union. Therefore he asked for a vote on the Council's feelings on the two alternatives. The council voted as was expected and neither alternative received a majority. After additional discussion, one of the council women moved that a public hearing be held on this issue before a formal ordinance was presented to Council. The motion passed and the public hearing was arranged.

At the public hearing, the opposition to the curbside collection alternative failed to materialize. Henrietta Higginbotham, the head of the local chapter of the American Association of Retired Persons (AARP), expressed her group's views, which were obtained by sampling their membership. While a small percentage of AARP was concerned about the physical problems of carrying their trash to the curb, they were not as concerned about this problem as they were of the possibilities of increased collection costs. Most of the remaining comments spoke out against a sanitation rate increase and were in favor of any proposal which would prevent such increases.

With the public hearing, the sentiment changed on council. Four of the five members who originally favored the second alternative switched their support to the curbside collection alternative. With a vote of 10-4 in favor, the city council then passed an ordinance to provide for curbside collections.

With the passage of the ordinance, the Mayor made a few concluding remarks thanking the Council for their support on this matter. "I think we've accomplished something significant tonight. We have restored fiscal stability to one of our city's vital departments. In doing this, we have avoided increasing the financial burden of government on our citizens. At the same time, we have asked our citizens to help us directly in keeping our costs under control. The encouraging response to this proposal demonstrated in both the public hearing and council chambers gives me a great deal of confidence in keeping our city on the track of fiscal responsibility."

Case 5

Richmond Memorial Hospital*

In November 1975, Mr. John N. Simpson, Senior Vice President and Administrator of Richmond Memorial Hospital (RMH), was looking over the statistics shown in Exhibits 1 and 2 concerning the RMH emergency room operations. It appeared that these might represent the culmination of many factors that affect emergency health care delivery; and he wondered if such statistics could be used to prepare forecasts for various planning purposes.

Richmond Memorial Hospital was a nonprofit community hospital dedicated to providing modern health care for the community that it served in the northwestern section of Richmond, Virginia. Since first opening its doors in January 1957, the hospital had established a fine reputation in the community and was recognized as being a well run, effective organization. Associated through lease agreements with RMH was the Sheltering Arms Hospital, the only hospital in the state dedicated to providing care for those financially unable to pay for their care. Together these hospitals formed the second largest medical complex in the City of Richmond. As part of the service to the community, RMH oper-

*This case was written by Mr. W. Blaker Bolling, Candidate for the degree of Doctor of Business Administration at The Colgate Darden Graduate School of Business Administration, University of Virginia, under the supervision of Associate Professor Curtis J. Tompkins. Copyright ©1976, by the University of Virginia Graduate Business School Sponsors.

ated an emergency room (ER) that was open 24 hours a day, 365 days a year. Since this facility was placed in operation soon after the opening of the hospital, the ER had experienced a dramatic increase in utilization and consideration was now being given to expanding the facilities, which were becoming cramped—especially during peak periods.

Mr. Simpson knew that similar dramatic increases in ER use had been experienced at many hospitals in the United States. A number of factors were recognized to be involved in this increased use of hospital emergency departments including population increases, a decrease in the number of general practitioners, the unavailability of physicians at night and on weekends, an increasing proportion of the population without a family physician, public awareness of the ER as a source of care, and benefits covered by certain health insurance plans. Although these were important factors, Mr. Simpson knew that trying to relate them to the operations at RMH would be quite difficult if not impossible.

As he glanced over the data, he noticed that both the number of patients receiving care at the emergency room and the number of those admitted to the hospital through the ER (a subset of those visiting the ER) appeared to have peaked. However, this slight decline was largely attributed to the recent opening of other hospitals in the city. The effects of operations in other hospitals in the same marketing area were not new to Mr. Simpson as he remembered what had happened when a nearby major hospital had temporarily curtailed its ER operations in the mid-sixties and slightly later when another hospital opened its new ER facilities. He was concerned about the effects in 1975, however.

Much of the care provided in the ER was not of an emergency nature. Indeed, the emergency room at RMH (and those at most other hospitals) were being used increasingly for episodic, non-acute cases by the community desiring weekend and evening health care services. This posed a dilemma for the RMH administrator. On one hand, RMH was dedicated to providing high quality care to the community; on the other hand, use of the ER by non-acute cases and the resulting difficulty in assuring continuity of care could result in the provision of less than desirable care. Although RMH was now pioneering in innovative ambulatory care outreach facilities within its primary service area in an attempt to address some of these problems, the ER remained a problem for Mr. Simpson.

As he studied the ER utilization data, Mr. Simpson felt sure that there were underlying patterns that could be useful in scheduling personnel, in budgeting, as well as in developing longer-range plans for facilities. Previous studies had provided some indication of how the visits were distributed by day of the week and time of day. Mr. Simpson now desired to have good methods for short- and long-range forecasting. Some previous work using seasonal regression methods had provided fairly good monthly forecasts for awhile but these had been abandoned as the forecasts became increasingly unreliable.

Mr. Simpson wondered if some of the new forecasting methods might be of assistance but was concerned with which, if any, to choose and how to test them for performance. Given the changing structure of the community, the new hospitals, the outreach facilities, etc., he wondered if any forecasting method could be used or whether he should rely on intuition. Was there some relationship between ER visits and admissions that could assist him in his evaluation?

EXHIBIT 1

Visits to the Emergency Room
(Average Number Per Day For Each Month)

Month	1960	1961	1962	1963	1964	1965	1966	1967	1968	1969	1970	1971	1972	1973	1974	1975
Jan.	28.80	31.41	41.83	49.67	56.70	61.90	76.51	72.25	76.67	77.58	96.32	92.39	107.16	108.45	103.48	98.84
Feb.	30.44	32.14	39.14	47.68	57.46	61.89	76.89	67.64	69.24	80.42	91.18	101.75	100.38	98.86	102.11	100.00
Mar.	31.45	34.48	43.16	52.90	57.22	73.45	82.32	74.41	79.51	82.80	91.10	97.06	102.23	98.81	113.87	95.26
April	38.03	41.30	47.16	55.56	66.66	77.03	81.53	82.13	75.33	92.60	96.43	101.87	108.80	110.97	115.63	101.33
May	36.93	43.80	53.74	54.70	71.03	89.80	85.45	78.83	84.22	101.61	108.97	108.84	115.16	114.61	114.29	109.16
June	40.46	46.90	54.43	58.63	74.63	89.10	88.23	88.33	95.16	108.80	107.63	116.57	115.80	117.07	114.23	112.07
July	44.29	47.96	54.74	64.64	73.41	92.67	93.83	88.45	95.12	107.96	110.26	117.39	123.06	118.13	119.58	107.77
Aug.	44.09	52.96	57.41	66.45	72.80	97.38	90.12	91.80	96.80	114.45	119.06	118.87	122.13	118.90	113.39	107.29
Sept.	41.60	51.23	56.03	61.20	72.73	92.26	81.16	88.03	97.13	105.36	117.97	112.63	120.13	122.07	116.03	104.86
Oct.	39.00	43.22	54.41	59.67	65.67	91.16	81.70	79.54	86.61	102.22	106.81	110.00	104.87	108.71	107.23	100.77
Nov.	37.36	41.33	49.80	61.76	67.46	79.56	72.66	80.50	82.20	94.76	96.47	100.17	103.93	105.30	100.60	
Dec.	39.83	41.06	49.64	56.87	63.00	80.12	68.64	77.93	90.67	87.51	91.26	98.23	107.03	95.84	94.26	

EXHIBIT 2

Admissions to the Hospital Through the Emergency Room
(Average Number Per Day For Each Month)

Month	1960	1961	1962	1963	1964	1965	1966	1967	1968	1969	1970	1971	1972	1973	1974	1975
Jan.	8.00	7.03	9.54	11.41	11.22	11.35	15.96	12.93	13.00	13.64	15.35	15.71	14.16	14.00	13.00	14.26
Feb.	7.82	7.82	10.46	10.55	10.64	11.57	14.82	12.96	11.37	14.21	15.00	16.21	13.79	11.96	15.89	13.68
Mar.	8.74	7.77	10.61	12.12	10.80	14.87	14.67	12.22	12.41	13.16	15.29	16.00	13.45	11.52	13.45	13.13
April	8.93	8.90	9.43	10.66	12.03	13.30	13.13	13.03	11.26	14.46	14.83	16.57	13.43	13.90	13.93	12.30
May	7.96	9.87	10.45	10.16	10.83	15.70	12.29	10.80	11.16	13.70	13.58	13.32	14.90	14.10	13.19	12.35
June	7.20	8.10	9.86	9.46	10.90	13.16	11.76	12.20	12.20	14.33	14.30	16.57	13.80	13.03	12.87	13.07
July	7.64	8.38	10.12	8.93	10.83	13.93	11.45	11.80	13.35	13.70	13.94	15.81	13.90	13.52	13.97	14.10
Aug.	8.35	8.77	9.74	10.35	10.67	13.58	12.48	11.51	12.74	13.48	14.58	14.90	12.16	12.94	11.71	12.43
Sept.	8.16	9.53	10.93	8.96	11.00	13.90	12.10	12.56	12.50	14.06	16.53	16.17	12.63	13.33	12.63	12.97
Oct.	8.41	9.38	11.00	10.16	10.96	15.22	12.41	12.58	11.35	14.83	14.74	14.90	12.55	13.45	12.61	11.55
Nov.	7.10	8.30	10.30	10.86	11.00	14.03	11.60	12.63	12.66	13.90	14.87	15.40	10.97	14.13	12.77	
Dec.	8.48	8.38	11.54	10.19	10.58	15.41	11.80	11.41	10.83	11.06	13.29	14.65	12.68	13.03	11.90	

EXHIBIT 3

Determination of Expected Overtime Costs

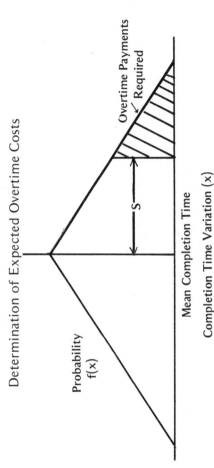

Probability f(x)

Overtime Payments → Required

S

Mean Completion Time

Completion Time Variation (x)

x = The Deviation of Completion Time from the Mean (+ deviation = work completed after mean time)

S = The allowable deviation in completion time before overtime payments begin

U = The upper limit of deviation from the mean completion time

O_t = Overtime costs per hour per truck

$f(x)$ = Probability of variation (z) from the mean completion time = $\begin{cases} -mx + b \text{ when } x > 0 \\ mx + b \text{ when } x \leq 0 \end{cases}$

m = Slope of the probability distribution function

b = The intercept of the probability distribution function

C_0 = The total expected overtime cost per day

$$C_0 = C \ O_t \int_S^U (x-S)f(x)dx \qquad C_0 = O_t \int_S^U (x-S)(mx+b)dx$$

$$C_0 = \left\{ \frac{mU^3}{3} + \left[\frac{b-Sm}{2} \right] U^2 - SbU - \frac{mS^3}{3} - \left[\frac{b-Sm}{2} \right] S^2 + S^2 b \right\}$$

THREE

PRODUCTIVITY/PERFORMANCE MEASUREMENT

Management Control Systems in Libraries[*]

Libraries, like many other nonprofit institutions, have traditionally lacked adequate management controls. This lack can be traced to several factors. A major reason is the absence of any real pressure on library administrators to develop adequate control systems. Libraries seldom, if ever, face competition, and consequently librarians have little to motivate them to be concerned with either effectiveness or efficiency.

In general, the boards of trustees of public libraries and the administrators of colleges and universities have put little or no pressure on libraries to be efficient. Libraries are seldom a center of controversy, and boards and administrators have had little inclination to look at the internal workings of the libraries under them. This fact has been pointed out by Robert Munn:

> It has often been observed that administrators devote most of their attention to matters at either end of the spectrum and have little time for those in the middle. In the academic world, the library is definitely in the middle. It is unlikely to be the cause of either a crisis or a coup. It will not, on the one hand, trigger a riot nor, on the other hand, will it bring in a multi-million dollar grant. In short, the library is one of those

*This technical note was prepared by Leslie E. Grayson and Henry W. Wingate, respectively, Professor of International Business Economics, Librarian-Assistant Professor. Copyright ©1975, by the University of Virginia Graduate Business School Sponsors.

academic sleeping dogs which the harassed administrator is quite content to let lie.[1]

This observation holds equally true for public libraries.

Although lack of motivation is the major cause of the inadequate controls which exist, the absence of clearly defined objectives and the difficulty in measuring output in libraries have contributed to the failure to develop control systems. This difficulty in measuring output has led libraries often to use input as a measure of output. Most annual reports of libraries offer as evidence of the success of the past year the amount of expenditures for the year. This is, of course, in sharp contrast to the practice of profit-making enterprises. A corporation's annual report almost invariably begins with a statement of the past year's sales and earnings. Of course, expenditures are important to the corporation also, but they are of negative consequence. The lower they are in relation to sales, the better. A case in point, which is not at all atypical, is reflected in a recent annual report of a major university library. The opening sentences of the report are:

> This was a landmark year for the University Library. For the first time, expenditures for books and binding rose above one million dollars, reaching $1,160,402.

Like a corporation, a library gets something in return for its expenditures. It gets books and the services of people to catalog them. It gets periodicals and the services of people to bind them. It gets microfilm and manuscripts and government documents. It is what is gained that is the measure of success, not the cost, and it is necessary that a library recognize this if it is to become truly concerned with its effectiveness and efficiency.

MEASURES OF EFFECTIVENESS

Any library, regardless of its type, serves a well-defined clientele. An academic library exists to serve the students and faculty of the college or university of which it is a part. A public library exists to serve the population of the city or county in which it is located. A special library exists to serve the needs of the organization to which it belongs. Because

---

[1] R. F. Munn, "Bottomless Pit, or the Academic Library as Viewed from the Administration Building," *College and Research Libraries,* XXIX (1968), p. 52.

of the well-defined constituencies, it has been traditional for libraries to measure their effectiveness (how well their objectives are accomplished) in terms of the number of the constituency served over a given period of time. This is usually stated as a circulation figure; that is, the number of books lent over a given time period.

In most libraries, measures based on circulation are reasonable in that they do relate directly to the goal of serving as large a percent of the constituency as possible. However, given the library's three functions of education, information and recreation, it is clear that a gross circulation figure in itself falls short of being an adequate measure of a library's effectiveness.

As a measure of effectiveness, a gross circulation figure gives little indication of how well the "information" function is being performed. Often, a library user seeking information on a particular subject will find the data he needs while in the library or will telephone the reference department. In neither case will a book be circulated, and the circulation figure will be unaffected by the user.

With regard to the "recreation" function, gross circulation will be affected by borrowers of novels and other nonresearch material. However, much of the recreation function involves users leafing through books and magazines within the library. Here, again, the circulation figure is unaffected.

The research or "education" function of a library also presents problems in that much of the research may be performed within the library. In many public libraries, the majority of users are school-age children working on school projects. Such use of the library depends to a large extent on the adequacy of the school libraries. If the school libraries are inadequate, the "education" function of the public library may loom larger than any other function.

Although it is clear that a gross circulation figure falls short of being a good measure of a library's effectiveness, it is the easiest figure to obtain and to understand. For these reasons, most public libraries rely on circulation figures to measure their effectiveness. Exhibit 1 presents data from the annual report of a fairly representative public library. This statement is the library's main measure of effectiveness. The statement shows that 472,384 books were borrowed from the library system in 1973, or an increase of 2.7 percent over 1972. While this gross figure should probably be related to the size of the population served, few small- to medium-sized libraries do so.

Effectiveness measures other than circulation figures can be and are used by libraries, but they have not proven very helpful. Because circulation figures give no indication of the use of books and periodicals

EXHIBIT 1

Circulation and Book-Stock Report
Fiscal Year 1973

Circulation			
	1973	1972	Increase (Decrease)
Main Library	169,493 Vols.	171,930 Vols.	(1.4%)
Branch A	183,659	177,771	3.3%
Branch B	24,129	23,961	0.7%
Branch C	21,998	20,608	6.7%
Bookmobile	73,105	65,556	11.5%
Total	472,384 Vols.	459,826 Vols.	2.7%

Book-Stock			
	Oct. 31 1973	Oct. 31 1972	Increase (Decrease)
Main Library	64,332 Vols.	60,250 Vols.	6.8%
Branch A	33,293	30,619	8.7%
Branch B	8,077	6,391	2.6%
Branch C	9,297	7,811	19.0%
Bookmobile	22,297	20,969	6.3%
Total	137,296 Vols.	126,040 Vols.	8.9%

within the library, such measures as daily entrance count and the average daily seating capacity utilized (requires hourly head counts) are sometimes attempted. In these instances, however, the effort expended in gathering the data often cannot be justified.

Effectiveness measures in academic libraries are not very different from those of public libraries. However, since in-library research is a very important function of an academic library, circulation figures are probably not as valid an indication of a college library's effectiveness as they are for a public library.

MEASURES OF EFFICIENCY

While libraries have not traditionally been very interested in developing output measures of effectiveness, they have shown even less interest in measures of efficiency (how well resources are used in producing outputs). There has been very little pressure put on libraries directors to be cost conscious, and cost accounting is all but nonexistent in libraries. After a brief flurry of articles in the 1930s,[2] cost accounting in libraries has been largely ignored. This lack of interest can probably be traced directly to libraries' traditional apathy toward operating efficiency. John Millett's observation that "librarians rate the importance of their jobs in the light of the size of their book collections, the number of their employees, and their total expenditures"[3] is quite correct. There is, of course, no reason to develop cost information when the objective is to attain the highest level of expenditures possible. Cost accounting only becomes of interest when there is an interest in increasing the level of output in relation to the resources expended.

In lieu of a cost accounting system, the measure of efficiency most often used in libraries is the number of books added over a certain period of time. Figures for a typical library appear in Exhibit 1. Actually, this is more of an effectiveness measure if one of the goals of the library is to increase the size of its collections.

University libraries have been as slow to develop efficiency measures as public libraries. A portion of the annual report of a university library is shown in Exhibit 2. It is apparent that none of the output measures listed relates to inputs (e.g., the number of books cataloged is not related to the cost of operating the cataloging department). Until outputs are related to inputs, measures of efficiency cannot be said to exist.

IMPROVING THE PERFORMANCE MEASURES OF LIBRARIES

The development of useful measures of performance for libraries depends on the ability of library administrators to:

1. Clearly define the objectives of the library and to rank those objectives in priority order.
2. Formulate quantitative measures of effectiveness and efficiency which relate directly to the objectives.
3. Set standards of performance stated in quantitative terms.
4. Disseminate actual performance data among libraries of similar type and size for purposes of comparison.

[2] Fremont Rider, "Library Cost Accounting," *Library Quarterly* VI (October 1936) and Robert A. Miller, "Cost Accounting for Libraries," *Library Quarterly* VII (October 1937).

[3] John A. Millett, *Financing Higher Education in the United States* (New York: Columbia University Press, 1952), p. 123.

EXHIBIT 2

University Library
Statistical Report, 1972

Department	1972	1971	Increase (Decrease)
Acquisitions			
Books Purchased	4,911	6,019	(18.4%)
Periodical Titles Received	795	775	2.6%
Cataloging			
Books Cataloged	7,781	8,279	(6.0%)
Books Reclassified	1,856	880	110.9%
Circulation			
Books Circulated	27,745	24,984	11.1%
Reference			
Questions Handled	3,335	2,800	19.1%
Expenditures			
Total Library	$254,052	$220,198	15.4%
As percent of total			
University budget	5.1%	4.7%	

It is actually more important that the objectives of a nonprofit organization be clearly stated in quantitative terms than it is for a profit-oriented organization. In a business, profit serves as a very good quantitative measure of both effectiveness and efficiency. In the absence of such a single, overall measure, it is essential that a library establish objectives and quantitative measures which will indicate how well those objectives are being accomplished and how well its available resources are being expended.

The overriding objective of any organization, profit or nonprofit, is to satisfy its customers or patrons. In a business, profit is directly related to the degree of customer satisfaction. If a business cannot provide as much or more customer satisfaction than its competitors, the customers will see to it that the business will, sooner or later, fail. But libraries are monopolies, and unless library service is so poor as to encourage complaints, it is not necessary that a library concern itself with the question of customer satisfaction.

To measure adequately the effectiveness of a library, it is essential that a measure be developed that reflects the degree of customer satisfaction. While there are many problems related to the use of circulation data for measuring effectiveness, in most cases circulation provides the single best measure of effectiveness. If the proposition can be accepted that satisfied customers use the library and borrow books from the library, then circulation can be said to measure the degree of customer satisfaction.

The use of gross circulation figures fails to provide any means by which standards can be set. For this reason, the circulation figures must be related to the population the library serves. This can be done in two ways. The circulation can be stated on a per capita basis, or if the number of *different* borrowers over a particular time period can be ascertained, a percentage of population using the library can be derived. The first of these methods is easier, and it is often used by larger libraries. Exhibit 1 shows that with a population of around 81,000 a per capita circulation figure of 5.8 books per year can be derived. While this method does relate the gross circulation figure to population, a small percent of heavy borrowers distorts the figure. While 5.8 books per capita were lent by the library system in 1973, a large proportion of the population never used the library.

With regard to circulation, perhaps the most appropriate measure is the *percent* of population using the library system. This measure is seldom used because it requires data on the number of *different* users borrowing books over a certain time period. However, if data processing equipment is used in maintaining circulation records (as it is in many large libraries), it would not be difficult to issue each user a card with a unique number and to collect data at the end of each period on the number of different cards used in borrowing books.

Although little research has been done in the area, it is well known that most public libraries serve a relatively small percent of the population. Children, housewives, and retired people, for example, are generally heavy users, while working men and the poor tend to be light users. Using a percent of population measure would permit the establishment of very well-defined objectives which could be stated in terms of increasing the percent of population using the library. For example, if the current month's use is 25 percent of the population, the library might set as an objective an increase in monthly use to 30 percent of the population.

Developing quantitative measures of efficiency is not as difficult as establishing measures of effectiveness. The resources available to a library can be stated in financial terms, and the outputs are generally stated in quantitative terms such as number of books circulated, number of books purchased, or number of books cataloged.

When a library does become interested in measuring the efficiency of its operation, it needs some semblance of a cost accounting system by which to set standards against which current performance can be measured. It is mainly in the technical processes of acquisitions and cataloging that cost accounting can be put to good advantage. Some library activities, most notably reference work, defy costing. A reference question may take one or two minutes or several hours of a librarian's time. But most of a library's activities are routine and standard costs can be developed.

The first step in setting up a library cost accounting system is to define the cost centers. These are acquisitions, cataloging, circulation, and reference. The total expenses of nonproductive units, such as general office and janitorial, would then be allocated to the cost centers. These overhead costs added to the direct labor and direct material costs of each center would represent the full cost of operating each center. By dividing this full cost by the number of units produced (books ordered, books cataloged, books circulated), the cost per unit can be determined. Over a period of time a standard cost per unit can be developed, and each month's production can be measured against standard.

Only when a large number of libraries see fit to develop similar quantitative measures of performance will it be possible to establish standards by which an individual library can evaluate its own effectiveness and efficiency. The formulation of standards would, of course, also require accurate disclosures by a number of libraries of their performance data.

CONCLUSION

As is the case in many other nonprofit institutions, the financial administration of libraries has generally not been subject to close scrutiny or tight cost control. While the competitive nature of the marketplace makes it incumbent on profit-oriented enterprises to strive to obtain a return on the resources expended, institutions such as libraries operate under no such impetus. A business which cannot operate in such a way that its expenditures-return relationship is favorable will not survive. Yet a library which cannot operate so that its expenditures are reasonable in relation to the goods and services procured is frequently or generally rewarded with a larger appropriation.

It would appear that libraries have less reason to be exempt from the development and use of output measures of effectiveness and efficiency than many other nonprofit organizations. Libraries serve a very well-defined clientele, and tangible outputs exist in the books acquired, the books cataloged, and the books circulated. While some activities, such as reference service and in-library reading, are very hard to measure, most of a library's activities are measurable and can be related to inputs.

Case 6

Charlottesville
Fire Department*

In December 1976, the Research Triangle Institute (RTI), in collaboration with the National Fire Protection Association (NFPA) and the International City Management Association (ICMA), issued preliminary findings of an 18-month evaluation of fire protection delivery arrangements in a nationwide sample of 1400 fire departments. Charlottesville Fire Chief Julian Taliaferro immediately began using the RTI criteria to measure the effectiveness and productivity of the Charlottesville Fire Department, in relation to similarly constructed fire departments in cities of comparable size nationwide.

BACKGROUND

The Charlottesville Fire Department protected both the City of Charlottesville and part of Albemarle County. The city itself included some 10.4 square miles, a population of approximately 56,000, and property valued at $766,143,984 (true market value).[1]

*This case was prepared by S.Y. Young and C.J. Tompkins, April 1977. Revised by C.J. Tompkins, April 1979. Copyright ©Curtis J. Tompkins.

[1] For the purposes of this study, the University of Virginia student population, buildings and ground have been included in these totals. While certain parts of the University are technically in the county, the areas are in fact within city limits, and therefore correspond more closely to measures of protection for the center city area than for that of the county.

Fire Department resources included five (5) engine companies, one (1) aerial ladder, sixty-eight (68) paid personnel and a volunteer force that functions in an auxiliary capacity.

Albermarle County itself had no paid fire department. Protection was maintained through a network of six (6) volunteer companies numbering two hundred-fifty (250) persons. The county also had, for a number of years, a verbal agreement with the city that the latter would automatically respond to fire alarms originating within a specified thirty (30) square mile area of the county, comprised mostly of that urbanized portion surrounding the city. This area had a population of approximately 19,800 and property valued at $202,365,670. While there were no county volunteers located within this area, those in close proximity would respond to fire alarms there.

The county contributed to the annual budget of the city fire department in proportion to the services it was rendered. In fiscal year 1977 this amounted to $163,303 of a total budget of $831,629. The county also maintained one (1) engine company located at the main fire station, this being the engine the city normally used to respond to county fires. Therefore, it can be seen that the city fire department served two distinct regions; the city itself and a portion of Albemarle County. Chief Taliaferro's study attempts to evaluate and compare levels of fire protection provided by the city fire department to each area.

MEASUREMENT CRITERIA

RTI reduced all departments studied to 4 categories: fully volunteer, mostly volunteer (50 to 90 percent), mostly paid (50 to 90 percent) and fully paid departments. The departments were then further divided by size of population and type of community protected, whether center, ring, or fringe. A center city was described as an urban area with a population greater than 25,000 having considerable fire hazard and a paid fire department. A ring city was defined as a suburban community with a population of less than 100,000, and with a fire department composed of some volunteer personnel. A rural, low density community on the edge of an urbanized or suburban area was considered to be a fringe city. Exhibit 1 shows the "effectiveness measures" developed by RTI for each type of department and population size.

The city of Charlottesville was classified as a center city of population between 25,000 and 100,000 with a fully paid fire department. It may be noted in Exhibit 1 that RTI offered no category for a center city with a mostly paid force. This is ideally what Charlottesville would be considered, but since that classification did not exist, the next most accurate one was chosen. Chief Taliaferro felt the fully paid description to be closest to the true situation as over 90 percent of all fire alarms were handled with available paid personnel.

The 30 square miles of Albemarle County protected by the city was classified as a ring city of a population between 5001 and 25,000 with a mostly volunteer force. The force was considered mostly volunteer because, while the city did respond to fire alarms in the area, its function was considered to be auxiliary to county volunteer companies that also responded to alarms in the area. Criticality of city response depended upon response time for county units and the seriousness of the fire. The city would normally respond to alarms with one engine company and three firefighters, but would usually be outnumbered by volunteer equipment and personnel.

RTI evaluated all departments as related to measures of effectiveness and productivity, using information gathered from years 1973, 1974, and 1975. Most of the figures used are averages for the three-year period and all are corrected for inflation.

Effectiveness was described as the extent to which the incidence of fire, loss of life, personal injury, and property loss was minimized. The seven measures used to operationalize the concept were:

1. Number of fires per 1,000 of population protected.
2. Dollars of property loss per capita.
3. Dollars of property loss per $1,000 of market value of property.
4. Dollars of property loss per fire.
5. Number of civilian injuries and deaths per 100,000 of population protected.
6. Number of civilian injuries and deaths per 100 fires.
7. Number of firefighter injuries and deaths per 100 fires.

Productivity was defined by RTI as the measure of the relationship between results obtained and resources utilized. Rather than rely strictly on levels of effort (expenditures) to measure fire department costs, RTI preferred to speak of *total cost*, defined as the sum of expenditures and dollar property losses.

Indicators used to reflect productivity were:

1. Expenditures per capita
2. Expenditures per $1,000 of market value of property

EXHIBIT I

Comparison of Fire Service Delivery by

Column	A	B	C	D	E	F	G	H
Productivity	0-5000 Population Protected				5,001-25,000 Population Protected			
Measures	Ring		Fringe		Ring			
	Fully Vol.	Mostly Vol.	Fully Vol.	Mostly Vol.	Fully Vol.	Mostly Vol.	Mostly Paid	Fully Paid
Total Cost per Capita Points for:								
—Upper 25%	41.15	115.99	52.74	177.62	23.32	30.77	40.46	60.41
—Median	18.69	84.35	26.37	97.31	15.58	28.75	22.92	35.92
—Lower 25%	13.29	64.03	15.56	50.03	10.18	18.36	22.28	26.35
Total Cost/ $1000 Market Value of Property Points for:								
—Upper 25%	*	*	4.88	3.49	4.58	2.05	2.59	2.30
—Median	*	*	2.49	3.04	1.39	1.38	1.53	1.77
—Lower 25%	*	*	.89	2.49	1.07	.96	1.13	1.25
Total Cost/Fire Points for:								
—Upper 25%	3504.33	9009.96	3657.59	3047.87	5059.96	3638.99	5054.43	6644.25
—Median	2002.86	7934.05	2054.53	2780.17	2558.14	2635.54	3433.89	3615.31
—Lower 25%	896.85	3462.47	1322.28	1919.33	1572.06	1467.69	2401.90	2324.66

Comparison of Fire Department Effectiveness Measures

	A	B	C	D	E	F	G	H
Prevention No. of Fires/1000 Population Protected: Points for:								
—Upper 25%	22.98	23.26	14.31	49.56	9.48	15.95	22.94	16.99
—Median	9.20	9.49	10.77	25.61	5.94	9.43	9.75	10.37
—Lower 25%	6.08	5.21	5.87	17.84	2.69	6.63	4.91	3.28
Suppression $ Property Loss per Capita Points for:								
—Upper 25%	20.38	81.32	30.22	42.61	16.04	11.98	10.72	10.26
—Median	7.62	13.03	13.80	30.18	8.06	7.69	7.85	6.68
—Lower 25%	3.19	3.94	5.53	8.70	5.63	5.10	3.67	3.65
$ Property Loss per $1000 Market Value Points for:								
—Upper 25%	*	*	4.30	1.46	1.60	.75	.73	.60
—Median	*	*	1.34	.97	1.02	.50	.58	.34
—Lower 25%	*	*	.64	.62	.58	.34	.10	.15

Population Protected, City and Department Type

Column	I	J	K	L	M	N	O	P
Productivity		5,001-25,000		25,001-100,000 Population Protected				100,000 Pop. Prot.
Measures		Fringe		Center		Ring		Center
	Fully Vol.	Mostly Vol.	Mostly Paid	Fully Paid	Mostly Vol.	Mostly Paid	Fully Paid	Fully Paid
Total Cost Per Capita Points for:								
—Upper 25%	10.75	36.31	60.89	44.17	47.91	46.70	38.08	57.34
—Median	6.54	24.99	32.14	33.10	27.03	33.05	33.27	36.74
—Lower 25%	3.66	17.03	20.26	23.12	16.15	24.43	24.68	33.61
Total Cost/$1000 Market Value of Property Points for:								
—Upper 25%	*	2.82	*	5.99	*	5.92	2.97	7.10
—Median	*	2.53	*	1.66	*	3.45	2.19	3.47
—Lower 25%	*	1.72	*	1.01	*	1.88	1.67	2.31
Total Cost/Fire Points for:								
—Upper 25%	3188.75	5338.68	6419.81	4134.84	3598.50	4893.40	4866.57	4292.02
—Median	1206.57	3338.98	4071.51	3041.19	2940.36	3321.04	3562.64	3230.81
—Lower 25%	798.90	2122.61	2331.71	2373.46	2553.19	2566.30	2472.18	2308.63

Effectiveness Measures

	I	J	K	L	M	N	O	P
Prevention No. of Fires/1000 Population Protected Points for								
—Upper 25%	12.56	18.10	20.19	19.23	12.99	12.42	13.00	17.89
—Median	3.90	10.87	9.19	12.78	7.44	9.32	10.25	11.80
—Lower 25%	1.57	4.66	4.23	7.24	4.01	6.58	7.97	9.59
Suppression $ Property Loss per Capita Points for:								
—Upper 25%	9.64	19.70	12.39	14.96	19.15	11.35	13.82	14.65
—Median	4.17	9.72	11.40	10.40	10.35	7.05	7.28	12.29
—Lower 25%	2.51	4.76	7.95	5.39	3.98	4.94	5.52	7.11
$ Property Loss per $1000 Market Value Points for:								
—Upper 25%	*	1.29	*	2.10	*	.94	.74	1.80
—Median	*	1.17	*	.54	*	.68	.52	1.05
—Lower 25%	*	.54	*	.31	*	.52	.33	.64

Column	A	B	C	D	E	F	G	H
Productivity	0-5000 Population Protected				5,001-25,000 Population Protected			
Measures	Ring		Fringe		Ring			
	Fully Vol.	Mostly Vol.	Fully Vol.	Mostly Vol.	Fully Vol.	Mostly Vol.	Mostly Paid	Fully Paid
$ Property Loss per Fire								
—Upper 25%	1156.97	6542.52	2796.83	2110.77	2501.04	1647.40	1309.42	923.30
—Median	740.33	1277.13	1485.71	1202.92	1937.45	938.21	816.19	826.68
—Lower 25%	473.75	767.00	784.68	704.83	1214.82	438.51	318.45	439.50
Civilian Injuries & Deaths/100,000 Population								
—Upper 25%	23.92	*	0	33.66	7.15	21.73	*	16.10
—Median	0	*	0	0	0	7.93	*	10.02
—Lower 25%	0	*	0	0	0	0	*	0
Civilian Injuries & Deaths/100 Fires								
—Upper 25%	3.49	*	0	1.94	.54	1.79	*	1.42
—Median	0	*	0	.31	0	.85	*	.37
—Lower 25%	0	*	0	0	0	0	*	0
Firefighter Injuries & Deaths/100 Fires								
—Upper 25%	5.09	.79	1.22	.65	4.89	2.65	2.66	7.82
—Median	.54	0	0	0	1.47	.58	1.17	.38
—Lower 25%	0	0	0	0	0	0	0	0

3. Total cost per capita
4. Total cost per $1,000 of market value of property
5. Total cost per fire

After obtaining all measurement figures for each fire department, an average of each was computed for those departments considered to be in the lower 25 percentile of service delivery (more effective), those at the median or average level of delivery, and those in the upper 25 percentile or less effective level of service delivery. Those were the figures used for comparison in this study, target figures being those in the lower 25 percentile.

CHARLOTTESVILLE'S PERFORMANCE

As shown in Exhibit 2, the number of fires per 1,000 of population protected in the city averaged 10.68 for the 1973-1975 period; this pushes the city above the lower 25 percentile figure of 7.24. Chief Taliaferro believed the difference might be attributed to the fact that Charlottesville did not have a well developed fire prevention program. In 1977 there was only one fire prevention officer, and therefore the program was conducted on a somewhat hit-and-miss basis. The Chief felt

Column	I	J	K	L	M	N	O	P
Productivity Measures		5,001-25,000			25,001-100,000 Population Protected			100,000 Pop. Prot.
		Fringe		Center		Ring		Center
	Fully Vol.	Mostly Vol.	Mostly Paid	Fully Paid	Mostly Vol.	Mostly Paid	Fully Paid	Fully Paid
$ Property Loss per Fire								
—Upper 25%	1730.96	2277.62	3708.09	2210.82	2388.40	1119.69	1215.07	1465.76
—Median	730.83	1402.66	1213.64	1111.97	1640.15	950.89	791.35	
—Lower 25%	498.46	731.31	834.40	393.94	1004.74	441.52	517.50	
Civilian Injuries & Deaths/100,000 Population								
—Upper 25%	0	19.59	*	28.48	20.22	18.87	22.05	40.30
—Median	0	0	*	19.09	2.89	15.80	13.83	23.54
—Lower 25%	0	0	*	13.84	0	9.57	6.36	12.08
Civilian Injuries & Deaths/100 Fires								
—Upper 25%	0	1.77	*	2.23	1.67	2.94	2.33	3.07
—Median	0	0	*	1.66	.29	1.62	1.65	1.80
—Lower 25%	0	0	*	.86	0	.80	.69	1.41
Firefighter Injuries & Deaths/100 Fires								
—Upper 25%	5.00	2.71	*	4.14	7.40	2.27	4.03	5.63
—Median	2.33	.92	*	2.51	2.96	1.03	3.33	3.49
—Lower 25%	0							

more time spent on public education and prevention programs would decrease the figure substantially.

The county figure of 2.98 compared favorably with the more effective target 6.63. This would be due to the low population density in the county which provided for less fire hazard than a high density area such as the city. The Chief expected this figure to rise as population and age of structures in the county increased.

Property loss per capita and per $1,000 of market value of property for the city are both higher than the median figures. This is in part due to the relatively low average manning of 2.6 firefighters per engine company. The number of firefighters immediately present at a fire would help determine the number and type of suppression activities that could be initiated. The longer certain activities must be delayed, the greater the chance of increased property loss.

In contrast, the property loss per fire for the city was below the median. This was in part due to the fact that Charlottesville had relatively little industry as compared to other cities of the same size. More industry would increase the risk of industrial fires, where property loss is normally greater than in dwelling fires (the type with the greatest frequency in Charlottesville).

EXHIBIT 2

Charlottesville Fire Department
Effectiveness Measures

Effectiveness Measures	Albemarle County / Charlottesville	Target More Effective (Lower 25%)	Median	Less Effective (Upper 25%)
Prevention				
Number of Fires/1000 of Population Protected	2.98 / 10.68	6.63 / 7.24	9.43 / 12.78	15.95 / 19.23
Suppression				
$ Property Loss Per Capita	27.47 / 10.90	5.10 / 5.39	7.69 / 10.40	11.98 / 14.96
$ Property Loss Per $1000 of Market Value	2.69 / 1.25	.34 / .31	.50 / .54	.75 / 2.10
$ Property Loss Per Fire	9219.00 / 1021.00	438.51 / 393.94	938.21 / 1111.97	1647.40 / 2210.82
Civilian Injuries and Deaths Per 100,000 Population	5.05 / 35.71	0.00 / 13.84	7.93 / 19.09	21.73 / 28.48

	Col 1	Col 2	Col 3	Col 4
Civilian Injuries and Deaths Per 100 Fires	1.79	.85	0.00	1.70
	2.23	1.66	.86	3.34
Firefighters Injuries and Deaths Per 100 Fires	2.65	.58	0.00	1.70
	4.14	2.51	1.07	.84

Levels of Effort

	Col 1	Col 2	Col 3	Col 4
Expenditures Per Capita	21.02	15.02	8.08	5.28
	31.75	24.77	20.92	8.61
Expenditures Per $1000 Market Value of Property	1.44	.98	.51	.52
	3.22	1.84	.86	.62

Productivity Measures

	Col 1	Col 2	Col 3	Col 4
Total Cost Per Capita	30.77	28.75	18.36	32.76
	44.17	33.10	23.12	19.51
Total Cost Per $1000 Market Value of Property	2.05	1.38	.96	3.20
	5.99	1.66	1.01	1.42
Total Cost Per Fire	3638.00	2635.00	1467.00	10,993.00
	4134.00	3041.00	2373.00	1,827.00

A comparison of property loss per capita and per $1,000 of market value of property would indicate the county to be high above the less effective range. But these figures are somewhat misleading. The property loss totals used here are averaged for the three-year period 1973-1975. In 1973 and 1974 there were two large industrial fires in the county, one where loss was estimated at $270,000, the other at $750,000. Without these two fires, property loss would have been substantially less for both years. For example, in 1973 loss was actually $97,000. Chief Taliaferro believed these two catastrophic fires inflated what property loss might routinely have been. Calculations with these two fires deleted showed property loss indicators to fall, although they still hovered in the less effective range (i.e., per capita, $9.38 and per fire $3,102).

Also, when using property loss figures in terms of per capita and per fire, Chief Taliaferro believed it was important to keep in mind the low population density of the county area (19,800 total) and also the low number of fires occuring in the county (i.e., 59 in 1975 as opposed to 598 for the city). Another contributing factor to higher property losses in the county was the longer response time experienced; meaning the fire was already somewhat advanced by the time the engine company arrived.

Civilian injuries and deaths per 100 fires were very high for Charlottesville as compared to other cities of its size. One reason may be the way in which injuries and deaths were reported in Charlottesville and other cities, a factor for which the RTI survey makes no allowance. Chief Taliaferro indicated that the Charlottesville Fire Department reported any civilian injury at the scene of a fire, however slight. Other cities may have reported the same way, or they may report only those injuries of a more serious nature. Those departments who follow the latter policy would compare more favorably in this measure than the former.

Grouping together injuries and deaths may also have distorted the meaning of rating. Charlottesville averaged one death due to fire per year. The year 1975 saw 19 injuries and one death. Considering some injuries were probably slight, do those figures carry the same meaning as do 19 deaths and one injury?

Civilian injuries and deaths were also relatively high in the county. This again may be due to the reporting procedure. Also involved may be longer response time averaged for county alarms. Chief Taliaferro felt that possibly 25 percent of injuries could be related to this last factor.

The fighter injuries and deaths per 100 fires for the city were extremely low—well below the lower 25 percentile figure. This was due in part to mandatory protective clothing and required training for the firefighters. Also fewer injuries were reported in this fire department than may be the case in others.

Those explanations would also apply to firefighter injuries and deaths in the county as related to city firefighters. But the county figure was high as compared to the city figure probably due to the county volunteers that would respond to these fires. Volunteer firefighters normally wore less protective clothing and had fewer training hours, two factors that would increase chances of firefighter injuries.

Fire Department expenditures per capita and per $1,000 of market value of property were low for both the city and county. But low expenditures do not automatically indicate efficiency. For a comparison with the target figures it must be kept in mind that while expenditures were lower than the 25 percentile, property loss figures were higher. This would indicate that the fire department was not as effective in the provision of fire protection as it might have been—whether this be due to resource misallocation or underfunding, a more likely factor in this case.

The extremely low expenditure per capita for the city might also relate to an additional factor. It must be kept in mind that the target figure for Charlottesville corresponds to that for a fully paid department and that Charlottesville was not strictly all paid, as there was an auxiliary force available. It seems probable that if Charlottesville had not had this auxiliary force, the city would have had to hire additional personnel at added cost.

TOTAL COST

The concept of total cost, while more informative than that of expenditures alone, may be somewhat misleading in its implications. As a combination of property losses and expenditures, it purports to be a productivity measure of effectiveness and efficiency where maximum productivity is achieved when total cost is minimized. RTI admitted that the calculation is indifferent to tradeoffs between property loss and fire department expenditures.

For example, the same total cost could be achieved both by a department with low expenditures and high property losses and one with higher expenditures and lower property losses. Chief Taliaferro believed that a service-oriented agency such as a fire department cannot be indifferent to these tradeoffs. The departmental goal of minimizing property loss due to fire must be part of any productivity measure. Chief Taliaferro was not certain that equal total costs reflect equal productivity when one department may spend more money, but have a good suppression record, and another may spend a minimal amount, but have a history of high property loss.

Chief Taliaferro thought the productivity concept would be more useful if property loss and expenditure could be weighted in a manner to reflect departmental goals and objectives.

For the city, total cost per capita was low, a commendable figure upon first inspection. But closer examination shows that this figure was a combination of extremely low expenditures per capita and higher than average property losses.

Total cost per $1,000 of market value of property for the city was below the median for comparable fire departments. This again was the result of low expenditures and high property loss in this category.

Total cost per fire for the city was below the target figure mostly as a result of low expenditures as property loss per fire was closer to the median level.

In contrast to the city, total cost per capita and per $1,000 of market value of property for the county was above the median level. This was due to extremely high property loss in the county as discussed earlier.

Case 7

The Social Service Division of the University of Virginia Medical Center*

In March 1977, Miriam Birdwhistell, Director of the Social Service Division of the University of Virginia Medical Center, and Eleanor Crocker, Chief of Social Service-Psychiatry, met to discuss the short falls of the Division's current efforts to collect data for evaluation purposes. Birdwhistell and Crocker felt that the present system did not provide an adequate base of information on which to gauge effectiveness. They were interested in more effective data gathering for purposes of their own service and personnel evaluation. Additionally, they felt that for future funding and staff increases, the Federal and State governments might require the division to present detailed reports on what it was doing and how well the services were being delivered. A final impetus was the hospital's plans to institute an internal auditing system under which random cases would be reviewed to determine the quality of medical care patients were receiving; the social service aspect of the care would need to be measured along with the other services provided.

*Case prepared by Maura Connell, John Dickman, Robert Hirama, June McCormack and Curtis J. Tompkins, April 1977. Revised by C.J. Tompkins, April 1979. Copyright © Curtis J. Tompkins, 1979.

ORGANIZATION

Before 1970, each medical department of the University of Virginia Medical Center had its own social work staff. In 1970, the Division of Social Service was set up to centralize the hiring and supervision of this function. A corollary objective of the new organization was to increase the professionalism of the social service staff. The division was coordinated by a chairperson who was directly responsible to the Vice President for Health Sciences. The chairperson supervised five departmental chiefs who, in turn, supervised the social workers in their respective departments. The social work departments were: Medical-Surgery, Psychiatry, Pediatrics and Child Abuse, Children's Rehabilitation Center, and Children and Youth. A partial organization chart is shown in Exhibit 1. The staff deployment closely paralleled that which was in existence prior to 1970.

Most of the social work staff were state employees whose salary funding ultimately came from the Virginia State Legislature. Additional funds were channeled through the Medical Center's expense budget and outside sources such as HEW. The Children and Youth Department was supported almost entirely by HEW funds.

The chairperson and several chiefs had faculty appointments in conjunction with their Social Service status. While some lecturing was done, most of the teaching consisted of training medical and nursing students in the dynamics of the patient's social context. The chiefs of Pediatrics and Children and Youth were also involved in community education for the prevention of illness and child abuse. Although it was apparently expected that the majority of the chiefs' time would be spent in direct patient service, there were no clear guidelines for the allocation of their time among their various functions.

SERVICES

The purpose of social work in a hospital was to assist a patient and his family with the social/environmental adjustments precipitated or intensified by the patient's illness. The social worker helped the patient and family cope with the stresses that kept them from accepting or applying medical recommendations.

General services provided included the following:

EXHIBIT 1
Partial Organization Chart

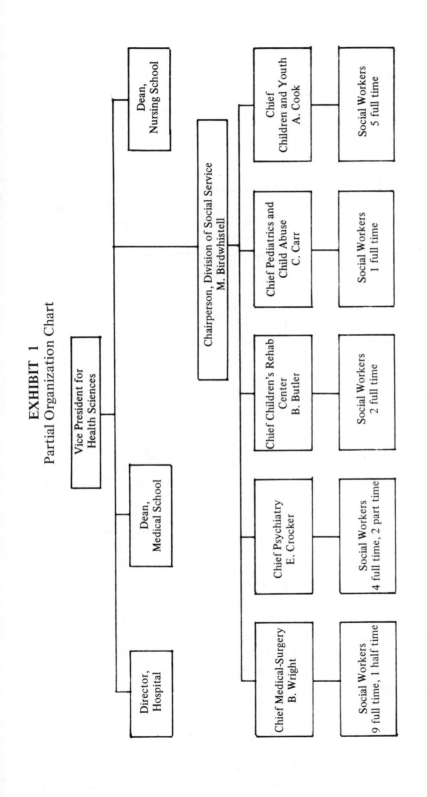

1. Emotional support and assistance to the patient and family in adjusting to the patient's illness
2. Assisting out-of-town families arrange housing and other needs
3. Arranging outpatient treatment
4. Coordination of and referral to needed community services
5. Discharge planning

The specific service provided naturally depended on the patient and the illness. Consequently, the various departments tended to emphasize certain services. For example, the Medical-Surgery department might have been involved with arranging outpatient treatment and community services, while the Psychiatry department might have emphasized family psycho-therapy. All of the above services, however, were provided to some extent by each department.

The referral of patients to the Social Service Division was accomplished by several means. The Quality Assurance Division of the hospital and the Social Service Division jointly developed a form (Exhibit 2) which was completed by the clerk upon admittance of the patient. As indicated on the form, patients with particular illnesses or circumstances were automatically referred. In addition, doctors, nurses and other medical staff could make a referral if the need for a social service became evident. The individual making the referral usually suggested the type of service warranted. The social worker then made an assessment of the patient and implemented the necessary aid.

In several of the departments, notably Pediatrics, the Children's Rehabilitation Center and the Psychiatry department, the social worker was part of an interdisciplinary medical team that worked with the patient. It was the social worker's responsibility to bring to the team the expertise in analyzing the family and social situation of the patient and its effect on a treatment plan. Implementation of the treatment plan involved the provision of social work services. Consequently, there was a close relationship between the social worker and the respective medical staff. The doctor had complete responsibility for the patient and medical unit. He participated in establishing case priorities and the kinds of services that were to be provided; follow-ups on patients were reported to the doctor. The prime responsibility of the social worker was to the medical team involved in the patient's treatment.

REPORTING SYSTEM

There were two primary methods of communication and reporting within the Social Service Division: meetings and the filling out of forms.

EXHIBIT 2
Inter-Departmental Referral Form to Social Work

Name_____ UVA No._____

     (last)   (first)   (middle)

Address _____

Date Admitted _____ Initial LOS_____

Service_____ Location_____

Admitting Diagnosis _____

Reasons for Referral (check all that apply):

1. Patient 62 or over living alone or with invalid   _____
2. Suspected child abuse/neglect patient under 18   _____
3. Suspected abuse/neglect patient over 18   _____
4. Patient or relative unable to give information at admission _____
5. Patient/family needing lodging assistance for extended treatment _____
6. Patient transferred from nursing/foster home or institution _____
7. Chronically ill patient, rehospitalization anticipated _____
8. Patient's condition likely to cause increasing impairment _____
9. Adult patient unable to care for self _____
10. Social worker/social agency named in chart or by patient _____
11. Patient/family requests Social Work referral _____
12. Patient needs special equipment at home _____
13. Patient/family having difficulty adjusting to illness _____
14. Patient with multiple handicaps _____
15. Patient with diagnosis of terminal illness _____
16. Parents after death of child in hospital _____
17. Patient with diagnosis of substance abuse _____
18. Patient with psychiatric diagnosis _____
19. Repeated ER visits when need for medical treatment is questionable _____
20. Patient not complying with medical regimen _____
21. Patient with disfiguring condition _____
22. Obstetrical patient when
    a. adoption requested _____
    b. abortion requested _____
    c. complicated pregnancy/delivery _____
    d. infant transferred to NICU _____
    e. baby with birth defect _____
    f. patient is mentally retarded _____
23. Financial assessment _____
24. Other _____

Referred by _____   Date _____

Disposition:

A. _____ Case being evaluated for services.

B. _____ Case evaluated. No action indicated.

C. _____ Other.

While some of these methods were consistent among the five departments, there was significant diversity. A brief description of the various communication techniques follows.

Reporting

The method of record keeping that was common to all departments[1] was the practice of entering notes on the patient's medical chart. There was no particular format for the social worker's entry, and notes were not necessarily recorded for each patient encounter. The referral document, if one existed, was not included in the file, and no effort was made to evaluate the social service by comparing the worker's "progress notes" with the original assessment. Social workers' notes were scattered through the medical record rather than being kept in one place. The final type of form filed in the patient's medical record was a discharge summary which suggested the type of post-discharge social work to be done. Again, follow-up evaluations of the social service were rarely made after discharge since the record was sent to the hospital's central files, which made recall inconvenient. The medical charts were normally reviewed only in the event that a chronic patient was readmitted to the hospital.

Aside from the medical record, few formal notes were kept on the patients. It appears that only Anne Cook of Children and Youth maintained actual files; the other chiefs kept "scratch notes" and entries on their calendars.

In terms of reporting, only one form was currently being used: The UVA Social Work Reporting Form (Exhibit 3). The social workers (except those in Children and Youth) filled these out at the end of each month based on tallies from their calendars. The reports were turned in by the chiefs to Ms. Birdwhistell who used them to get an idea of the amount of work being done by each group and how their time was being spent. At one time the data had been fed into a computer, but there was currently no methodical compilation or analysis of the information. The data provided by the chiefs tended to be quite general; breakdowns of specific services and time involvements were not made. The chiefs did not feel that the forms were very useful as presently processed. It appeared that only Eleanor Crocker of Psychiatry used the forms as an aid in supervising her staff.

Because there was some dissatisfaction with the current reporting system, some independent efforts were being made within various

---

[1]This pertained to Children and Youth only when a client was admitted to the hospital.

groups. Corinne Carr of Pediatrics had traditionally made reports only on patients who had required two hours or more of her time during a given month. She had recently begun to record all patient encounters in the hope of being able to isolate the more routine services that could be assigned to a clerical worker. In Medical-Surgery, two social workers had been asked to set up a reporting system in response to the hospital's planned internal audit. They were attempting to provide a documented assessment, objective, plan and evaluation of service for each patient. Bertha Wright, the chief of Med-Surg., believed the procedure was too complicated to implement on a large scale.

Meetings

There were basically four types of meetings attended regularly by the Social Service staff. The first type were meetings with the co-members of the interdisciplinary teams to which the social worker was assigned. The purpose of these encounters was usually to discuss specific patients that were being treated at the time; these normally occurred at least once a week. Secondly, the chiefs met once a week for about one and a half hours to review procedures, plans and progress. A third type of meeting were those held by a chief and her staff. These were for supervision, planning or evaluation purposes. It is noted, however, that the only formal evaluation of social workers occurred once a year; at that time, a state evaluation form was filled out and discussed. Finally, administrative meetings were held once a month and were attended by the chiefs and a representative (social worker) from each department; matters of general importance to the Social Service Division were discussed here. Recently, the Accountability Committee had begun attempts to set up a reporting system for the division. This action was in response to the hospital's internal audit plan and was an effort to incorporate assessment, objective, plan and evaluation procedures into a form.

DEVELOPMENT OF AN EVALUATION SYSTEM

In trying to design a system to evaluate effectiveness, Birdwhistell and Crocker realized it was important to clarify the desired purposes of the evaluation. They developed the following list of goals and specifications for the proposed evaluation system:

I. Proper Utilization of Staff
   A. The evaluation system should make it possible to allocate staff to the departments within the division on the basis of need. At present, the demand on social workers in some departments is much greater than in others.
   B. The evaluation system should enable management to determine what type of personnel are needed. Currently, it appears that social workers are doing a large amount of clerical-type work.
   C. The evaluation system should enable management to more effectively match the special education and skills of different social workers to differing tasks. This would increase the efficiency and quality of services provided.
   D. The system should allow the evaluation of individual workers. At present, it is difficult to make a useful and well documented evaluation.

II. Overall Division Effectiveness
   A. The evaluation system should tell management exactly what the division is doing. Currently, management has only a general knowledge of what services are being provided.
   B. The evaluation system should allow management to determine whether the services are actually producing the results desired as stated in the division's objectives.
   C. The evaluation system should provide a sound basis for management's choice of services to be rendered, given a limited amount of resources.

III. The evaluation system should allow management to meet the requirements of governments, hospital auditors and others who will assess the division.

IV. The evaluation system should also help the division identify problems with interfacing organizations. For example, it could allow Social Service management to make suggestions for improvements in hospital or community agency services that would ultimately make the division more effective in meeting its objectives.

EXHIBIT 3

UVA Social Work Reporting Form

Patient's Name _____ UVA No. _____

Month _____ yr. _____
New _____
Reopen _____
Carried over _____

Patient's UVA Number   □-□□□□□□
Residence_____ _____
Birth Year   □□
Sex 1. male 2. female 3. unknown   □
Employment Status   □□
Medical Payment Status   □□
Patient Service Assignment   □□
Working Medical Diagnosis _____
Referral Date   □□□□□□
Source of Referral   □□
Reason for Referral   □   □   □
                Date Admitted   □□□□□□
For   Date First Seen by S.W.   □□□□□□
in-patients   Date Medically Ready for Discharge   □□□□□□
only   Date Discharged   □□□□□□
Services Provided   □   □   □   □
                                                   □   □   □   □
Total Time   □□
Total Fee (charged by S.W.)   □□□
Social Work Diagnosis   □□□
                                                         □□□
                                                         □□□
Service Outcome _____
Disposition 1. Remaining Open 2. Closed 3. Deceased   □
                                 Social Worker _____

Instructions for UVA Social Work Reporting System

Patient's Name and UVA Number

This item was placed at the top for confidentiality reasons. Please cut off before turning the form in. It would be wise to keep them (not indefinitely) until a system for chart review is implemented. All the committee would have would be the date, patient's number, and the social worker's name. In order to pull the chart, the patient name will need to be supplied by the worker.

Month, Year—New, Reopen, Carried Over

Month and year relates to the month in which you are reporting. Obviously, the forms turned in this month will be dated Nov., 1975. The other three items relate to the status of the case in your caseload at the time of the initial monthly contact.

Patient's UVA Number

Fill in the *last* six boxes unless the patient is in the Towers and doesn't have a UVA number. In those instances, the letter is placed in the first box followed by six numbers.

Residence

Write in the city and state.

Birth Year

If the patient was born in 1942, put 42 in the two available boxes.

Sex

Self-explanatory.

Employment Status

Select the most appropriate description and place the corresponding number in the boxes.

01	Preschool	06	Unemployed
02	Going to school	07	Unemployed due to illness
03	Keeping house	08	Disabled
04	Working full time	09	Retired
05	Working part time	10	Incarcerated

Medical Payment Status

Select most appropriate source of payment for this particular visit.

01	Medicare	06	CCB
02	Medicaid	07	CHAMPUS
03	Referred Medicaid	08	None
04	Cash fee	09	Unknown
05	Private insurance	10	Other

EXHIBIT 3 (CONTINUED)

Patient Service Assignment
   Please refer to attached list.

Working Medical Diagnosis
   This is *not* a request to be very specific, accurate or to include all the diagnoses. It would be helpful, if you know the patient's primary medical diagnosis, to please write it in.

Referral Date
   Self-explanatory.

Source of Referral
   Select appropriate source:
   01   UVA Physician (includes attendants, house staff, and students)
   02   Nurse
   03   Patient
   04   Family of patient
   05   Community agency
   06   System (i.e., all HCC patients have to be seen by a social worker)
   07   UVA Social Worker
   08   Ward Clerk
   09   Other
   10   LMD (local medical doctor)
   11   Quality Assurance Screening (admissions)

Reason for Referral
   Select most appropriate reason(s) in order of importance per your social work assessment.
   1. Need for social work assessment.
   2. Psychological functioning.
   3. Assistance with adaptation to illness.
   4. Need for discharge planning.
   5. Need for facilitating services.
   6. Consultation with other staff.

In-Patient Data
   Self-explanatory.

Services Provided
   There are boxes available to indicate as many as 8 out of the 10 services.
   1. Social work assessment   3. Casework with family of pt.
   2. Casework with patient   4. Marital therapy

5. Family therapy	8. Chart, letter, telephoning
6. Parent counseling	9. Collateral contacts*
7. Group work	10. Consultation with other staff

Total Time

This indicates the total time spent on patient-related activities during the course of the month. Please record in 15 minute time units, i.e., 4½ hours is equal to 34 time units.

Total Fee

This is defined as the total fee for social work services charged to that patient in the month, whether or not the Division of Social Work receives it. In settings where a single fee is charged a family, allocate a portion of that fee for social work.

Social Work Diagnoses

See attached sheet. Select up to three diagnoses and record them in order of importance.

Service Outcome

Select appropriate outcome.
1. Service provided/case closed
2. Service initiated/case continuing
3. Assessment completed/referral for needed service
4. Service provided/follow-up will be initiated in the future
5. Assessment completed/service not needed
6. Patient declined service

Disposition

Self-explanatory except for deceased. If a patient died in this month but additional services are needed by the family, keep the case open until all services are completed, then record deceased.

---

*Collateral refers to contacts with other professionals in the medical center as well as agencies and professionals in the community concerning a patient.

EXHIBIT 3 (CONTINUED)
Social Work Diagnosis

100 Psychological functioning
101 Personal adjustment problems
102 Family relationship problems
103 Marital conflict
104 School problems
105 Employment problems
106 Child protection
107 Family planning
108 Adoption counseling
109 Abortion counseling
110 Alcoholism
111 Drug problem
112 Sterilization request
113 Adult protection

200 Assistance with adaption to illness
201 Acceptance of illness and/or needed treatment
202 Understanding medical recommendations
203 Assistance in obtaining treatment, medical equipment, payment of medical care

300 Need for discharge planning
301 In own home or relative's home
302 Nursing home
303 Boarding or rest home
304 Psychiatric facility
305 Other institution
306 Other

400 Need for facilitating services
401 Lodging
402 Transportation
403 Food
404 Clothing
405 Medicine
406 Medical equipment
407 Referral to resource for financial help for living expenses
408 Referral to resource for financial help for medical needs
409 Referral for community health services
410 Referral for training, school or employment help
411 Referral for protective services
412 Information re: resources, facilities
413 Referral for community mental health resource
414 Other

Patient Service Assignment

01 Adult Psychiatric Clinic
02 Allergy Clinic
03 Arthritis Clinic
04 Anti-Convulsive Clinic
05 Amputee Clinic

06 Child and Adolescent Clinic (C&A
07 Children and Youth (C&Y)
08 Cystic Fibrosis Clinic
09 Chemotherapy
10 Cardiac Clinic
11 Cerebral Palsy Clinic
12 Cardiac Care Unit (CCU)

13 Diabetic Clinic
14 Dermatology & Syphilology (D&

15 Emergency Room (ER)
16 Endocrine Clinic
17 Employee Health

18 Family–Community Medicine
19 Facial Deformity Clinic

20 Gastro-Intestinal Clinic
21 Burn Unit
22 Gynecology (GYN)

23 Handicapped Children's Clinic
24 Hemodialysis Unit (Renal)
25 Hemotology Clinic
26 Hypertension Clinic

27 Learning Disability
28 Lupus Clinic
29 Medical Clinic
30 Medicine
31 McIntyre III

32 Muscular Dystrophy Clinic
33 Myelomeningocele Clinic

34 Neurology
35 Neurosurgery
36 Newborn Special Care Unit
    (NBSC)
37 Obstetrics (OB)
38 Orthopedics
39 Orthopedics (Towers)
40 Opthamalogy (EYE)
41 Otolaryngology (ENT)

42 Pain Clinic
43 Pediatric Surgery
44 Psychiatric–Davis 2
45 Psychiatric–Davis 3
46 Psychiatric Consult
47 Pediatrics
48 Pulmonary Clinic
49 Plastic Surgery

50 Radiation Therapy
51 Renal Clinic
52 Rheumatic Fever Clinic

53 Screening Clinic
54 Scoliosis Clinic
55 Surgery

56 Thoracic-Cardio-Vascular

57 Urology
58 Surgery Clinic
59 Ent Clinic
60 Plastic Surgery Clinic
61 Eye Clinic

75 Bloomfield

99 Social Work Division

FOUR

PLANNING

Adaptive Forward Planning[*]

During the early 1980s the number of nonprofit organizations engaged in systematic, long-range corporate planning will be significant; this confident prediction is based partially on first hand observations of several well managed nonprofit institutions such as the United Way of America and the YMCA. Yet, in the 1970s, most nonprofit organizations lagged far behind many for-profit corporations in their strategic, long-range planning practices. Most nonprofit organizations suffered from a malady sometimes called "annualitis," the myopic preoccupation with plans and activities for the next year, but minimal regard for long-term, strategic implications or opportunities. One of the primary revolutions in management of nonprofit and public sector organizations during the next five years will be considerable attention to what Peter Drucker has called "strategic planning—the entrepreneurial skill."[1]

The movement toward a more proactive, strategic approach to management from a typically reactive, tactical mode is being fostered by volunteer board members who are themselves engaged in strategic planning in their corporations, by nonprofit organization managers who are being educated to the need for such planning, and by the increasing avail-

*This note was written by Curtis J. Tompkins, Copyright © 1978 by C.J. Tompkins.
[1] Drucker, Peter J., *Management: Tasks, Responsibilities, Practices*, Harper and Row, 1974. (In particular, see Chapter 10).

ability of timely information and analytic capabilities vital to the planning process. Nonprofit managers are increasingly less willing to accept the consequences of allowing external factors, by default, to determine their organizations' destinies.

A challenge faced by many nonprofit organizations during the late 1970s and early 1980s is one of determining how to go about strategic, long-range planning. While the concept is increasingly appealing, the most effective process for organizing and conducting an organization's strategic planning process is not generally understood. However, there are some tested principles and practices that are emerging and seem worthy of consideration by managers of nonprofit organizations. The purpose of this paper is to summarize some of the basic considerations, elements and approaches that are being used with some degree of success by several progressive nonprofit organizations. It is important to emphasize at the outset that there is no single, absolute best process for strategic planning; rather, each organization must develop its own tailored process. That process will require a fairly high degree of conceptual skill as well as reasonable amounts of technical and human skills on the part of managers engaged in the process.

Short-term planning and activities should be accompanied by an awareness of the longer-term implications, the "futurity," of those plans and actions. The strategic, long-term plan becomes a backdrop and a framework for shorter-term, tactical decisions. Truly successful long-range planning must be comprehensive, integrating all areas of responsibility within an organization. It is very important that the long-range planning process be open, dynamic, flexible and continuing; typically, the long-range plan of an organization should be carefully reviewed, evaluated and updated annually. The planning process, in this sense, should be "adaptive" rather than static. Perhaps, then, the best term for this process would be "adaptive forward planning," as suggested by Paul, Donavan, and Taylor[2] and others.

BASIC INGREDIENTS AND CHARACTERISTICS

The basic theory of adaptive forward planning has been stated by Vancil and Lorange[3] as follows: "Using a time horizon of several years,

[2]Paul, R.N., N.B. Donavan, and J.W. Taylor, "The Reality Gap in Strategic Planning," *Harvard Business Review*, May-June, 1978, pp. 124-130.
[3]Vancil, R.F. and P. Lorange, "Strategic Planning in Diversified Companies," *Harvard Business Review*, January-February 1975, p. 81.

top management reassesses its current strategy by looking for opportunities and threats in the environment and by analyzing the company's resources to identify its strengths and weaknesses." The simplicity of this statement is deceiving, for the successful practice and implementation of adaptive forward planning require considerable top executive involvement and staff time, expertise in forecasting, development and maintenance of an information base, a system for monitoring key external and internal factors, and a degree of comprehensiveness that may not have existed previously in many nonprofit organizations.

A key first step in adaptive forward planning is the clear definition of who the organization's *constituents* are and will be during the next 5-10 years. This is not always an easy thing to do. Indeed, many hours of discussion and analysis have been spent on this step by conscientious board members, executives, and others involved in projecting where the nonprofit organization should be going and what it should become. To the extent there is lack of understanding or agreement within the organization about its present and future constituencies, to that extent ambiguities will occur in the remainder of the planning process.

The important *needs* of an organization's constituents should be identified. An acceptable balance among these needs must be articulated so that operating policies reflect the organization's true intentions relative to each constituent. The pattern described by an organization's operating policies is a very real indication of what an organization is trying to become.

Closely allied with the definition of constituents and identification of their needs is the development of a fairly specific statement of the *role and mission* of the organization. Once again, this step is often difficult for many nonprofit organizations and has been finessed by top executives who want to avoid dissension and time-consuming arguments. The executive may contend that the organization's role and mission is well known and well accepted. Often, the board chairman or executive will refer to the charter, the bylaws or the constitution of the organization when asked for a statement of role and mission. Such statements may prove to be of limited value for purposes of deciding future strategy. Broad statements such as "to do good for mankind throughout the world" are not sufficient definitions of role and mission. The organization's past, present and future roles and missions may be very different. The question of "what our mission should be" deserves periodic, indepth consideration as a vital part of adaptive forward planning.

Based on constituent needs and organizational mission, *long-term goals* are established for the organization. These goals should not be hopes, but should be realistic, attainable indications of what the organization as a whole is trying to achieve and to become. Specific organizational *objectives* supporting the general long-term goals are then developed. An objective should be specific, measurable, and attainable; the expected timing of an objective should be clearly stated.

An organization cannot be "all things to all people." Some of its activities may be deferable; others may be critical and considered absolutely nondeferable. *Priorities* must be established for an organization in terms of specifying the relative importance and deferability of its objectives. Failure to recognize and articulate relative priorities can significantly hamper organizational effectiveness. An organization with muddled or unrealistic priorities is likely to fail to achieve according to its real potential.

It is vital to the planning process to have the ability to *measure results* and to use those measures to realize whether expectations are being fulfilled or not. Peter Drucker has made the following strong statement in this regard:

> In strategic planning, measurements present very real problems, especially conceptual ones. Yet precisely because what we measure and how we measure determine what will be considered relevant, and determine thereby not just what we see, but what we—and others—do, measurements are all-important in the planning process.[4]

A *five-year planning horizon* is typical in many good long-range planning programs; however, the selection of an appropriate planning horizon depends heavily on the type of organization and its environment. The United States Postal Service has begun to consider what its business should be 20 years from now. A local human service organization has decided to use a five-year planning horizon. An academic department at a major land-grant university is attempting to plan over a seven-year horizon; another academic department, in the same field of study at another university uses a three-year horizon.

Whatever the planning horizon, the long-range plan should be *reviewed and revised* annually, reflecting changes in planning assumptions and premises. This requirement is sometimes difficult to sell and implement within a nonprofit organization which may be short-staffed and inundated with short-term demands and crises. The work involved in developing an organization's first comprehensive, long-range plan may leave key participants in the planning process somewhat weary. Yet, it is a very costly trap to allow excuses, reasons and alibis to justify failure to

---

[4] Drucker, op. cit., p. 128.

engage in continuing, adaptive forward planning. Most environments and our understanding of those environments are changing sufficiently to mandate an annual indepth review and revision of the plan.

ACTIVITIES INVOLVED

An organization's plan should state *what* an organization is going to do, *how* it is going to proceed, and *when* it will take action, developed in relatively broad terms for the more distant years and in specific terms for the closer years. Present services, products and activities should be appraised to determine future potential and future hurdles. Then, possible future services, and ideas for services should be considered; possible directions for future growth should be identified. Organizational strengths and weaknesses should be analyzed in terms of components of capability such as human resources, physical facilities, specialized experience and expertise, technological superiority, supply and market positions, financial capability, the organization's momentum in its present fields of activity and the organization's flexibility—its ability and willingness to adapt and change. These strengths and weaknesses should be compared to those of the organization's present and future competitors.

All organizations compete for resources, personnel and markets. Some organizations are "passive competitors," but, like it or not, they still are in competition for one thing or another. The more aggressive competitor may be more likely to recruit the more capable staff members, to gain a larger share of available resources, and to receive more recognition and acceptance among its constituents. Adaptive forward planning can be the cornerstone of effective management in a competitive, changing environment.

While good planning does not substitute facts for judgment, factual ground work should be the basis for a good plan. "Brainstorming" sessions and "retreats" are not ways to get the factual work done. Information needs to be continually gathered about the organization's environment. This "intelligence acquisition" should provide pertinent information about social and cultural changes, demographic shifts, the economic environment, government policies, the technological environment and markets and competition. At the outset of an adaptive planning program, the task of environmental scanning (as it has been called) may seem to constitute an unreasonably burdensome requirement, but it does not have to be so. Few organizations can afford to institute a

comprehensive, sophisticated "environmental information system" during the early stages of development of an adaptive forward planning
program, but most organizations can justify gradually increasing their
attention to key influences in the environment.

Forecasting changes in the organization's environment may seem impossible or, at least, difficult and frustrating. Yet, a manager explicitly
and implicitly makes assumptions about the future everytime he or she
makes a decision, and those assumptions or premises constitute a type
of "forecast." The better one's forecasts, premises and assumptions
about the future, the better his or her decisions. The strength and usefulness of an organizational plan are dependent, in part, on the accuracy
of the underlying forecasts. William Ascher has aptly stated that "undoubtedly policy-makers themselves are generally unaware of how important the forecasts really are in their ultimate decisions."[5] The need for
good forecasts in successful adaptive forward planning should be in-
tuitively apparent. The problem has been, and will continue to be, that
it is very difficult to forecast many environmental changes that will occur 3-5 years hence. Yet, it is increasingly unacceptable in many nonprofit organizations to ignore the futurity of short-term decisions; future
implications must be projected, considered and analyzed. Thus, forecasting must be a key activity within an organization's adaptive forward
planning program.

Most nonprofit organizations in the late 1970s were still relatively
casual about forecasting, compared with for-profit corporations. Many
opportunities to do forecasting were being foregone by nonprofit managers. However, notable exceptions were beginning to emerge, and a
gradual realization of the need for and the possibility of forecasting
seemed promising.[6] A survey of forecasting methods and management
considerations are presented in footnote 7.

One approach to the difficult areas of environmental analysis and
forecasting is to develop a set of position papers which deal with alternative organizational strategies under several possible future scenarios.
By involving representatives of various key constituencies in the process
of reviewing, editing and revising such position papers, the decision
maker may be able to gain more insight and more confidence about the
validity of forecasts, assumptions and premises.

[5] Ascher, William, *Forecasting: An Appraisal for Policy-Makers and Planners,* The John Hopkins University Press, Baltimore, 1978, p. 4.

[6] The case study on *Richmond Memorial Hospital* is an example of a situation where past
experiences may serve as the basis for predicting the future, especially in forecasting the demand for services.

[7] Tompkins, Curtis J., "Business Forecasting," chapter in the *Encyclopedia of Professional
Management,* McGraw-Hill, New York, 1978.

In most nonprofit organizations, meaningful involvement of key constituents in the organizations' planning process usually proves to be politically beneficial and technically helpful. However, methods employed to gain such meaningful involvement vary considerably among organizations. Some organizations have outside constituents on their long-range planning committees; others solicit comments and suggestions from outside constituents about planning assumptions, but do not otherwise allow intimate involvement in the internal planning process. The degree of outside constituent involvement in long-range planning depends on the organization's marketing philosophy and on the trade offs between the specific risks and benefits associated with such involvement.

A long-range planning committee should be established within the organization and should report to the chief executive officer of the organization. This committee should make sure that people who will be responsible for accomplishing the objectives at the operational objective level, do participate in the establishment of organizational objectives. The committee should focus on a limited number of goals, perhaps no more than seven or eight. Typically, a long-range planning committee in a nonprofit organization would have the following responsibilities:

1. Organizes and reviews pertinent literature.
2. Reviews, modifies and approves the proposed long-range planning approach proposed by the committee chairman and the organization's chief executive.
3. Meets to prepare the role and mission statement of the organization for board consideration.
4. Determines expectations held by key internal and external constituents for the organization, and factors this information into the preparation of the organization's role and mission statement.
5. Plans the schedule for long-range planning.
6. Collects (or directs staff members to collect) data necessary for forecasting and decision making.
7. Reviews critical data regarding future trends, community needs, and capabilities of the organization.
8. Determines the critical issues for the organization.
9. Finalizes recommendations of organizational goals and implementation strategies.
10. Evaluates actual achievement of the organization against the plan, and determines areas of success and problems.
11. Recommends revisions in the organization's process and schedule for long-range planning.

Adaptive forward planning is time consuming. It should not be an "add on" or overtime type of duty for an executive. It is important that the chief executive be directly involved in the planning process. If top anagement is truly committed to achieve the best possible results from strategic planning, that commitment should be demonstrated by real involvement, with special focus on underlying assumptions and trends.

BENEFITS OF ADAPTIVE FORWARD PLANNING

One of the payoffs from adaptive forward planning should be the filling of the so-called "strategic gap"—the disparity between the organization's future potential and "status quo results" that would probably occur without good planning. One of the action results from effective planning should be the replacement of organizational weaknesses with organizational opportunities. Thus, good adaptive forward planning should minimize the disparity between organizational potential and what the organization actually achieves, on a continuing year-to-year basis.

A value of good planning is that it helps to keep executives from panicking when reverses happen or dips occur. Adaptive forward planning does *not* assume there will be ideal conditions or "smooth sailing." Unexpected things *will* happen, but they in no way affect the practicality of planning. Indeed, as an executive becomes involved in adaptive forward planning on a continuing basis, he or she becomes increasingly attuned to the possibilities of environmental change and consequently is better prepared mentally and emotionally for such change than might otherwise be the case.

Effective adaptive forward planning, by virtue of being comprehensive, fosters and supports better integration of the various parts of an organization. It becomes one of the common threads that strengthens an awareness of the inter-relationships of the subsystems within the organization. Good planning does not "staple together" the plans of the departments or divisions within an organization; rather, it weaves a fabric that should be stronger than a simple collection of individual plans. As such, it should provide a balanced approach to the organization's future in which the parts of the organization increasingly seek to fit their activities more effectively into the larger pattern portrayed by the overall plan and its underlying assumptions and premises. Looking at it the other way, the chief executive can better judge individual policies and practices by evaluating how they relate to other policies and to organizational goals through the adaptive forward plan.

Through the process of adaptive forward planning, an executive can better judge how consistent a proposed strategy is with respect to the current environment and, more importantly, with respect to the environment as it appears to be changing.

The organization which fails to conduct adaptive forward planning incurs "opportunity costs" (i.e., fails to close the strategic gap). In that sense, there are risks involved in failing to plan. In a related but somewhat different sense, good adaptive forward planning provides a relatively comfortable opportunity for the decision maker to evaluate the risks associated with alternative strategies. Major areas of managerial choice are usually identified while there is still time to explore a variety of alternatives, and resource requirements are discovered well before the last minute. This should result in a more acceptable degree of risk for the organization than would otherwise be true.

LEVELS OF PLANNING AND NECESSARY SKILLS

Most of the attention in this paper has been on strategic planning for the organization as a whole. At that broadest of all levels of planning, the organization addresses several questions including:

1. What should be the mission(s) of the organization?
2. What should be the service (market) scope of our operations and why do we believe we can be successful in our endeavor?
3. On what basis do we undertake some projects and programs and exclude others?
4. On what basis do we say YES to some proposals and NO to others?
5. On what basis do we decide to drop an existing program or project?

Paul, Donavan and Taylor[8] point out a common weakness of many plans as follows:

> Most plans say nothing about "folding a bad hand," but they should because it is inevitable that bad hands will turn up in any extended period of time.

At a more specific level of planning (often called programming, planning and budgeting), the following questions pertain:

[8] Paul, et al., op. cit.

1. What multi-year programs, projects or groups of related activities should we consider?
2. Which programs best contribute to the accomplishment of our organizational mission(s)?
3. Which projects best reflect our competitive advantages?
4. How shall we allocate our resources among projects?

The most specific level of planning deals with individual responsibility unit planning and control (often called operations management), addressing such questions as:

1. What short-term activities should we undertake?
2. How shall we assign responsibility and motivate and control behavior?

A good discussion of these three levels of planning and of the relationships among them is presented by Dermer.[9] An effective, adaptive forward planning system should interrelate these three levels so that in practice they are mutually supportive and reinforcing.

At the broadest level of planning, organization structure and management philosophy should be considered. Should we adopt a matrix approach to management? Should we decentralize? Can we use a management by objectives process throughout the organization? Is zero-base budgeting an appropriate activity for our organization? To the extent these questions of *how* we manage are treated as strategic level considerations by top management, the organization will tend to be strong and healthy. This requires significant *conceptual* ability on the part of top management. Perhaps no other managerial activity requires as much conceptual skill and creativity as does strategic planning.

As the level of planning becomes more specific, less conceptual skill is required and more technical and human skills are needed by the managers involved. Resource allocation methodologies and interpersonal skills become increasingly useful as planning becomes more specific. In 1955, Robert L. Katz first discussed the "skills of an effective administrator" in this regard,[10] and 20 years later, he reflected on his earlier perceptions.[11] He concludes that, whereas technical and human skills

[9] Dermer, Jerry D., *Management Planning and Control Systems: Advanced Concepts and Cases*, Richard D. Irwin, Homewood, Ill., 1977.

[10] Katz, Robert L., "Skills of an Effective Administrator," *Harvard Business Review*, January-February, 1955.

[11] Katz, Robert L., "Retrospective Commentary," Chapter 2 in *Harvard Business Review on Management*, Harper and Row, 1976.

can be learned and strengthened throughout a manager's career, conceptual skill is an innate ability that is much more difficult to enhance and develop. Thus, a manager who has been successful as a first-line supervisor and as a middle-level manager may not be successful as an upper level administrator where more conceptual skill is needed. One of the managerial activities where conceptual strength or weakness may be most apparent is strategic planning.

In evaluating a manager's performance, it is often difficult (and sometimes impossible) to prove whether organizational success or failure should be attributed to the organization's plan, to the manager's executive of the plan, or both. As Paul, Donavan and Taylor have stated,[12] "a poorly *executed* plan can produce undesirable results just as easily as can a poorly *conceived* plan." In other words, a manager with good conceptual ability may produce an excellent plan but fail to achieve expected results because of weak human or technical skills. The other side of that coin would be the situation where strong human and technical skills compensate for a weak plan, to produce outstanding results in spite of the poorly conceived plan. This latter type of situation has appeared to be the case in many successful nonprofit organizations.

CRITERIA FOR EVALUATING
THE PLANNING PROCESS

To assure a high likelihood of successful planning in a nonprofit organization, the board member, top executive, or chairman of the organization's adaptive forward planning system should consider the following questions and suggestions:

1. Does the planning head have the most appropriate temperament, training and attitude to be effective in his role?
    This person should be objective and open to new ways of doing things. In addition to having good conceptual skill, the planning head should not be afraid to say that "this is right and that is wrong," with an indifference to the personal implications of fact finding and objective analysis. This is often a rare individual in many organizations; yet, the success of the entire planning process

[12] Paul, et al., op. cit.

depends heavily on having such a person be responsible for the planning activities of the organization.

2. Does the director of the adaptive planning process have continual, balanced contact with the various aspects of the organization?
The resultant plan should reflect a team approach, with balanced influence and participation from all parts of the organization.

3. Is top management intimately involved in the planning *process*?
Top management should avoid making the plan an end in itself and should pay special attention to the assumptions and trends underlying the plan.

4. Is the plan geared to *events* rather than to a strict timetable that ignores the possibility of legitimate reasons for changing the absolute timing of activities?
Plans that recognize the dependence of action on certain events occurring are likely to be more successful than those that are inflexible in this regard. For example, a good plan may state "If Event Y happens we will institute Service Z" or "We will develop Phase 3 when contributions reach Level X."
The key words in these event-oriented statements are *if* and *when*.

5. Does the plan provide explicit criteria for abandoning a project?
This point was mentioned earlier in this paper.

6. Is there an effective monitoring system for key areas of organizational activity and environmental change to permit the organization to make "on course corrections" during the year with a minimal amount of effort?

7. Is the plan reviewed thoroughly each year, and does the organization make a new updated five-year (or other appropriate planning horizon) plan each year?

8. Is the long-term plan internally consistent? Does each program plan fit into an integrated pattern?

9. Has the planning committee determined the key influences in growth and other changes in the organization's markets?

10. Have the strengths and weaknesses of the organization been accurately evaluated?

11. Have the strengths and weaknesses of the organization's *competitors* been appraised?

12. Have the capacities of the various organizational functions to support the plan, been projected far enough ahead?

13. Are the organizational goals and objectives consistent with the current and future needs of the organization's constituents?

14. Are the organization's goals and objectives appropriate in view of available resources?

15. Does the plan involve an acceptable degree of risk? What provisions have been made for future reverses?
16. Is the planning horizon appropriate?
17. Have all reasonable alternatives been considered?

In some organizations there is confusion about the relationships and differences among forecasting, planning, and budgeting. The aim of forecasting is to show what future trends and conditions will or might be; planning aims to take advantage of those trends and conditions. Budgeting involves forecasts, coordination and control of future management actions; planning encompasses budgeting and goes into the what, how and when of those actions, and considers a longer period of time than does the budgeting process. In many nonprofit organizations, budgeting has been the predominant planning activity, and the resultant myopic management has hindered the effectiveness and progress of those organizations.

Case 8

Common Cause*

TIME TO END THE FLIM-FLAM

One of the most moving lines in the Declaration of Independence appears at the very end of that document. In support of the Declaration, the signers say, "... we mutually pledge to each other our lives, our fortunes, and our sacred honor." Down the years, many Americans have followed them in that pledge. We have had our full share of rascals and cynics in American history, but we have also had our share of those who gave their lives, literally and figuratively, to make this nation a model for all mankind. They believed the words of the Declaration. They not only pledged but gave their lives, their fortunes, and their sacred honor. All to what end? To create government with a "For Sale" sign on it?

Perhaps at a less critical time in our history we could tolerate rascality in high places. But not now. Our country is in deep trouble. We cannot tolerate the dominance of courthouse politics, the shady deal and the crass payoff. It is time for the citizen to stand up and say "Enough!" It is time to end the flim-flam and put our political institutions into working order. It can be done.[1]

*This case was prepared by Stephen J. Zimmerly under the supervision of Professors Christopher Gale and Leslie E. Grayson of the University of Virginia. Copyright ©1974, University of Virginia Graduate School of Business Administration Sponsors.

[1] John W. Gardner, *In Common Cause*, W.W. Norton & Co., New York, 1972, p. 43.

In July, 1972, Roger Craver, Director of Development for Common Cause, was considering new avenues for increasing the membership of the two-year-old organization. Mr. Craver felt that the "bread and butter" membership renewals, consisting mainly of better educated, higher income, generally middle-class whites, was saturated. Since he was sure that further extensive mailings to this group would not generate the added members that Common Cause needed, he had explored the possibilities of appealing to other major segments in American life, including disadvantaged groups, retired people, blue-collar laborers, civil service workers, military personnel, youth groups, and academics.

After some hesitation, Mr. Craver decided that youth groups offered the most feasible segment from which to generate new members; however, despite the fact that he and his colleagues at Common Cause had developed considerable experience and expertise in understanding the needs of their current constituency, he felt somewhat at a loss as to what appeals and methods would most effectively attract young people to Common Cause.

THE BEGINNING OF COMMON CAUSE

When John Gardner, now Chairman of Common Cause, was Secretary of Health, Education and Welfare (HEW), he became convinced that the only way to revitalize governmental institutions was through an active citizenry. Common Cause, organized by Gardner in 1970 to work within the system for the benefit of the average person, was meant by its founders to become "the citizen's lobby." Common Cause exemplified the hard-hitting, relentless, and successful citizen action that was sweeping the United States in the early 1970s. According to the Common Cause people, they proved that the average person could "fight city hall" . . . and win! They did it, they maintained, by combining widespread citizen concern with the professional lobbying techniques previously used by special interest groups, business, and labor. As John Gardner stated their purpose: "We deal with the basic issue that underlies all others—whether citizens will have access to their own government and whether we can call our government to account."

Mr. Gardner was a well-respected "establishment" man; before he became Secretary of HEW, he was President of the Carnegie Corporation. Since he was deeply involved in many aspects of American society, he was able to enlist the aid of several nationally known individuals as board members, including Mayors John Lindsay (New York) and Carl Stokes (Cleveland), Leonard Woodcock (President of the United Auto Workers), The Rev. Jesse Jackson (civil rights leader), Betty Furness (consumer protection consultant), and Andrew Heiskell (chairman of Time, Inc.).

Washington skeptics, having seen the birth and death of many citizens. organizations, predicted that Common Cause would be an unmitigated disaster. Accordingly, Mr. Gardner thought that a first year's membership goal of 100,000 was optimistic. However, mail poured in at the rate of 1,000 letters per day, and this goal was surpassed in only twenty-three weeks. At the first anniversary, Common Cause had 200,000 members. This compared with the 155,000 members of the better known League of Women Voters.

ORGANIZATION

Common Cause had only a small staff of trained lobbyists and public relations experts. Volunteers provided the driving force of the organization at both the national and local levels. At any given time in the Washington headquarters, it was not unusual to see a wide variety of people digging through the mounds of mail and computer printouts that threatened to inundate everything and everyone. There was a constant sense of urgent excitement coupled with the more mundane realization that some "staffer" was always dispersing change to pay a volunteer's bus fare. Because of its volunteer nature, Common Cause had internal communications and staff turnover problems. On-the-job training was minimal and work assignments were casually based upon personal preferences. The walls virtually bristled with memos, posters, slogans, and instructions. Visitors often commented that moving through the offices was more like swimming than walking. Effectiveness of the local chapters varied a great deal from state to state and from locality to locality. All local chapters were staffed exclusively by volunteers. Chapter activity was conducted in "bursts"; when an issue caught on there was feverish activity frequently followed by extensive periods of lull.

AGENDA

Common Cause was a nonpartisan organization, but as a lobby it did take a firm stand on issues. To determine the priorities of the members, the first newsletter contained a list of fifteen proposed areas of action; the letter encouraged members to indicate which of these issues they felt should be pursued by the organization. Because of the difficulties encountered in gauging the opinions of the rapidly growing membership, a similar "referendum" was held in June 1971 (Exhibit 1 lists the results of that second questionnaire). The choice of questions for the referendum had been developed from a set of goals established by the Board of Governors. In addition to the more formal channels, many members expressed their feelings through letters they sent to the national headquarters in Washington or by local meetings. However, local autonomy in issue selection was not allowed. Common Causes's Governing Board, composed of 60 persons elected by the membership at large and 20 persons elected by the Board, made the decisions as to which issues would be joined, as well as how and when.

The agenda issues that were to be the major areas of concentration were quite broad. The new organization needed, however, quickly to establish a record of success. To do this, Common Cause mounted extensive campaigns for the 18-year-old vote and against the Supersonic Transport (SST) aircraft. Both congressional votes in 1972 went as Common Cause had lobbied, and those "instant victories" were used to attract additional members and jell the present ones into a cohesive unit.

In reviewing the requirements for successful lobbying, Mr. Gardner developed these conclusions:

> The first requirement for effective citizen action is stamina. Arthur Vanderbilt said court reform is no sport for the short-winded. The same

EXHIBIT 1

Selection of Issues by Members, July 1971

Issue	% of Respondents Who Favor
Overhaul and revitalize government	94.5%
Protect and enhance the environment	89.5
Improve criminal justice system	89.4
Withdraw all U.S. forces from Indochina	85.4
Help eliminate poverty	79.7
Fight sex and race discrimination	74.6
Make government accountable	53.3
Tax reform	20.9
Arms control	6.5

Source: Common Cause records.

is true of citizen action. The special-interest lobbies never let up. The second requirement is an informed public. The special interests flourish in the dark. Officials begin to respect citizen action when they discover that citizens are watching and the media are reporting what the citizens see. The third requirement is focused action. The gravest weakness of many high-minded citizens is random indignation. They must pick a few targets and mobilize strength, numbers, and money in order to have an impact. The fourth requirement is the creation of inside-outside alliances. An effective citizen group doesn't sit outside Congress, or any government body, lobbing mortar shells over the walls. There are ready allies inside for any forward-looking movement, and they have to be found. The fifth requirement is a professional cutting edge. It's a peculiar quirk of high-minded people to believe that only the wicked need good lawyers. Citizens must be prepared to match professional skill and knowledge with their opponents.[2]

INTO ACTION, 1972

By the beginning of 1972, Common Cause had accomplished its short-term objective of keeping alive and was now ready to turn to the longer term issues of the war in Indochina, campaign finance monitoring and reform, Congressional reform (i.e., the end of the seniority system and the end of closed hearings), and equal rights for women.

Common Cause slated its major activity in 1972 toward the monitoring of campaign spending. It had sued both political parties to restrain them from violating the law which prohibited individual contributions of more than $5,000 to a political candidate. It lobbied, sued, and prodded; finally Congress passed a new campaign-spending law which took effect on April 7, 1972. Armed with this law, Common Cause investigated over 200 candidates for possible violations. TRW, Inc. was also sued for violating a law which prohibited campaign gifts by government contractors. All of those actions were resolved in favor of Common Cause. However, as Fred Wertheimer, who directed the campaign-monitoring project, explained, the new law did not change the enforcement mechanism: "It didn't change the fact that government officials had to go to court to prosecute offenders and never did."

Common Cause favored financing the nation's elections with public subsidies and tax credits instead of large private contributions. Mr. Wert-

[2] Elizabeth Drew, "Conversation with a Citizen," *The New Yorker*, pp. 35-55, July 23, 1973. (Reproduced by permission).

heimer observed "We live in a corrupted political system: It allows people who want preference from the government to provide financial aid to precisely those people who are asking for a favorable political decision. The new law helps deal with this problem. It is comprehensive in its requirement of disclosure and we want to get compliance with it; we want to force candidates to make their financial resources clear."

The major legal battle, however, was with the Committee to Re-elect The President (CRP); the CRP was a privately organized group working for Richard Nixon's re-election. Common Cause sued this group to make public a list of those who contributed to Mr. Nixon's campaign before April 7, 1972, the effective date of the new campaign-financing disclosure law. While technically the CRP would not have to give out this information, there were many pieces of evidence that indicated that there were irregularities in the committee's methods.

Taking legal action was only one of Common Cause's three methods of operation, and it was generally considered to be a means of last resort. Most of Common Cause's efforts went into lobbying through either the professional staff in Washington or a groundswell of public sentiment as expressed in letters and phone calls from citizens to their representatives in Congress. The professional lobbying effort was concentrated in Washington where it performed in much the same fashion as any other lobby. Members of Congress were bombarded with information in support of Common Cause's issues and the message that it represented over 200,000 citizens.

The professional staff was generally credited by the press nationwide and by the inner sanctums of the Washington power structure as doing an excellent job on the missions it had undertaken (see Exhibit 2), but the only way that Common Cause could effect change was through the force of an active membership. To harness the power of that membership, Common Cause developed an intricate system known as the Washington Connection.

THE WASHINGTON CONNECTION

The Washington Connection was primarily a telephone-based activist hot line. The country was broken down by states and the states by congressional district. At the Washington office of Common Cause there were two functions—staff and line. The network staff was composed of two managers (who helped with procedures and problems) and four

EXHIBIT 2
Press Coments About Common Cause

"It's heartening to see a calm, unfrantic movement here working to improve American politics, not to destroy or freeze it. Beside our daily dose of bad news, the momentum Common Cause is gaining is good news indeed."

— Flora Lewis
Washington Post

"The aim of Mr. Gardner's effort is not to found a new party or win a particular campaign. His hope is to freshen the springs of political life, to recruit new talent for both parties and at every level of government, to concentrate attention on the issues that are genuinely significant, to sponsor needed reforms. It is a bold and ambitious undertaking which Mr. Gardner and his colleagues are attempting. Self-government lives by that kind of boldness and ambition."

— The New York Times

"Democracy just doesn't flourish in the half-light. The public has a right to know exactly how its public servants are performing and how its interests are being served. Americans realizing democracy's great short-changing through secrecy can be grateful that Common Cause's strong shoulder will be placed against bolted government doors."

— Palm Beach (Fla.) Post

"So you're skeptical about making fundamental changes in the system from within. So now you don't know where to turn. Tell you what. Take a look at Common Cause, the 200,000-member 'citizen's lobby.' . . . It was Common Cause that forced the Nixon Campaign Committee to disclose where its money came from all during 1971 and up to March 9, 1972. . . It was Common Cause that forced TRW, Inc., a $200,000,000 a year defense contractor to dissolve a political fund collected from its employees. The message was not lost on other corporations. It was Common Cause that fed hundreds of newspapers and TV and radio stations all the details about how much money candidates for President, Congress, and the Senate were collecting, and more important, just where it was coming from. And that's just a start."

— The National Observer

"The country has a pressing need for restructuring its political and economic institutions and for a healthier new set of priorities. Common Cause can play an important role in this task."

— Sacramento (Calif.) Bee

Source: Common Cause records.

area supervisors (each of whom was responsible for the network activities in at least ten states). The line function was headed by a state team leader who was the knowledgeable person about that state. Specific responsibilities were: know all Common Cause issues and national actions; know the Common Cause membership in the state; know local populations, industries, and communities; know current state issues; know local media personnel; and develop and maintain good working relations with the members of the state volunteer team which the leader headed. The members of the state volunteer team performed the other line functions. They were more generally known as district liaison volunteers, and they were the primary contact (by telephone) between Common Cause headquarters and members in a congressional district. These teams were the link in the lobbying program, and success was directly related to how much stimulus and enthusiasm could be passed from Washington to the states and how much information could be passed back to Washington.

On a day-to-day basis, the Washington Connection was used to establish a Common Cause organization in each congressional district (see Exhibit 3 for membership information). What was, in effect, established was a telephone net that allowed each member to be contacted during an "alert." Rapid communication during an "alert" was the basis of all the planning. An alert" situation was defined as one in which the national office decided that immediate member action (rallies, letters, and phone calls to legislative representatives leading to media publicity) was needed to implement a Common Cause project or support an issue. The considerable outflowing of public opinion that was generated during an alert was an important lobbying tool used by the professional staff at the congressional level.

DISTINCTIVE ATTRIBUTES

In defining the difference between Common Cause and the previous, more traditional reform movements, Mr. Gardner said,

> I think the old-style good-government movement had two failings. First, they imagined that we might achieve a kind of static perfection of governmental processes and then we could all relax and be happy under a good government. They didn't understand that somebody always has too much power and somebody always has too little, and that if you drive the bad guys out of power, the good guys who replace them will

soon get accustomed to power and grow to love it and may eventually abuse it. So the struggle never ends. The other failing of the old good-government movements was that they felt themselves to be above politics. But politics is the only forum in which we can resolve our differences. As long as equally worthy people have incompatible goals, somebody has to mediate—unless you want things decided by the whim of a dictator or unless you want to shoot it out. The politicians are our mediators. We have to rehabilitate the whole notion of politics as the kind of free market in which we resolve conflicting purposes. It's always untidy. It will always be grubbier than we might want it to be. But we can't afford to scorn it. . . . There are some extraordinarily good, resilient, effective people in politics. At the other extreme are the crooks and the exploiters. And in the middle are a lot of unheroic types who will respond to pressures, good or bad. Citizen action tries to work with the good guys, immobilize the crooks, and stiffen the spines of the unheroic.[3]

MEMBERSHIP BUILDING

The officers of Common Cause were convinced that a strong, active, growing membership was essential to lobbying success. The larger the membership, they reasoned, the more public pressure Common Cause could control and the more money it would have to support its activities. Additionally, an increased membership would provide a wider base of support and thereby dispel the elite image that some detractors tried to associate with Common Cause. Consequently, a great deal of effort went into recruiting membership, exemplified by the fact that about one-third of all revenues received went into obtaining new members (see Exhibit 4 for a breakdown of the 1972 budget).

Roger Craver's main job as Director of Development was to ensure the continued growth of Common Cause. Mr. Craver, who had an extensive background in public relations, direct mail advertising, and college and university fund-raising projects, began by evaluating the results of past campaigns as well as determining the current economic resources of the organization.

The total 1972 budget for all activities was projected at $3.4 million (see Exhibits 5 and 6 for 1971 operating statements). This was split into three funds: The Program Fund, the Readiness Alert Fund, and the New Membership Revolving Fund. The Program Fund was financed en-

---

[3] Elizabeth Drew, op cit.

EXHIBIT 3
Membership by State, July 1973

State	No. of Members	State	No. of Members
Alabama	530	Montana	532
Alaska	339	Nebraska	713
Arizona	2,040	Nevada	341
Arkansas	513	New Hampshire	1,294
California	38,539	New Jersey	9,751
Colorado	3,593	New Mexico	1,095
Connecticut	6,194	New York	33,823
Delaware	745	North Carolina	2,731
District of Columbia	4,765	North Dakota	334
Florida	5,351	Ohio	7,941
Georgia	1,737	Oklahoma	810
Hawaii	728	Oregon	3,091
Idaho	313	Pennsylvania	11,316
Illinois	10,254	Rhode Island	1,164
Indiana	2,542	South Carolina	478
Iowa	1,884	South Dakota	295
Kansas	1,582	Tennessee	1,447
Kentucky	1,192	Texas	5,607
Louisiana	653	Utah	647
Maine	849	Vermont	1,075
Maryland	8,058	Virginia	5,708
Massachusetts	12,120	Washington	4,433
Michigan	6,466	West Virginia	509
Minnesota	4,876	Wisconsin	3,686
Mississippi	204	Wyoming	230
Missouri	3,415		
		Membership Total	218,523

Source: Common Cause records.

tirely from the $15 renewal payments of members. This supported the regular legislative-lobbying program, field operations, the newsletter and other publications, and the headquarter's administrative expense. Total 1972 expenditures were projected to be $2.2 million.

The Readiness Alert Fund was financed by contributions in excess of the $15 dues. The 1972 average revenue per member was expected to be about $17.50; therefore, an average of $2.50 per member or $500,000 was available for this Fund. These funds were used to operate the 1972 Campaign Monitoring Project, for lobbying of delegates at the two na-

Exhibit 4
1972 Budget of $3,463,000

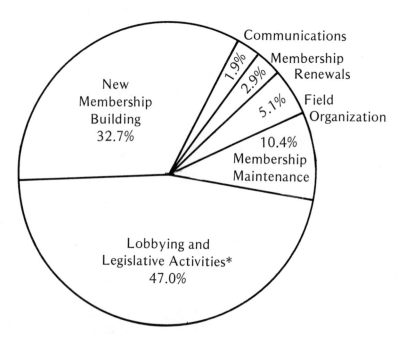

Percentages of Lobbying and Legislative Activities Funds:

Campaign financing and campaign monitoring	22.6%
Open up the system and Congressional reform	29.2%
State issues and state reform	15.9%
End the war	14.9%
Equal rights and state ratification	5.9%
Other Legislative issues	11.5%
Clean water	
D.C. home rule	
Busing	
Welfare reform	
Consumer protection	
No-Fault insurance	
Child care	
Gun control	
Miscellaneous	
Total "Lobbying and Legislative Activities"	100.0%

Source: Common Cause records.

EXHIBIT 5

Statement of Revenue and Expenditures and Changes in Fund Balance
(Year Ended December 31, 1971)

Revenue

Memberships	$3,522,544
Contributions	664,851
Grant from Stern Fund	43,000
Other	23,281
	$4,253,676

Expenditures

Salaries	$ 884,627
Payroll taxes and employee benefits	85,082
Postage and mailing	683,179
Printing and publications	611,856
Membership mailing lists and advertising	495,653
Consultant fees and expenses	416,056
Computer processing	334,401
Telephone and telegraph	172,010
Office rent	109,786
Staff travel	92,228
Furniture, equipment and leasehold improvements	68,403
Special projects	55,835
Office supplies and expenses	47,907
Stern Fund project	36,976
Other	90,951
	$4,184,950
Excess of revenue over expenditures	$ 68,726
Fund balance beginning of period	249,388
Fund balance end of period	$ 318,114

Source: Common Cause records.

tional political conventions, and for the Peace Action Center. Money in the Readiness Alert Fund could be designated by the governing board for special projects that couldn't be funded from the regular Program Fund.

The New Membership Revolving Fund financed membership building efforts. The $15 dues from *new* members were plowed back into this fund. Mr. Craver thought that it cost $10.25 to obtain a new member. On the other hand, it cost an average of $.99 to renew a membership; a

EXHIBIT 6

Statement of Assets, Liabilities and Fund Balance
December 31, 1971

ASSETS	
Cash	$206,356
Certificates of deposit	200,000
Prepaid expenses	60,167
Total assets	$466,523
LIABILITIES AND FUND BALANCE	
Liabilities	
Accounts payable	$109,145
Other	39,264
Total liabilities	148,409
Fund balance	318,114
Commitments	
Total liabilities and fund balance	$466,523

maximum of four renewal notices would be sent (costing in total $1.40), while some members renewed their membership automatically.

In establishing the 1972 membership goal, Mr. Craver felt that a total membership of 200,000 was necessary to finance the current level of activities; however, as Mr. Craver said, "Our goal is to get as many as possible."

Methods of Membership Recruiting

In the past, membership drives had been somewhat limited. Free publicity, newspaper stories, brochures, and some direct mailings had resulted in the initial flood of 200,000 members. However, since 1970, Common Cause had really only been able to hold a steady position. Roger Craver was quite worried about future prospects. He said, "Lots of us here are worried about the future; we will have to do something or else we will slowly wilt on the vine."

Consequently, during June 1972, Mr. Craver had placed a full page advertisement (Exhibit 7) in the Sunday edition of each of the following newspapers: *New York Times, Washington Post, San Francisco Chronicle, Christian Science Monitor,* and *National Observer.* He felt that these papers were circulated in areas that offered the most potential; however, to judge by the returned coupons, total ad expenses exceeded total direct memberships by $10,000. Paid newspaper ads did not seem to be effective in attracting additional members. Other alternatives that he had under consideration were public service announcements on radio and television; aside from the production costs, these were free, but they were most often aired only during low audience rating times. In addition, there were several restrictions on content that led Mr. Craver to feel that this means of advertisement was of little use to Common Cause. As a result, membership procurement relied mostly on direct mail. Mr. Craver maintained that this was the only consistently effective way of gaining new members.

Historically, January, February, and September had been the best months to use direct mail. Mr. Craver had conducted an extensive test to measure the responses to each of eight different membership ad packets. The most successful one was a 6" X 9" envelope (eventually sent to one million people) with the outside caption:

> FOR SALE: THE UNITED STATES GOVERNMENT
> All Bids Will be Handled in Secrecy.
> Details Are Sealed In This Envelope.

Inside was a four-page letter from John Gardner which was a hardhitting injunction against the evils in government (excerpts are contained in (Exhibit 8). This mailing generated 113,000 new members. The 6" X 9" envelope, however, was expensive; Craver was pleased to discover that a small and cheaper package, sent to five million people, produced comparable results. He estimated that Common Cause's present middle-class, well-educated, and high-income white market was potentially 16 million people, representing over 20 million households. Total package costs (lists, labor, printing, and postage) were $153,744 per million in quantities exceeding one million. Subscription and membership lists were purchased from other groups and organizations which often had many of the same people; one major disadvantage of these was the annoyance caused current members by duplicate mailings. The list purge, or "cleaning" process at Common Cause was expensive, but Mr. Craver was not entirely certain as to the magnitude of the problem, except to say that it was noticeable at a rate above 5% duplication.

EXHIBIT 7

They laughed when we started Common Cause.

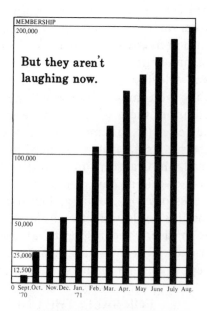

MEMBERSHIP

But they aren't laughing now.

0 Sept.Oct. Nov.Dec. Jan. Feb. Mar. Apr. May June July Aug.
'70   '71

It's no secret that when we started Common Cause a little over a year ago, the idea of a citizen's lobby was regarded with considerable amusement in and around the Capitol.

(One Washington wit promptly disposed of the idea by dubbing it "John Gardner's Lost Cause".)

But now we have some people over there worried.

Because when you grow in one year from 0 members to 200,000 members, it indicates that something may be stirring "out there" where the people are. And when those members are concerned enough to become activists, and to pay $15 a year in dues to support the work of the organization, then you know that something is happening out there.

Everybody's organized but the people.

What's happening is that these Americans have begun to realize that many of our political and governmental institutions are eaten out with corruption, or are so rigid and unresponsive that they can no longer cope with the nation's problems.

They sense that "money talks" through powerful amplifiers for the special interests, while the unorganized citizens can't even get near the microphone.

They are deeply disturbed by the wall of secrecy behind which more and more government business is being conducted.

They see, all too clearly, that the people are being lied to and manipulated and bilked by the institutions that were created to serve them.

They are tired of feeling helpless as individuals and they are finally getting together and doing something about it.

Why outside pressure is needed.

The political structure of this country is so badly in need of repair that even if the ideal man were to be elected to the presidency in 1972, and even if he were to have a vastly improved Congress to work with, it would still not be enough to solve the nation's most serious problems.

By election day, the deals will already have been made, the I.O.U.s will have been signed, another coalition of special interests will have been put together, and the strings will have been firmly attached to the winning party.

That is why conventional politics are not going to cure what ails us.

We are up against something much deeper.

There has got to be an outside force to bring pressure to bear against the sensitive areas that are now "off limits" to both parties, to open up the doors and windows of government at every level and let in the fresh air and light.

That is what Common Cause is all about.

A national citizen's lobby.

Common Cause is something different.

It is not a third party but a third force in American life.

It is concerned not with the advancement of special interests, but with the well-being of the nation.

It regards its membership not as a voting bloc, but as a cadre of well informed and determined activists whose influence in their communities is far greater than their numbers.

It combines "constituency clout" back bone with a cutting edge of professionals in Washington, including four of the best lobbyists on Capitol Hill working full time.

For the first time, the people are sitting in on the insider's poker game.

Our track record so far.

"Early this year Common Cause sued the major political parties, seeking to have them enjoined from violating campaign spending laws now on the books. In late August a judge rejected a motion to dismiss the suit and in the process posed a monumental problem for politicians who don't like to account publicly for their campaign monies. . ."
—The Flint, Mich. Journal

". . . The only way the parties can head off this suit is to write a tough campaign spending bill in Congress on . . ."
—D. J. R. Bruckner column, Los Angeles Times

". . . Dummy committees and hidden contributors must be forbidden, to prevent special-interest groups from 'investing' in candidates with the expectation of profitable returns. Our friends at Common Cause are on the right track toward curbing this national scandal. They deserve support. They're your friends too."
—St. Petersburg, Fla. Times

"Partly because of massive anti-war lobbying by John Gardner's Common Cause, the White House is far more concerned over an end-the-war amendment to the 1971 military procurement bill in the House than it admits."
—Evans and Novak column, Washington Post

"—Common Cause is acknowledged to have been the chief citizen organization lobbying for the Constitutional Amendment to give 18-year-olds the right to vote.

"—Common Cause is credited by members of Congress and the press with helping produce the first real crack in the archaic seniority system in Congress.

"—Common Cause has stamina. And professionalism. Already 200,000 and growing every day, it has been praised as the best organized, most determined movement of its kind in the history of the country."
—Wabash, Ind. Plain Dealer

". . . Common Cause is doing a job that the public needs, that neither party has done nor can do, and a job, moreover, that can only lead to better government."
—Hutchinson, Kansas News

"Common Cause deserves a world of credit for the tremendous job it played in rallying opposition to the SST. . ."
—Senator William Proxmire

"John Gardner forthrightly calls his Common Cause a 'Peoples Lobby', and is beginning to move mountains."
—Architectural Record

Only an aroused and organized citizenry can revitalize "The System" and change the nation's disastrous course.

Common Cause believes that most of the country's problems today stem from the failure of the people to involve themselves in the political process.

It believes that politics and government must become "everybody's business."

You have seen what Common Cuase has been able to accomplish in one year with only 50,000 members, then 100,000, then 200,000.

Imagine what a revitalizing effect it would have on the government if we were one million strong.

Join us in Common Cause and help make it happen.

We cannot and should not depend on big contributors. The money to support our work must come from the members themselves.

We therefore ask you to enclose a check for $15 with your membership application.

ALTERNATIVE MARKETS

Roger Craver felt that the youth of America had changed greatly during the early 1970s. He detected what he thought to be a shift away from the "radical approach" to one which could be described as "working within the system." If this were true, he felt, young people would find Common Cause to be an organization "tuned-in" to their needs. After all, he reasoned, Common Cause's credo was one of gradual changes in government which would return more power to the people.

However, Mr. Craver foresaw several potential problems if he pursued the youth market. First, he was concerned that substantial influx of young people into Common Cause might conceivably antagonize large segments of the existing membership, especially the older, less active members. He felt that some campus activity could be characterized as "shirt-pocket agenda"—that is, highly volatile but not necessarily long-lived. If this happened, Common Cause headquarters would probably lose control of the membership which would result in the disintegration of the organization. As it was, Common Cause was relatively homogeneous, and Mr. Craver did not want to develop internal factions and conflicts. Mr. Craver was also afraid that the good name and lobbying effectiveness of Common Cause would be ruined if a few kids staged a hippie demonstration in the name of Common Cause.

Second, there was a matter of economics. He felt that the regular $15 membership fee might be too high for young people, but it cost $7 a year to service a member with newsletters, administrative overheads, etc. This meant that direct mail, newspapers, and other expensive means of attracting members could not be used to attract youth. This left volunteer person-to-person selling as the only other alternative he saw, but Common Cause had no contacts or representatives on the thousands of high school and college campuses across the nation.

On the other hand, the youth market offered great potential. Mr. Craver estimated that appropriate potential members might number as high as nine million in college and 18 million in high school. Youth also represented activism. Common Cause would increasingly need to rely on its members taking action on the issues. Volunteers were always in short supply to perform the telephone, administrative, and research tasks. If Common Cause were to expand its scope of activities into state and local reform, a greatly increased number of volunteers would be needed. There was also the good chance that a person who joined Common Cause as a youth might be an active, dues-paying member for years. Mr. Craver felt very strongly about this point, but he could not guess as to how many would remain for how long. Thus he did not know

EXHIBIT 8

Excerpts From a Common Cause Mailing

From: John Gardner
Chairman, Common Cause

Dear Fellow Citizen:

It can't happen here, you say? But it *is* happening here. Every day. And that's not just opinion. That's indisputable fact.

When one man pays out over two million dollars to presidential and Congressional campaigns (yes, it's a fact!), the United States Government is virtually up for sale.

When qualified men and women cannot run for political office because they refuse to take special-interest contributions (and that's a fact!), I say our government is up for grabs to the highest bidders.

When appointments to high office, business favors and favorable legal decisions are purchased behind the scenes by giant corporations (and that's a fact!), I say our system desperately needs cleaning up.

When Congressmen who have holdings in banks serve on the Banking and Currency Committee (and that's a fact!), I say some of our lawmakers are serving their own needs and not the needs of their constituents.

When our legislators resist open meetings and decide on public issues behind closed doors, I say that secrecy is a convenient means to cover up a multitude of sins.

What has been most disturbing about these violations of our democratic system is that until recently so many Americans were willing to accept them as matters they could not control. There's a new spirit in the land, now, a determination by the people to fight back. And now there is something you, the ordinary citizen, can do to have a voice—an effective voice—in decisions of government.

---

what short-term deficit spending might mean in long-term members.

Therefore, Mr. Craver felt that it was best to run some sort of market test that could be controlled in such a way that if he was not successful, he could terminate it without having created a great deal of confusion and anxiety among the current members. Mr. Craver decided to talk to approximately fifteen college representatives and a number of political science and civics teachers at the high school level. He, at the same time, wanted to test a new membership price of $7.50. If it costs $7.00 a

You can join Common Cause. . . .

When you are a Member of Common Cause, you help achieve these and the many other things we work on not only through your membership dues—although that helps greatly—but with a willingness to act when there is a need to act.

As a Member, you receive *Report from Washington* 10 times a year, filling you in on the issues and advising you when and how you can take action on them. Members write, wire, even telephone their Congressmen. Some visit their Congressmen in person. They also write to their local newspapers on the issues—and talk to local editors and news directors of TV and radio stations. Often, they get their clubs or lodges or unions to discuss and pass resolutions on the issues. What and how much you do is, of course, up to you. . . .

I urge you to be our next new member. There is a Common Cause Membership Form enclosed for you. When you return it to enter your membership, you join over 200,000 Americans in one of the most important citizens' movements this country has ever known. Membership dues are $15 a year. This helps pay for our broad legislative and program activities and for the publication of *Report from Washington* which is available only to Common Cause Members.

So if you have been discouraged by what's been happening in and to our country in recent years—don't be. Join Common Cause.

If you have been skeptical, saying there is nothing you can do to rid our governmental institutions of corruption—don't be. Join Common Cause.

If you want action, action to get this country back on the right track— don't just sit there. Join us. We need you. You need Common Cause.

Together, we *will* make democracy work.

> Sincerely,
>
> John Gardner
> Chairman

---

year just to service a new member with newsletters and the like, that only left $.50 for acquiring new members. A prime consideration was the development of a low-cost method for attracting youth. Mr. Craver felt direct mail was prohibitive, that media space and time was too expensive, which left it up to point-to-point, people-to-people contact, point-of-purchase, and other methods which frankly had proved unsuccessful in the past, although to a different audience.

Case 9

The College of
William and Mary*

In August, 1975, Mr. Ben Carnevale, director of men's intercollegiate athletics at the College of William and Mary (W&M), was deciding how to meet his own responsibilities within President Graves' objectives for the W&M athletic program in the light of limited and uncertain revenues. These objectives were to: (1) achieve a reputation of high quality in intercollegiate athletics; (2) develop the non-revenue intercollegiate sports programs for both men and women; (3) provide maximum support for the intramural programs; (4) balance the overall athletic program without reducing the strength of the revenue sports; and (5) achieve these objectives with an athletic program operating in the black.

BACKGROUND ON WILLIAM AND MARY

The College of William and Mary was founded in 1693 (the second college in the American colonies after Harvard) by King William III and Queen Mary II of England to train young men and clergy for the Church

*This case was made possible through the cooperation of the College of William and Mary. It was prepared by Mr. William D. Monday, Jr., under the supervision of Professor Derek A. Newton as the basis for class discussion and not to illustrate either effective or ineffective handling of an administrative situation. Copyright © 1975 by The Colgate Darden Graduate Business School Sponsors of the University of Virginia.

of England at a school of "good Arts and Sciences." The school severed formal ties from Britain in 1776. In 1779, Thomas Jefferson, the College's most distinguished alumnus, reorganized the school's curriculum and in so doing created the first truly American university. William and Mary became state supported in 1906, coeducational in 1918 and, by modern definition, achieved university status in 1967. It was the first college to establish an intercollegiate fraternity, Phi Beta Kappa (1776), an Honor System (1779), and the elective system of study (1779). The College was located in the beautiful and historic city of Williamsburg, Virginia, where it constituted an integral part of the restoration of Colonial Williamsburg. The focal point of the 1,200 acre campus was the Sir Christopher Wren Building (1695), the nation's oldest academic building still in use.

William and Mary was governed by a chancellor and 17-member Board of Visitors under the direction of the General Assembly of the Commonwealth of Virginia. The president, Thomas A. Graves, reported to the Board for the supervision and operation of the College. Exhibit 1 gives a partial organization chart for the School. W&M was unique as the only state institution in the country with both high academic standards and a small enrollment. While many schools were growing to reach university status, W&M strove to retain its image as a small college. According to Mr. Graves:

> William and Mary is a state university of national character and contribution, that is highly selective, coeducational, full-time and residential with primary emphasis on liberal education at the undergraduate level, dedicated to the development of the "whole individual."

In 1974-1975, the enrollment was 5,800 full-time students, of which 4,850 were undergraduates. The student body was 70% in-state (by direction of the Board of Visitors); half male and half female. Thirty percent of the students received financial aid totalling $1.5 million. The 1974 entering class had a mean Scholastic Aptitude Test score above 1,200 points (300 above the national average) and over half had participated in four or more extra-curricular activities in high school. Mr. Van Voorhis, assistant to the president, characterized the student body as: "independent study and research oriented, well-balanced and non-career specialized; although dedicated to the educational experience, the students are extensively involved in extra-curricular activities."

The operating expenses for 1974-1975 for the entire college totalled $19,800,245. Sources of funds included:

EXHIBIT 1
The College of William and Mary
Partial Organizational Chart

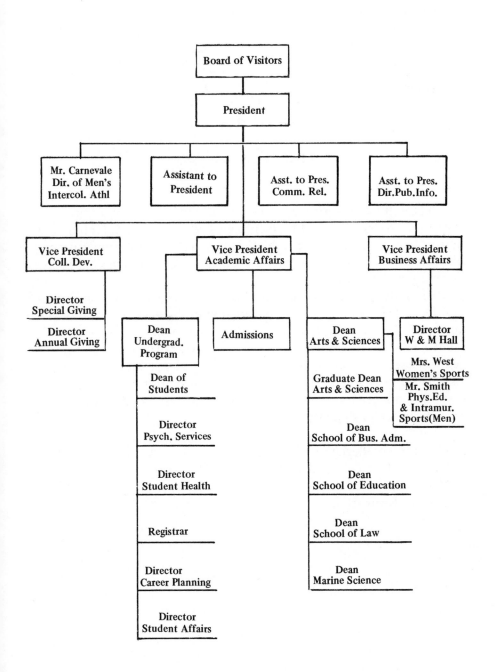

General Funds (tax sources from the state)		$ 8,531,631
Special Funds:		
Federal Grants	$ 946,177	
Other:		
Tuition and Fees	6,450,225	
Auxiliary Enterprises[1]	3,872,212	11,268,614
Total		$19,800,245

ATHLETICS AT W&M

Athletic programs were administered at W&M by three departments: men's intercollegiate athletics; men's physical education and intramurals; and women's intercollegiate athletics, physical education and intramurals. Funds to support the athletic programs came from various sources as described below.

Each undergraduate student at W&M was charged a "tuition and general fee." The amount of tuition varied with the in-state or out-or-state status of the student. The "general fee," constant for all students, included $88 for an "athletic and recreation fee." The revenue from this fee was used to support the men's and women's athletic programs, the intramural program, and various recreational or cultural activities. The operating budget for 1974-75 for these activities, based on the $88 fee charged to 4,850 students was as follows:

Men's Intercollegiate Athletics	$355,604
Women's Intercollegiate and Intramural Athletics	48,185
Men's Intramural Athletics	2,400
Student Recreation:	
Dances and Special Events	3,675
Concerts	3,150
Lectures	1,575
Band Funds	3,675
Overhead (2% to the State)	8,536
Total	$426,800

[1] Auxiliary Enterprises were university services such as housing, dining facilities, and student health which were required to be self-supporting.

The athletic and recreation fee for 1975-76 was set by the Board of Visitors at $110. The comparative distribution of this fee for the two years is shown below:

Athletic and Recreation Student Fee

	1974-75	1975-76
Intercollegiate Football	$37.50	$ 36.00
Intercollegiate Basketball	9.00	
Men's Non-Revenue Sports	10.00	20.00
Women's Non-Revenue Sports	10.00	20.00
Men's & Women's Intramural and Recreation Sports	.50	6.00
Supporting Activities for Men's Athletics	17.00	24.00
Total Amount for Athletics	$84.00	$106.00
Student Recreation (dances, concerts, lectures, band)	$ 2.00	$ 2.00
State Overhead charge of 2%	2.00	2.00
	$88.00	$110.00

For 1975-1976, the $36.00 of the athletic and recreation fee allocated to support intercollegiate football and basketball was in the form of a mandatory season ticket that entitled each student to attend all home football and basketball games.

Other funding sources included gate receipts, radio and television rights, program advertising and sales, stadium concessions and designated private gifts. This latter source was administered by the William and Mary Athletic Educational Foundation (AEF). The following table shows these actual amounts for 1972-1973 and 1973-1974.

	1972-73	1973-74
Football Receipts	$146,085	$237,025
Basketball	31,961	34,990
Miscellaneous Concessions and AEF Contributions	170,283	199,087
	$348,329	$471,102

The AEF was an organization of alumni and friends of the College whose contributions went directly to the Men's Athletic Department to pay for grants-in-aid and other expenses. Mr. Barry Fratkin, the full-time executive director of the Foundation, coordinated all types of solicitations in support of the W&M athletic program (e.g., contributions, courtesy cars, advertisements). The Foundation comprised an Executive Committee directed by a president, and seven regional vice presidents whose main function was to coordinate the fund raising activity. The Foundation was not an advisory body on policy decisions, although several major contributors made informal suggestions to college personnel periodically.

The athletic facilities comprised William and Mary Hall, Blow Gymnasium, Adair Gymnasium, Cary Stadium, six tennis courts and seven playing fields. The three programs, physical education, intramural, and intercollegiate, used the facilities so extensively that few facilities were available for students choosing to pursue an independent and unstructured recreation program.

Department of Men's Intercollegiate Athletics

Mr. Ben Carnevale was appointed director of men's intercollegiate athletics at William and Mary in July 1972 after a department reorganization had moved the former director of men's intercollegiate athletics, Mr. Hooker, to the post of director of the William and Mary Hall facility (an athletic complex housing the athletic administration office and the basketball arena, but also rented out for concerts). Mr. Carnevale was greeted by new head coaches in both revenue sports, football and basketball, appointed the previous spring by President Graves. Both programs were floundering in terms of attendance, won-loss records and in their ability to support themselves financially.

As director of men's intercollegiate athletics, Mr. Carnevale reported directly to President Graves and was responsible for the administration of the men's intercollegiate athletic department, including scheduling, budgeting, allocation of grants-in-aid, and overall supervision of the fifteen men's intercollegiate sports programs. In implementing the sports programs, Mr. Carnevale was responsible for following NCAA and Southern Conference guidelines.[2] A brief description of these programs as of 1975 follows (Southern Conference participation is maked by an asterisk):

---

[2]Members of the Southern Conference were: Appalachian State University, The Citadel, Davidson College, East Carolina University, Furman University, Virginia Military Institute, University of Richmond, and The College of William and Mary.

Football*—11 game schedule—Single ticket price $7—Home field Cary Stadium (15,000)—average home attendance, 12,000—Natural turf—portable bleachers at each endzone—usually played 5 conference games per year and four or five home games—100 participants.

Basketball*—25 game schedule—Single ticket price $3—Home site William and Mary Hall (10,700)—average home attendance 4-5,000—Tartan floor—usually about 14 games played at home—11 to 12 games against conference opponents—14 participants.

Track and Field*—W&M competed in Cross Country (8-10 meets), Indoor (10-15 meets) and Outdoor (12 meets) Track—A conference championship meet was held for each—W&M totally dominated the conference in this sport for the past decade—W&M Hall featured an indoor Tartan track where one or two meets are held each year—The outdoor facility was inside Cary Field Stadium surrounding the football field. It contained an eight lane Tartan surface, bordering high jump, long jump, pole vault, shot-put, discus, javelin and triple jump facilities—50 participants.

Baseball*—30 game schedule—Home field Cary Field Park—Stands held about 150 people—12-14 games against conference opponents—W&M has not been very successful in baseball during the last decade—Attributable to lack of full-time head coach (until 1974)—Record of late has hovered around the 12-18 mark—25 participants.

Soccer*—11 or 12 game schedule—Usually 4-6 conference games—About half the games played at Home—Soccer field was a part of the Intramural field complex—In its eighth year at W&M and usually team was among the top three in Conference—About thirty players on roster.

Lacrosse—11 or 12 game schedule—Home site Cary Field Stadium—Opponents were mostly from region of Maryland to North Carolina—Season's record had been around 6-5 for the past seven years—finished in the top 20 nationally in 1974—About 40 participants.

Gymnastics—12 meets—Home site was W&M Hall—Finished 3rd in the Southern Region of the National Association in 1974-75—with 9-2 record—9-3 in 1973-74—About 20 participants.

Swimming*—12-15 meets—Home site was Adair Pool—About half the meets were at home—Among the top four in conference competition—A conference championship meet was held—About 30 participants.

Wrestling*—18 matches and about four "open" meets a year—About four conference matches per season—A conference championship meet was held—winners advance to Nationals—Home site was either W&M Hall or Blow Gym—Team had finished either first or second the last eight years in Conference title meet—About 25 participants—Finished 17th in the Nation in 1974.

Fencing—12-14 Competitions a year—Matches at home were held at either Blow Gym, W&M Hall or Adair Gym—Record had been up and down over the last several years—Usually around the .500 mark—About 15-20 participants.

Tennis*—20-25 Matches—Home site was Adair Courts (6 composition surfaced outdoors)—Lights installed for night play—About 10 conference matches—A conference championship was held—W&M among the top four in Conference over the past several seasons—About 15 team participants.

Golf*—15 matches—About half the matches were against Conference opponents—A Conference championship was held—Home site was Williamsburg Country Club—Team had finished next to last in Conference the past several years—About 10 participants.

Rifle*—12-15 matches—A conference championship was held—Home site was Rifle range underneath Cary Field stands—About half the matches were at home—Team usually among top four in Conference—About 10 participants.

In addition to its Southern Conference affiliation, W&M was also a member of the Eastern College Athletic Conference (ECAC). The obligation to that group was secondary to the Southern Conference. The primary purpose behind joining the ECAC was basketball and track scheduling. The ECAC wan not a conference in the usual meaning but a regional concept which encompassed all three college divisions within its geographical boundaries.

The Southern Conference presented the "Commissioner's Cup" to that member whose overall intercollegiate program was the most successful during the past year's competition. The award had been made for the past six years; W&M had won it four times and in the last two years finished second and third respectively.

W&M's home game attendance figures in football and basketball during the past few years would rank among the top three in the Southern Conference. Exhibit 2 gives the won-lost record for W&M in football and basketball for the past ten years and the 1975-76 schedule.

Mr. Carnevale's major responsibility was the supervision of the head coaches of the 15 sports and their respective staffs. In this capacity he developed and supervised a budget for each sport, generally by raising the previous year's budget as he saw necessary. Head coaches participated in this process to the extent that they negotiated the final budget figures and any requests for special expenditures with Mr. Carnevale. Once a budget figure for each sport was determined, the head coach was given free reign to allocate it as he saw fit. Although Mr. Carnevale attempted to retain a balanced sports program, he tended to favor the

EXHIBIT 2

Won-Lost Record in Intercollegiate Football and Basketball 1965-1975

	Football	Basketball
1974-75	4-7	16-12
73-74	6-5	10-18
72-73	5-6	10-18
71-72	5-6	10-17
70-71	5-6	11-16
1969-70	3-7	11-16
68-69	3-7	6-20
67-68	5-4-1	6-18
66-67	5-4-1	14-11
65-66	6-4	13-12

1975-1976 Football and Basketball Schedules

Football	Basketball	
Univ. of No. Carolina	Appalachian State*	Furman*
East Carolina Univ.	Eastern Connecticut*	Virginia Tech.
Univ. of Pittsburgh	George Washington	Richmond*
The Citadel	The Citadel*	East Carolina Univ.
Ohio Univ.*	Wake Forest	Old Dominion*
Rutgers Univ.	Dickinson*	VMI*
Furman Univ.*	Wagner*	Virginia Tech.*
Virginia Tech.	Iowa	Davidson
Virginia Military Inst.	Princeton	The Citadel
Colgate Univ.*	Washington College*	Virginia*
University of Richmond*	Old Dominion	Richmond
	East Carolina Univ.*	Rutgers*
	Virginia Military Inst.	

*Home games

track program which had achieved national prominence. As a consequence, Track received approximately 60% of the $40,000 grant-in-aid money allocated to non-revenue sports. Exhibit 3 gives the intercollegiate athletic budget for 1974-75 and projections for the next three years. Exhibit 4 gives the grant-in-aid figures for 1974-75.

In evaluating the performance of his coaches, Mr. Carnevale considered won-loss records relative to the respective level of competition and the

EXHIBIT 3

Men's Intercollegiate Athletic Budget

	First Projection 74-75	Revised Projection 74-75	Actual 74-75	75-76	Projected 76-77	77-78
Undergraduate Enrollment			4,850	4,900	4,950	5,000
REVENUES						
Revenue Sports						
Gate Receipts:						
Football	$165,000	$220,000	$232,000	$205,000	$ 210,000	$ 220,000
Basketball	40,000	40,000	36,700	50,000	55,000	60,000
AEF Contributions	110,000	110,000	124,000	240,000	200,000	200,000
Miscellaneous (net)	50,000	45,000	48,000	50,000	50,000	50,000
Student Ticket (@ $36.00)	*	*	*	176,400	178,200	180,000
Total Revenue Sports	$365,000	$415,000	$440,700	$721,000	$ 693,200	$ 710,000
Non-revenue Sports						
Student Fee (@$20.00)	*	*	*	98,000	99,000	100,000
Support of Men's Sports						
Student Fee (@ $24.00)	355,604	355,604	355,604	117,600	118,800	120,000
Other:						
Donations	10,000	10,000	10,000	10,000	10,000	10,000
Surplus	20,000	31,000	31,000	16,000	91,250	97,450
Total Revenues						
Current Fund Local	60,396	30,000	30,000			
TOTAL	$811,000	$841,604	$867,304	$962,600	$1,012,250	$1,037,450

*Figured in $355,604 (from student fees for support of Men's Sports items below) for 1974-75.

(5% increase each year)

EXPENSES						
Revenue Sports						
Football	$417,745	$434,745				
Basketball	97,776	98,776				
Administration, Medical, and Publicity Support*						
Total Revenue Sports	$515,521	$533,521		$618,200	$649,000	$681,000
Non-revenue Sports						
Track (Indoor, outdoor, and cross country)	$ 47,368	$ 47,368				
Wrestling	12,540	13,540				
Baseball	10,300	10,300				
Tennis	5,500	5,500				
Rifle	2,050	2,050				
Fencing	1,750	1,750				
Swimming	5,150	5,150				
Golf	3,400	3,400				
Gymnastics	11,300	11,300				
Lacrosse	3,500	3,500				
Soccer	3,250	3,250				
Total	$106,108	$107,108		$112,450	$118,100	$124,000
Supporting						
General and Admin.						
Expenses	$113,291	$123,395				
Publicity	37,360	37,360				
Medical	28,720	30,220				
Contingencies	10,000	10,000				
Total	$189,371	$200,975		$140,700	$147,700	$155,100
TOTAL EXPENSES	$811,000	$841,604	$851,000[1]	$871,350	$914,800	$960,000
Ending Balance, June 30						

*1/3 of Supporting Fee transferred to Revenue Sports Budget effective 1975-76.

[1] Breakdown of expenses was not available. It was known that operating expenses had exceeded the budget by $19,000, but salaries and grants-in-aid were under the budget by $10,000.

coaches' success at developing their programs. When hiring a new coach, Mr. Carnevale was careful to consider the fit between the coach's aspirations and the character of the William and Mary environment.

Mr. Carnevale arranged the scheduling for the 15 intercollegiate sports. A successful basketball head coach for many years at the Naval Academy and member of the Basketball Hall of Fame, Mr. Carnevale had been able to use his contacts to secure an away basketball game in 1976 with UCLA and an invitation for the W&M basketball team to compete in the Rainbow Classic in Hawaii. In football, W&M would typically play four home games and seven away games to profit from the larger gate receipts at other institutions.

Mr. Carnevale acted as liaison between his department and two external groups directly related to the athletic function, the AEF and the Faculty Committee on Athletics (of which Mr. Carnevale was a member). This committee was appointed by the president to advise the president and the Board of Visitors on athletic policy and to monitor the athletic budget annually before it was sent to the vice president for business affairs and to the Board of Visitors for final approval.

Working with Mr. Carnevale was the assistant athletic director and business manager, Mr. Edward Derringe (who also had part-time teaching responsibilities in the Men's Physical Education Department). Mr. Derringe assisted Mr. Carnevale with team travel arrangements, served as liaison with the ticket office,[3] and prepared a monthly budget report. Mr. Derringe also assisted Mr. Carnevale with the supervision of the head trainer, the sports information director, and the equipment manager.

Department of Men's Physical Education and Intramurals

The head of the Men's Physical Education and Intramural Department, Mr. Howard Smith, was selected for a three-year term (and could serve two terms) and reported to the dean of the Faculty of Arts and Sciences. An assistant department head was in charge of the intramural program in addition to his part-time teaching duties. (In 1975, the intramural director was also the head baseball coach.) The department faculty consisted of six full-time members (four with tenure) and seven part-time members (two with tenure). Eleven of the thirteen faculty members also coached a varsity sport. Thus, part of their compensation appeared on the men's intercollegiate athletic budget and part on the sep-

---

[3]The Intercollegiate Athletic Department paid a fee for the services of the ticket office, a function of the William and Mary Hall facility. The facility was operated as a separate entity by the director, Mr. Hooker, who reported directly to the vice president for business affairs.

arate men's physical education budget. The Men's Physical Education and Intramural Department had its own facilities separate from the women, except for the six tennis courts which were shared. In 1974-75, the operating expenditures for the Department of Men's Physical Education, funded totally from General Funds (i.e., state appropriations) were $183,547. Expenses for the intramural program were included in this figure.

The three major responsibilities of the Men's Physical Education and Intramural Department were listed in the departmental handbook as: (1) professional preparation of physical education teachers to serve in the public schools of the State of Virginia, (2) the instructional conduct of the activity program for all male students needing one or more semester activities for completion of graduation requirements, and (3) the organization of a broad intramural program for all male students, faculty and administration members.

Each student was required to gain four credits in a program of physical activity (one of which must be swimming). These requirements could be satisfied by electing an activity course offered by the men's physical education department, by participating for a season in a varsity sport, or by passing one of the skill tests offered. The intramural and recreational sports program was one of the more popular and well supported extracurricular activities among the student body. In 1972-73, over 3,100 students (756 women and 2,417 men) participated in an organized intramural program of over 34 different sports. Except for volleyball, the intramural program was segregated by sex.

Prior to the 1975-76 school year, the budget for the intramural programs was contained within the men's physical education budget which was a part of the overall university budget, funded from university fund sources (i.e., state funds, tuition and fees). Beginning in 1975-76, the intramural program was to have a separate budget.

Department of Women's Intercollegiate Athletics, Intramurals, and Physical Education

The head of the Women's Intercollegiate Athletics, Intramurals, and Physical Education Department, Mrs. Mildred West, also served a three-year term and reported directly to the dean of the Faculty of Arts and Sciences. Her staff consisted of eleven instructors[4] responsible for the

---

[4] Four of the eleven instructors were financed by local funds. Mrs. West had obtained for them the title of Acting Assistant Professor of Physical Education to avoid the title of "Coach."

EXHIBIT 4
William and Mary Grants-in-Aid 1974-1975

	Full[1]	Partial	NCAA Limit	W&M Cost
Football	77	9	105	$231,545
Basketball	11	0	18	36,200
Baseball	0	4	19	2,200
Gymnastics	0	3	12	1,500
Soccer	0	1	19	500
Tennis	1	2	8	4,400
Track	3	21	23	23,536
Wrestling	0	13	19	4,656
				$305,031

[1] A full grant-in-aid at W&M was worth $2,700 to an in-state recipient and $4,000 to an out-of-state recipient. Some Southern Conference schools, especially the University of Richmond and East Carolina University, were developing their programs to approach the NCAA Division I level in "full" grants-in-aid in football and some other sports.

physical education and intramural program, and 10 varsity sports. The women had their own facilities (including control of the only pool suitable for varsity competition and the only six tennis courts on the campus).

Mrs. West explained that the objective of her department was to provide a *total* program for women. Those with no experience could learn a sport in physical education classes; those with some experience could play a sport in intramurals; and those who were highly skilled and competitive could participate in varsity sports.

The intercollegiate athletic program for women at W&M began in 1920. From 1965 to 1974, in response to the rising needs and interests of women students, the women's athletic program experienced expansion as reflected in the following data:

1. The number of student participants in varsity athletics had grown from 100 to 312,
2. the number of varsity events sponsored had grown from 44 to 138, and
3. the teams fielded had increased from 5 varsities, 1 junior varsity, and 2 interest groups to 10 varsities, 5 junior varsities, and 2 interest groups.

On the other hand, the coaching staff and financial support had not been increased proportionately. Mrs. West also noted that the portion of student athletic and recreation fees spent on athletics for 1974-75 was $404,289. Women contributed 50% of that amount but received only 12%.

Mrs. West developed her budget by asking her coaches to submit their individual requests to her. After discussions with each of them she submitted the total departmental budget to the vice president for business affairs for approval.

Exhibit 5 gives Mrs. West's actual and projected budgets through 1978. It was prepared with the following items in mind: (1) the estimated costs of operating and staffing the existing programs; (2) the cost of adding gymnastics as an intercollegiate sport for women and the cost of expanding the track and field program; (3) the costs for gradual compliance with Title IX in the provisions of comparable athletic facilities, staffing, and fundings for both sexes; and (4) the cost of grants-in-aid for women, assuming Title IX would require them.

Mrs. West explained that in hiring faculty members she looked for a physical educator first, one who could also coach a sport. She believed that many men's athletic programs tended to hire a coach first, and then place him in some classes to teach, often in a sport in which he had little interest. Mrs. West discouraged her staff from concentrating on a particular sport. She stated that she had no desire to hire coaches with aspirations of developing a "national power" in one sport at the expense of other women's sports. She evaluated the performance of her coaches through students and peer estimates of their ability to teach fundamental skills and develop a broad program.

Looking to the future, Mrs. West shared with Mr. Smith the expectation of a merger of the men and women's physical education departments. She, however, was apprehensive about a merger for two reasons. First, it would divorce women's intercollegiate sports from women's physical education, currently both part of an integral program. Second, it might force the women to adhere to the men's coaching philosophy and undermine the women's emphasis on physical education. Nor did Mrs. West wish to become involved in recruiting women athletes with grants-in-aid, since part of the women's philosophy was to provide a program for the existing students rather than to bring skilled students into the program.

FORMULATION OF ATHLETIC POLICIES

A 1961 statement on athletic policy by the Board of Visitors outlined several policies allowing for the broadening of intramural sports and en-

EXHIBIT 5
Actual and Projected Budgets for the Women's Athletic Program
1974-1978

| | Actual | | Projected | |
	1974-75	1975-76	1976-77	1977-78
Administrative Expense*	$24,709	$48,500	$ 64,220	$ 81,550
General Expense**	4,607	10,300	10,950	11,935
Sports:				
Archery	0	0	0	0
Badminton	450	1,108	1,200	1,320
Basketball	1,700	3,875	4,000	4,400
Dance	1,404	1,515	1,700	1,870
Fencing	1,100	1,785	1,900	2,090
Golf	1,400	2,060	2,200	2,420
Gymnastics	0	1,125	2,750	3,425
Hockey	2,300	3,207	3,350	3,685
Lacrosse	2,000	3,100	3,300	3,630
Mermettes	1,405	1,610	1,800	1,980
Swimming Team	2,000	3,205	3,400	3,740
Tennis	1,800	3,020	3,200	3,520
Track & Field	200	1,105	1,200	2,000
Volleyball	900	1,485	1,600	1,760
Misc. Sports	1,110	2,000	2,500	2,750
M&O of Physical Plant	400	700	1,100	1,210
Special Events	1,200	1,500	1,500	1,500
Contingencies	0	1,000	1,500	1,500
GRAND TOTAL	$48,685	$92,200	$113,370	$135,885
Grants-in-Aid (10 Full Grants if required by Title IX)	$ 0	$40,000	$ 40,000	$ 40,000

*Includes salaries for teacher/coaches (with one additional person added in second, third, and fourth years), secretary, student assistants, and publicity staff.
**Includes supplies, social security and insurance.

couraging the varsity teams to be competitive at the Southern Conference level.

In November 1973, Mr. Carnevale faced a potential $60,000 deficit as he planned the men's intercollegiate athletic budget for 1974-1975.[5]

[5] This deficit was reflected in the budget as a requirement for funds from the college account entitled Current Fund Local. Subsequent to this projection, the anticipated receipts from an additionally scheduled football game, and an actual surplus $11,000 greater than anticipated, lowered the projected deficit to $30,000. (See Revised Projection for 1974-1975 on Exhibit 3.)

Costs were rising significantly; revenues were remaining constant. President Graves recognized the need for a comprehensive evaluation of the athletic program in view of the fact that there had not been one since 1961. Therefore, in January 1974, at the direction of the Board of Visitors, President Graves appointed a special committee comprising faculty and students to "identify measures to augment and better distribute revenues so that the present quality and scope of the athletic program can be maintained."

THE STUDY

The Committee decided to consider, not only the question of how to finance the athletic program, but also the question of its very existence and goals at the College. Over a period of several months, the Committee held separate conferences with men and women coaches and instructors, the directors of men and women intramurals, representative men students, the Board of Directors of the Alumni Society and the AEF, the chairmen of the Faculty Admissions Committee and the Affirmative Action Committee, and the vice president for college development. The Committee also developed, distributed and tabulated a questionnaire sampling attitudes and opinions about athletics held by students, faculty, staff, alumni and AEF members. The major findings of this poll were:

1. Students and faculty favored reduced expenditures for the revenue sports. Alumni and AEF members favored increased funding to make W&M competitive among universities in the South.
2. Students and faculty favored reducing the amount of the student fee which supported men's revenue sports. Alumni and AEF members favored increasing the student fee proportionally to cover, in part, the rising costs of the revenue sports.
3. Faculty favored discontinuing the AEF, and using donations from alumni and friends to benefit the College as a whole. Alumni and AEF members favored increased support for revenue sports through increased AEF donations.
4. All groups agreed that football should be self-supporting from gate receipts, and that women's non-revenue and intramural athletics could be supported from other sources.
5. All groups agreed that basketball should be self-supporting, and that the non-revenue and intramural programs should be supported from other sources.

6. All groups, except for AEF members, agreed that women's athletics deserved more financial support, commensurate with their needs. AEF members believed women's athletic programs currently received about the right amount of support.
7. All groups agreed that the men's non-revenue sports were important and deserved additional financial support.
8. The faculty for men's and women's intramurals favored increased support from student fees.
9. Students favored grants-in-aid based on need for men and women. Faculty favored eliminating grants-in-aid. No clear preference on this issue was expressed by alumni and AEF members.

Based on their interviews, discussions and the questionnaire results, the Committee came to the conclusion that two different policies on athletics were possible to articulate for W&M. These policies became known as "Program I" and "Program II."

Program I.   Program I would be "planned, developed, and administered primarily for the educational and recreational benefit of the student participants." The athlete's presence at the College would not be "attributable to recruitment and subsidization for athletic ability. In all respects, but most notably in admissions, registration and financial aid, the student who decided to participate in intercollegiate athletics would be treated like all other students." The program would be supported largely by student fees; grants-in-aid for athletics would be discontinued, membership in the Southern Conference would be dropped, and a move to Division III status would be recommended. Program I would be in compliance with the current interpretation of Title IX guidelines.

Program II.   Program II would be "planned, developed, and administered for the benefit of the *College community.*" The athletic program would be designed to develop "a regional and national reputation in selected sports, and to enhance their reputation through a quality program and reasonably successful records . . . The undergraduate who participates will be the student-athlete whose dual role of student and athlete will both be recognized as significant. As an athlete the participant will often be recruited and sometimes subsidized for special skills and for potential service to the institution . . . some participants should receive preferential treatment on admissions and registration." Program II would not be in compliance with the current interpretation of Title IX guidelines without substantial modification. It would require football and basketball, the revenue sports, to be funded by gate receipts, contributions, miscellaneous revenue (advertising, concessions, TV contracts) and a student-ticketbook fee. At the end of a four-year transition period the need for the ticketbook fee would be re-evaluated.

PRESIDENT GRAVES' RECOMMENDATION

The committee concluded its report in October 1974. It urged the Board of Visitors "to adopt one of the policies and recommend one of the programs, which, in their best judgment, would be in the best interests of the students and the College as a whole."

President Graves thanked the committee for its proposals and prepared his recommendations. Several questions faced him. In the opinion of Mr. Van Voorhis, assistant to the president, there were substantial differences in opinion between those inside the College community and those on the outside, including to a significant degree, members of the alumni. Mr. Van Voorhis also noted that several of the older faculty, now in influential posts, were present at the College during a football scandal in 1951 involving falsifying high school transcripts. On the other hand, many of the concerned alumni were students at that time and witnessed a successful nationally ranked football team at the College.

The directors of the Alumni Society, the fund-raising body for the College, predicted disastrous consequences to the fund-raising program of the College if athletics were curtailed. Other alumni, however, said they would never contribute to the College until the athletic program was reduced in cost and size.

President Graves also recognized that the amount and the proportional division of the athletic and recreation fee was the subject of considerable controversy on campus. Students generally believed that the fee should not be increased, that the amount of the fee allocated to revenue sports should be decreased, and that women's and men's nonrevenue sports deserved more support from the fee.

One of the major concerns of the faculty that became a very real issue during the policy development was that the grant-in-aid money going to support revenue sports was a significant part of the total scholarship resources and therefore involved a heavy opportunity cost to the College.

Another major concern of the faculty and student body was the academic quality of athletes. On November 1, 1974, prior to submitting his recommendations to the Board of Visitors, President Graves approved a Special Admissions Review Committee to review all cases designated as "marginal" or "not acceptable" by the regular Admissions Committee procedures. The special committee included four faculty members.

In his recommendation to the Board of Visitors in November 1974, President Graves offered his own proposal. He wrote:

> I believe that a strong and competitive intercollegiate athletic program for men and women, as a part of the overall college athletic and recreational experience, can be fully compatible with the mission of the College, and can provide the College with the important opportunity of making a major contribution to both the student participants in athletics and to other members of the broad College community.

His recommendation was neither Program I nor Program II but his own proposal which was a third or middle ground. There were a few substantial differences from Program II, most notably one that would *discontinue* rather than *re-evaluate* the mandatory student ticketbook at the end of the four-year transition period. Dr. Graves' proposal also offered more support to intramurals and non-revenue sports and recommended a more moderate profile for the athletic programs than Program II, which had called for a program of national visibility. He believed that this action would put "teeth into the program," and place responsibility on alumni to support the program. The key points in his recommendation were:

1. The present admissions policy of the College will continue to provide special consideration, but not preferred treatment, for students with special skills who are recruited and who will receive grants-in-aid. These students will be allowed, insofar as practicable, to be accorded special consideration in registration in order to meet practice schedules.

2. The program must operate on a "continuing sound financial basis, in a manner that will neither divert scarce financial resources away from the primary educational mission and needs of the College, nor permit a deficit." The program was a direct challenge to the broader community to support the program through their increased contributions.

3. Schedules should aim to enhance the image of the College as an educational institution of regional and national standing.

4. Revenue producing sports could only be funded from contributions, gate receipts, radio and television rights, program advertising and sales, and stadium concessions. Student fees should not be used to support grants-in-aid.

5. Grants-in-aid for revenue-producing sports and non-revenue-pro-

ducing sports must be funded from the same sources. The non-revenue-producing intercollegiate sports and the intramural programs for men and women shall be supported by income from student fees, and by income from the revenue-producing intercollegiate sports when available.

6. Private gift income and endowment income shall not be used to support in full or in part the intercollegiate athletic program, except in those instances where gifts and endowments are specifically designated by the donor for that purpose.

7. Support in revenue sports would be decreased in price $10.50 (to $36.00).

8. If the men's intercollegiate program were not self-supporting at the end of the four-year transition period, it would be reassessed—specifically to determine the future of the revenue sports for possible reduction to Division III competition.

On Friday, November 22, 1974, at a 6:00 p.m. news conference, the Board of Visitors announced that it had voted to accept President Graves' recommendation "to upgrade the athletic program at William and Mary."

The following day, the William and Mary football team went into their final game a 7-point underdog, and toppled long-time rival University of Richmond 54-12. On Sunday, however, a crowd of students gathered on the lawn of the Wren Building to protest the Board of Visitor's decision. One banner read "W&M—a college *of* the students and faculty, *by* the Administration, *for* the ALUMNI."

IMPLEMENTATION OF ATHLETIC POLICIES

President Graves and Mr. Carnevale agreed that in order for the revenue sports to become self-sustaining, both AEF contributions and basketball gate receipts would have to double. Exhibit 6 gives a record of AEF contributions for the period 1963-1974. Early in December 1974, Mr. Carnevale asked Mr. Fratkin, who in July had been promoted from sports information director to executive director of the AEF, to commit to raising AEF contributions to $200,000 for each of the next two years. Mr. Carnevale received permission from Mr. Graves to allow the football and basketball head coaches to award the maximum number of grants-in-aid allowable under NCAA guidelines.

EXHIBIT 6

Athletic Educational Foundation Contributions 1963-1974

Year	Amount Raised	Number of Contributors	Average Contribution	Contribution to Athletic Budget
(Dec. 31)				
1963	$ 20,140	510	$39.49	
1964[1]	30,080	784	38.36	
1965[2]	39,395	1,080	36.47	
1966	40,905	930	43.98	
1967	46,460	1,129	41.15	
1968[3]	79,055	1,179	67.05	
1969	63,400	1,178	53.82	$ 54,000
1970	70,420	1,251	56.28	75,000[4]
1971	59,000	1,178	50.08	75,000[5]
1972[6]	67,190	1,150	58.42	60,000
1973[7]	105,540	1,118	94.39	75,000
1974	115,000			95,000
1975	200,000 (goal)			125,000
1976	225,000 (goal)			240,000 (commitment)
1977*				

Notes:
1. Marv Levy's first football team fall 1964—Coach of Year.
2. First Winning season in 12 years (6-4).
3. Full-time Executive Director, 3 winning seasons in a row.
4. President Paschall raised additional $18,000 to meet $75,000 commitment.
5. President Paschall raised additional $24,000 to meet $75,000 commitment. Change of coaches.
6. Change in Athletic Director, Football Coach, no special gifts.
7. Executive Director, Ben Carnevale's first year, promise of 30 scholarships if funds available.

*AEF expected their commitment would level off at $200,000 for 1977 and beyond.

In the ensuing 1974-1975 basketball season, W&M had its best season in 17 years, winning 13 of 15 home games. Student sentiment began to shift in support of a winning program. By March 1975, the head football coach had signed 30 high school athletes.

Despite a feeling of positive momentum from actions taken under the new athletic policy, Mr. Carnevale still experienced some uncertainty and uneasiness. His major concerns in August 1975, were:

1. *Faculty relations and admissions policy:*   W&M admissions policy stated that "an athlete must be capable of solid academic achievement." Coaches interpreted this statement as meaning being able to get through school; the faculty expected more.
2. *Student body sentiments:*   The W&M basketball team had generated a great deal of enthusiasm among students for "winners." This sentiment could easily shift with a losing season in football, basketball or track.
3. *The budget:*   Although the key to the new program's success would be a balanced budget, several sources of revenue for football and basketball were question marks. Gate receipts were susceptible to fluctuation due to rainy game days. The miscellaneous account covering TV rights, advertising and concession revenues was unpredictable. Finally, although AEF contributions appeared firm in the short run, could this level of contributions be sustained? By July 1975, the AEF had raised $173,000 toward its $200,000 goal.
4. *In-state recruiting:*   It cost William and Mary $1,300 a year more for an out-of-state grant-in-aid, yet the varsity coaches claimed they were unable to find enough quality athletes in Virginia, often having to compete with the Ivy League schools and private schools, such as Duke and Tulane. Would a winning tradition change this situation?
5. *Relations with other W&M athletic programs:*   Mrs. West needed more personnel and facilities. Several of her coaches were responsible for two or three sports in addition to their full-time teaching responsibilities. The women needed another indoor facility 72' X 100'; the men used four of the five current indoor facilities. Men's and women's intramural, recreational and physical educational needs, together with varsity teams' needs, placed high priority on building 24 more tennis courts. Cost estimates for 12 courts were placed at $310,000. Men's and women's varsity swimming teams needed an electronic timer for the Adair Gymnasium Pool. How should these needs be rank ordered? Where should the money come from?

FIVE

ACCOUNTING AND CONTROL

Cost Analysis for Nonprofit Organizations*

INTRODUCTION

The need for timely and accurate cost information by profit-oriented organizations has become so widely recognized that most of the contemporary literature on the subject is based on the premise that such a need exists. Consequently, the "cost-related" issues having the greatest practical significance to the profit-oriented sector are those related to the determination of relevant cost data, the establishment of a cost information system to provide these data, and the appropriate analysis of the resulting cost data.

The need for timely and accurate cost information by nonprofit organizations (including those in the public sector) has not yet become so widely recognized. It is no coincidence, however, that the 1970s have brought about an increasing awareness of the importance of cost accumulation and analysis to nonprofit organizations. Rising labor costs, economic uncertainty, double digit inflation, and the decline in the overall ability of nonprofit organizations to meet future financial needs, have all contributed to a rather rapid appreciation by the nonprofit sector for adequate cost information.

*Written by E. Richard Brownlee, II. Copyright © 1981, by the University of Virginia Graduate Business School Sponsors.

Probably the one event that occurred during the 1970s that contributed the most to the acceptance by managers of nonprofit organizations of the need for a satisfactory cost information system was the severe financial crisis experienced by New York City. To realize that a city such as New York, with its seemingly unlimited financial resources, was unable to meet its financial obligations, had a sobering effect on the entire nonprofit sector. Among other things, this realization prompted a demand by managers of nonprofit organizations and by the public they serve to know more about such financial matters as cost accumulation, cost analysis, and cost control.

The purpose of this chapter is to provide managers of nonprofit organizations with a foundation of fundamental cost concepts. Even so, most of the concepts discussed herein also have applicability to the profit-oriented sector.

COST CLASSIFICATIONS

The term *cost* is broadly defined as "the use or consumption of economic resources." These resources may be human resources, may exist in the form of real or personal property, or may be of a financial nature. Cost is usually expressed as a monetary value intended to represent the amount of a resource's use or consumption. Although costs may be classified in a variety of ways, some of the most common classifications pertain to: (1) cost behavior; (2) cost traceability; (3) cost controllability, and (4) cost origination.

Cost Behavior

Some costs vary in direct proportion to changes in the amount of services provided or activities performed, while some costs are not affected by such changes in levels of output. Still other costs may vary with changes in output but not in proportion to these changes. Four general cost classifications are often used to describe the behavior of almost all costs as they relate to volume changes. These are: (1) fixed costs; (2) variable costs; (3) semi-variable costs; and (4) semi-constant costs. Each of these cost behaviors is shown graphically in the following figures.

A *fixed cost* is one that remains constant as the quantity of services provided or activities performed increases. On a per unit basis, however, cost decreases as volume increases. Thus, to refer to a fixed cost as a

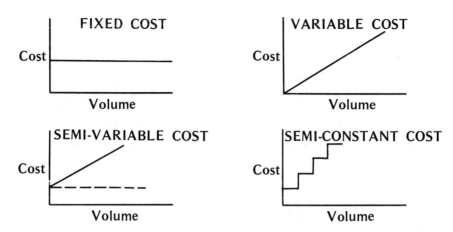

specific amount per unit of output is accurate at only one specific level of output. At a lower output level, the cost per unit is greater. At a higher output level, the cost per unit is less. Employees' salaries and rent on a building are examples of fixed costs.

A *variable cost* is one that changes in direct proportion to changes in volume. This means that the cost per unit of output will be the same regardless of the quantity of services provided or activities performed. Thus, a variable cost can be stated as a specific amount per unit without regard to any specific level of output. Examples of variable costs commonly include those pertaining to materials, water, and power.

A *semi-variable cost* is one that consists of both a fixed and a variable portion. Consequently, as the level of output increases, the cost per unit decreases but not in direct proportion to the increase in volume. For instance, if output doubles, the cost per unit decreases but by an amount less than half of its previous per unit cost. Semi-variable costs are probably more prevalent with profit-oriented organizations than with nonprofit organizations due to the existence in the profit sector of many employee compensation arrangements that are comprised of a fixed salary plus commissions. Utilities costs consisting of a minimum fixed charge plus an additional variable charge based on actual use or consumption are also examples of semi-variable costs.

A *semi-constant* cost is nothing more than a series of fixed costs. When graphed, it takes on the appearance of "steps" and is frequently referred to as a step-cost. Thus, a semi-constant cost is one that remains fixed over reasonably narrow ranges of activity and then increases to higher fixed cost levels as activity increases. The cost per unit of a semi-constant cost decreases as long as activity increases and the cost remains constant. As soon as a "step" occurs resulting in a higher fixed cost level, the cost per unit increases sharply and then begins to decrease until the next "step" occurs. For example, a medical clinic may need only one doctor to serve up to about thirty-five patients a day. Once the patient load exceeds this number, a second doctor is needed. When the daily patient load reaches about seventy, a third doctor is needed. The result is a series of fixed costs representing doctors' salaries that increase in amount each time the patient load increases by about thirty or thirty-five persons.

Direct Costs and Indirect Costs

The distinction between direct costs and indirect costs centers on the degree of their traceability to a specific segment or component of an organization. Those costs that are incurred solely for the benefit of a particular segment are known as *direct costs*. Strictly speaking, then, elimination of the organizational segment would result in the elimination of all the direct costs associated with it. On the other hand, indirect costs are those incurred for the benefit of many segments of an organization or even for the organization as a whole. In a hospital, the cost of staff personnel assigned to the cardiac unit represents the direct cost of operating that unit. The cost of maintenance personnel who repair and provide routine maintenance on all hospital equipment, the cost of the hospital administrators, and the cost of general clerical personnel represent indirect costs of operating the cardiac unit.

Full Costs and Incremental Costs

Most nonprofit organizations charge an amount for their services so as to provide for a recovery of their costs. A decision must then be made as to just what is meant by "costs" since there is really no such thing as "the cost" that will suffice for all decision purposes. This is true regardless of whether the organization is of the profit or nonprofit type.

Suppose that the administrators of the student health center of a large university were considering remaining open during the Christmas holidays in order to serve the medical needs of those students who remained at the university. Since the yearly student health fee paid by all full-time students was based on the assumption that the health center would be closed during all school holdiays, a decision to remain open during Christmas recess meant that a fee would have to be charged each student receiving medical attention at the health center during this period. In fairness to these students, it was believed that the holiday fee should provide only for the "recovery of costs."

While all student health personnel agreed with this concept of cost recovery, it was soon discovered that there were considerable differences of opinion as to what was meant by "costs." On one extreme were those advocating the use of "full costs." On the other extreme were those advocating "incremental costs." *Full costs* were all of the costs associated with operating the student health center for the year. These included administrative and staff salaries, supplies, drugs, rent for the building and certain equipment, utilities, and depreciation on the equipment owned by the student health center. (A discussion of the concept of depreciation and the rationale for its inclusion as a recognized cost is presented later in this chapter.) Those personnel advocating the use of full costs suggested that the annual amounts of these costs should be totaled and then divided by the average number of student visits to the health center during the previous three years. The result would be an "average full cost" per student visit. Students treated at the health center during the Christmas recess would be charged on this full cost basis.

Those student health personnel advocating the use of *incremental costs* believed that the full cost approach was untenable. They reasoned that most of the health center's costs would remain the same regardless of whether it closed or remained open during the Christmas holidays. All physicians and nurses were paid an annual salary and were expected to be at their offices doing research or other job-related activities during all but a few days of the Christmas recess. Clerical personnel were also paid an annual salary and received only a few days vacation at Christmas and New Years. Rent on the building and the leased equipment, utilities, and the amount of the depreciation recognized on the equipment owned by the health center would not be affected by a decision to keep the center open.

Advocates of incremental costing wanted to charge each student who used the services of the health center during the Christmas recess the amount necessary to recover whatever costs would be incurred by the center solely as the result of keeping it open during that time period. Such incremental costs would consist primarily of supplies, drugs, and a receptionist's salary since the regular receptionist's salary did not include any remuneration for working during those periods when the university was not in session. Charging students on this incremental basis would result in a much lower amount per visit than would be the case if full costs were used.

The correctness of any decision concerning cost determination depends primarily upon the objective(s) to be served. In the situation just described, the objective was to provide medical services to the students who remained at the university during the Christmas vacation, and to charge them a sufficient amount per visit so as not to affect the amount of the annual student health fee charged to all full-time students the following year. In other words, the student health center should be no better off or no worse off financially as the result of remaining open during the Christmas recess. Given this objective, the use of incremental costing would seem to be the most reasonable choice in this particular situation.

Controllable and Non-Controllable Costs

All costs incurred by both nonprofit and profit organizations should be controlled at some level within the organization. Once this is recognized, it becomes important to identify those individuals with the authority to determine the desired level of costs that need to be incurred in order to accomplish the organization's objectives. Many organizations are structured so that the managers of individual segments within the organization have complete authority to make decisions that affect the amount of all direct costs incurred by their segments. Quite often these same managers have little or no control over those costs that are "indirect" to their segments within the organization.

However, it is not possible to conclude that all direct costs are controllable and all indirect costs are non-controllable by all managers of all organizational segments or divisions. The reasons for this are twofold. First, it is not unusual for certain costs that are "direct" to a particular division to be controlled by someone with greater authority in the organization than that of division managers. Such costs are then non-controllable with respect to the division managers. Second, it is possible (although unlikely) that division managers may have some control over certain indirect costs incurred by the divisions. These would then represent controllable costs to the managers.

The importance of such a distinction in cost controllability lies in its application within an organization. Individuals should be held responsible for all costs over which they have control, and they should not be held responsible for those costs over which they do not have control. Two situations, then, should be avoided. First, not holding individuals responsible for costs over which they have control; second, holding individuals responsible for costs over which they do not have control.

Capital Costs and Operating Costs

An important distinction for both nonprofit and profit-oriented organizations to make is between capital costs and operating costs. The essential difference in these two types of costs lies in the period of time over which organizational benefits will be derived as the result of incurring these costs. *Capital costs* are those costs associated with the acquisition of both personal and real property expected to be used by an organization for more than a year. The "useful life" associated with such property can range from as little as two years for certain machinery or equipment to as much as forty or fifty years for some buildings. *Operating costs* are those costs associated with the everyday activities of an organization. These include salaries and wages, materials, supplies, rent, and utilities.

Since capital costs usually involve very large financial expenditures or commitments, the question often arises as to the proper manner of charging the day to day activities with the appropriate capital costs consumed during a given time period as a result of using the capital property previously acquired. An even more fundamental question deals with the need to charge *any* of such capital costs to the everyday activities. Both of these questions will be addressed later in the section on "Accounting Methods."

Joint Costs and Transfer Prices

Before concluding the section on "Cost Classifications," it seems appropriate to comment on two other cost-related problems that frequently arise in nonprofit organizations. As with previously discussed cost-related issues, these same two problems are present in profit-oriented organizations as well.

The first such problem deals with the treatment of *joint costs.* These are costs that benefit and are associated with two or more different activities within an organization. In a hospital, for instance, the salaries of the doctors and nurses who perform services for more than one division or other identifiable segment within the hospital represent joint costs. Similarly, the costs associated with the maintenance, repair, and cleaning of all hospital facilities, as well as the costs of the central clerical staff for the entire hospital, represent joint costs attributable to many or all of the divisions within the hospital.

The proper treatment of joint costs by the management of any organization depends on the particular situation under consideration and on the nature of the decision to be made. For instance, financial constraints might make it necessary for management to consider cutting back on the level of the organization's activities through the elimination of one of its present departments. In determining the resulting cost savings of such a change, only those costs that would no longer be incurred by the organization as a whole are relevant to the decision. Thus, all of the joint costs presently associated with the department under consideration must be carefully analyzed from a total organization point of view to see which of these costs, if any, would be eliminated. The remaining joint costs (i.e., those that would not change in total to the entire organization) would merely be allocated differently within the organization and, consequently, would not be relevant to the decision.

On the other hand, if management wished to determine the full cost of operating a specific department within the organization, then such cost should include an appropriate amount of the joint costs pertaining thereto. This requires an allocation of these joint costs to the different segments benefited by them. The method used to accomplish such a cost allocation should be selected with the objective of assigning the joint costs to the various activities in proportion to the benefits derived therefrom. In some situations, the allocation can be done quite meaningfully. In others, it can become quite arbitrary. In these latter situations, it must be realized that the resulting cost data are extremely "soft."

Another problem very similar to that of joint costs arises when one segment of an organization performs services for another segment of the same organization and wishes to be reimbursed for the "costs incurred" by charging a satisfactory *transfer price*. The determination of transfer prices within an organization should be made with full recognition of the effect that these prices will have on the relationship between the segments as well as on the degree to which inter-segment services are performed. The objective of establishing transfer prices is to motivate the managers of each organizational segment (division, department, etc.) to act in such a manner with respect to inter-segment services that the overall benefits to the entire organization are maximized. Put another way, transfer prices should be set so as to ensure that individual managers are motivated to act in a manner that works toward accomplishing the objectives of the organization as a whole, i.e., *goal congruence*.

Good arguments can often be made by the various department managers in support of what they believe to be "fair" transfer prices. Usually, the manager of the department providing the services tends to think more in terms of full costs while the manager of the department receiving the services tends to think more in terms of incremental costs. Although there are no easy answers to the transfer price problem, there is a recommended approach to its solution. First, transfer prices between segments of an organization should be established by individuals who are above these divisional levels. Second, transfer prices should be set so as to motivate those people associated with the individual divisions to act in a manner that is consistent with top management's objectives.

ACCOUNTING METHODS

Historically, most nonprofit organizations have used an accounting method referred to as a *modified cash basis*. Under this method, operating costs are charged to an organization's activities as cash disbursements are made, regardless of when the service was performed or the asset was acquired that gave rise to each cost. An exception to this rule, and the reason for the name "modified cash basis," is when capital assets are purchased. Here, the costs of these assets are not immediately charged to the period's activities because they are believed to have a useful life longer than a year. Such costs should, however, gradually be charged to the organization's daily activities. The process by which this occurs is known as *depreciation*. The next section entitled "The Concept of Depreciation" addresses this topic in more detail.

In recent years, an accounting method known as *accrual accounting* has gained considerable popularity with nonprofit organizations. The accrual method of accounting results in the recognition of costs when they are incurred, regardless of when the actual cash disbursements occur. Similarly, it results in the recognition of revenues at the time they are earned (i.e., when the services are performed), regardless of when the cash is received. This is unlike the modified cash basis that recognizes revenue when the cash is received rather than when the revenue is earned, and recognizes most expenses at the time the related cash disbursement is made.

The increased interest in the accrual method by nonprofit organizations is the result of the deficiencies inherent in the modified cash basis. Although these deficiencies have always been present, it hasn't been until recently that the financial difficulties experienced by numerous nonprofit organizations have accentuated the inadequacies of the financial information provided by the modified cash basis of accounting. Having made this same discovery many years ago, most profit-oriented businesses now use the accrual method of accounting. This is not meant to suggest that nonprofit as well as profit-oriented organizations shouldn't be concerned with the concept of cash-flow (i.e., actual cash receipts and disbursements), but rather that cash-flow usually does not provide a sound basis upon which to measure the overall financial consequences of an organization's activities.

THE CONCEPT OF DEPRECIATION

To most people, the term depreciation carries with it the connotation of something wearing out, falling apart, or in some fashion, physically deteriorating. In a business sense, accountants accept the idea that most capital assets (both real and personal property) do have limited useful lives to an organization because they do wear out or become obsolete. This means that organizations incur certain costs to acquire capital assets, use these assets over their useful lives, and dispose of them once they have worn out or become obsolete. Both the accrual and the modified cash methods of accounting recognize that the original costs of capital assets should be allocated to the periods that benefit from their use and that this allocation should be done on some systematic, rational, basis. Accountants refer to such an allocation process as *depreciation*.

The reason for an organization to recognize depreciation as a cost associated with its everyday activities (i.e., an operating cost) is that failure to do so will most likely result in charging an amount for the organization's services that does not generate sufficient resources to enable it to replace these capital assets once they lose their usefulness. In the past, some nonprofit organizations were fortunate enough to have almost unlimited financial resources available externally. Therefore, management felt that there really was no need to provide internally for the replacement of capital assets. In such cases, depreciation was often not recognized as an operating cost at all.

Since the days of seemingly unlimited capital availability appear to be gone, the failure to recognize depreciation as an operating cost is no longer supportable. In fact, the inflation that has occurred in the United States throughout the 1970s has brought about the recognition that during an inflationary period, even the recognition of depreciation based on historical costs is not sufficient to enable an organization to generate internally sufficient financial resources to replace those capital assets that are no longer useful. Such a realization on the part of management has resulted in the argument that the amount of depreciation recognized as an operating cost should be based on the replacement costs of capital assets and not on their historical costs. Although such "replacement cost" depreciation has generally been resisted by the accounting profession and has not yet been accepted by the Internal Revenue Service, the concept makes good economic sense from a management viewpoint.

THE USEFULNESS OF COST DATA

One of the most important uses of cost data by nonprofit organizations is in setting the prices to be charged for the variety of services performed. If prices are to be based on costs, then an organization must know just what its costs are. Only then can it make reasoned decisions about such issues as the use of full costs or incremental costs. Another point to consider is that many nonprofit organizations receive donated services and/or donated property, both of which enable them to provide their services at lower costs than would otherwise be possible. These organizations must seriously consider whether they can *reasonably* expect to continue to receive similar donations in the future. If not, then it becomes necessary for them to increase the prices charged for present services by an amount that will provide for the availablity of sufficient financial resources in the future when such services and/or property need to be acquired.

A second important use of cost data is in an organization's planning process. *Planning* is the means by which all organizations decide what actions must be taken now in order to achieve the objectives of the future. Since the environment within which an organization exists constantly changes, the organization's future goals and objectives must continually be reassessed. Thus, planning is very much a continuous process. Successful planning entails the collection and use of relevant data as the basis for present decisions so as to permit future objectives to be realized. Much of the data required in the planning process is cost-related.

A third important use of cost data is in the establishment of *budgets*, i.e., financial plans pertaining to various aspects of the organization. Typical budgets prepared by nonprofit organizations include:

Cash Budgets

Operating Budgets

Capital Budgets

Cash budgeting involves the projection of cash inflows and outflows over some future period of time. *Operating budgeting* pertains to the projection of services to be provided and operating costs to be incurred. *Capital budgeting* deals with the planned allocation of financial resources to the future acquisition of capital assets.

The budgeting process also provides a good means of forcing members of an organization to look ahead and to plan for the future. It often results in greater coordination among the many diverse aspects of an organization as the resulting budgets would otherwise not make sense in relation to one another. Finally, the budgeting process provides management with benchmarks (budgets) that may be used as a means of evaluating future performance of individuals within the organization and of the organization as a whole.

Performance evaluation, then, is another major use of cost data. Future performance can be measured by comparing the actual costs incurred with the budgeted costs. While the resulting cost variances certainly don't tell the whole story, they do provide an excellent means of identifying areas worthy of management concern.

Much has also been written lately about the use of another budgeting procedure by nonprofit organizations, that of *zero-base budgeting*. The objective of ZBB is to require each program within an organization to justify itself every so often and to provide a means for ranking specific program projects.

SUMMARY

The need for timely and accurate cost information by profit-oriented organizations has been recognized for many years. A similar need by nonprofit organizations is just beginning to be recognized. The recent interest in cost information on the part of these organizations is due in no small part to the serious financial difficulties experienced by New York City in the middle 1970s. In addition, inflation, competition for existing financial resources, and uncertainty about the availability of future financial resources have all contributed to the awareness of the importance of cost data.

Costs may be classified in many ways. These include:

Cost Behavior
   Fixed
   Variable
   Semi-Variable
   Semi-Constant
Direct and Indirect
Full and Incremental
Controllable and Non-Controllable
Capital and Operating
Joint Costs (and Transfer Prices)

Nonprofit organizations have traditionally used the modified cash basis of accounting. The deficiencies inherent in this method have led many organizations to adopt the accrual method of accounting in recent years. This change has enabled these organizations to distinguish revenues from cash inflows and costs from cash outflows, the end result being a better understanding of the financial affects of their activities. Regardless of which of these two accounting methods is used, however, consideration must be given to the costs associated with the consumption of capital assets. Accountants use the term depreciation to describe the process of recognizing such capital asset consumption costs. Although depreciation has traditionally been based on historical costs, the inflation experienced in the 1970s has given rise to the concept of replacement cost depreciation.

There are many important uses of cost information by nonprofit organizations. These include decisions regarding pricing, planning, various types of budgeting, and performance evaluation. The extent to which such data are being used is increasing. Like profit-oriented organizations, nonprofit organizations are realizing that it may no longer be possible to survive without adequate cost information, cost controls, and cost analysis.

Case 10

Charles W. Morgan Museum*

DISTRIBUTION OF SUPPORT SERVICE COSTS

In November, 1978 Cabot M. Davis was appointed Managing Director of the Charles W. Morgan Museum, succeeding Daniel Sharkey who had retired earlier that year after twenty-three years as head of the museum. Soon after he took over, Davis discovered a nagging problem which his predecessor never thought important enough to confront directly but which now threatened to disrupt the smooth operation of the museum. The problem concerned the distribution of the cost of certain activities which served four adjacent institutions (three schools and a research center) as well as the museum. Though the legal entity of the museum owned the land and facilities of all five institutions, and technically could direct their operation, in practice each was governed by its own board of trustees and operated under its own budget. The problem with cost distribution arose because the heads and business managers of the neighboring institutions complained that they did not understand the distribution and no one had ever been able to explain it satisfactorily. Furthermore, the distribution seemed to them to be unfair in several respects.

*Case prepared by Professor William Rotch, University of Virginia. Copyright © 1980, Colgate Darden Graduate Business School Sponsors.

Mr. Davis investigated and tried to understand the problem. However, the more he looked into it, the more complex and mixed up it seemed to become. He soon realized that it would not be wise to direct a solution, though he probably had the authority to do so. A good solution would be one that was acceptable to all the governing boards of the museum and neighboring institutions as well as their heads or directors. Therefore to provide a broad base of experience and representation he appointed a committee to analyze the situation and to recommend a method of distribution. The committee was to meet in August, 1979.

BACKGROUND

The Charles W. Morgan Museum had been established in 1875 by a generous bequest of one of the city's wealthier merchants. The bequest included a 52 acre site on the city's outskirts, a large mansion, a well selected collection of European paintings and sculpture and a modest endowment.

During the century that followed, the museum grew, constructing new buildings and adding to its collections. Also during that time four other institutions were established on the museum's land. In 1907 on the completion of a major new museum building the mansion became the site of a new school of art which had grown over the years to the 1970s. In the middle of the 30s an existing elementary school moved from its central city location to the museum's land. In 1951 a drama school was also established on the museum's land. Finally in 1956 a Center for Research on the Preservation of Art was established in its own building adjacent to the museum.

All of these institutions were supported primarily from donations, tuitions and fees. The museum and art school had modest endowments. The elementary and drama schools had to rely primarily on tuition. The research center was supported by grants and fees. All five worked separately to raise money from whatever private sources they could tap. The drama school was probably in the shakiest financial position, and in 1979 was particularly conscious of being caught between rising costs and a student body which could not afford tuition increases.

Over the years the museum had taken a leading role in providing support services for all five institutions. In 1979 these services fell into the following areas: Accounting; Switchboard; Purchasing and printing; Grounds maintenance; Heating; Service building; Security; and Administration.

In 1979 the total cost of these services amounted to slightly over one million dollars. Exhibit 1 shows the budgeted distribution for the most recent three years.

SERVICES PROVIDED

The following is a description of the services provided in the eight categories:

Accounting

The accounting department provided accounting services for all five institutions and consisted of eight people:

The Financial Officer who managed the department.

An Assistant, with particular concern for reconciliation of bank statements, distribution of investment income, insurance, and depreciation schedules.

Office Manager, who managed work flow and filled in for others as needed.

Two accounts receivable and payable clerks.

One payroll clerk.

Cashier, concerned with transfer and accounting for cash and deposits.

Ledger machine operator.

Switchboard

Though all five institutions had outside lines, there was a central switchboard which was manned during the day and which could connect a person calling a central number with any of the numbers in the institutions. Recently a more efficient system and a reduction in the hours of attendance had reduced the switchboard cost.

Purchasing and Printing

The four people in this department provided centralized purchasing for some of the supplies used by the institutions and did printing jobs as requested. The department also provided an internal messenger mail service including distribution of some outside mail that did not go directly to the institutions.

Grounds Maintenance

About twelve people worked on the grounds crew, doing three kinds of work. One kind was response to special requests from the institutions, for which they were charged directly. Another kind was "routine institutional" maintenance which clearly pertained to a single institution. (Mowing or raking that institution's grounds, for example.) The third kind was "general" maintenance which served all five institutions. Daily trash pick-up, leaf removal, snow plowing the common driveways, street repair and equipment maintenance were examples of the third kind of maintenance.

Heating Plant

All five institutions were served by one heating plant. The cost of running the plant was about 45% fuel expense and about 55% for the engineers running it and necessary repairs. The heat was distributed through steam lines which had meters to measure institutional consumption.

Service Building

The service building contained the heating plant (about 30% of the area) and shop areas used by the grounds crew. Included in the shop areas were an electrical shop and a carpentry shop. The carpenters and electricians were paid by the museum which charged other institutions for labor hours spent on jobs they requested. The building had been built in 1974 by the museum which, through a "depreciation" charge based on a fifty year life was slowly recovering its cost. The annual cost of the building, therefore, was the depreciation charge plus building mainenance.

Security

There was a security force which patroled the area and buildings 24 hours a day.

Exhibit 1

Distribution of Budgeted Support Service Costs (Distributed Dollars in Thousands)

	Total Budgeted Dollars	Museum		Elementary School		Art School		Drama School		Research Center		Other	
		$	%	$	%	$	%	$	%	$	%	$	%
Administration													
FY 1977-78	52,300	36.6	70.0	4.9	9.3	6.5	12.5	3.1	5.9	1.2	2.2		
1978-79	61,600	26.1	42.4	9.4	15.2	15.9	25.8	7.3	11.9	2.9	4.7		
1979-80	75,540	32.0	42.4	11.6	15.4	18.3	24.2	8.7	11.5	3.6	4.7	1.3	1.8
Accounting													
FY 1979-78	140,700	51.2	39.2	22.5	17.2	33.9	26.0	15.9	12.2	7.1	5.4		
1978-79	148,340	59.7	40.2	26.0	17.5	38.9	26.2	16.8	11.4	6.8	4.6	10.0	7.1
1979-80	168,390	83.4	49.5	22.2	13.2	33.3	19.8	16.1	9.6	9.1	5.4	4.2	2.5
Switchboard													
FY 1977-78	42,400	16.0	37.8	11.2	26.5	9.9	23.5	3.9	9.1	1.3	3.0		
1978-79	40,870	10.7	26.1	10.9	26.6	11.9	29.1	4.5	11.1	1.4	3.5	1.4	3.5
1979-80	35,930	8.7	24.2	7.7	21.3	10.3	28.7	3.1	8.6	1.5	4.1	4.7	13.1
Purch. & Printing													
FY 1977-78	68,000	35.7	52.5	13.2	19.4	12.2	17.9	3.7	5.5	3.2	4.7		
1978-79	68,410	26.5	38.7	14.7	21.5	14.9	21.7	6.7	9.7	5.6	8.2		
1979-80	72,910	21.0	28.7	18.9	25.9	18.1	24.9	8.0	11.0	6.9	9.5		
Grounds Maintenance													
FY 1977-78	269,500	116.2	45.7	46.1	18.1	66.2	26.0	22.7	8.9	3.2	1.2	15.0	5.6
1978-79	227,330	82.3	38.7	28.5	13.4	66.8	31.4	27.7	13.0	7.1	3.4	15.0	6.6
1979-80	235,440	87.2	37.0	39.6	16.8	69.7	29.6	33.1	14.0	5.8	2.5		

Exhibit 1 (continued)

	Total Budgeted	Museum		Elementary School		Art School		Drama School		Research Center		Other	
Heating													
FY 1977-78	229,310	112.0	52.0	20.2	9.4	45.0	20.9	24.2	11.2	13.9	6.4	14.0	6.1
1978-79	238,740	80.7	35.3	21.5	9.4	75.7	33.1	33.7	14.7	17.2	7.5	10.0	4.2
1979-80	273,820	112.4	41.0	25.2	9.2	69.3	25.3	38.4	14.0	19.8	7.2	8.8	3.2
Service Building													
FY 1977-78	26,500	12.7	45.7	4.6	18.1	6.2	26.0	2.3	8.9	.7	1.2		
1978-79	30,500	12.6	44.2	4.2	14.4	7.7	25.9	4.1	10.9	1.9	4.6		
1979-80	39,500	15.9	40.3	5.4	13.7	9.8	24.9	5.6	14.2	2.7	6.8		
Security													
FY 1977-78	174,000	131.9	78.7	14.6	8.7	3.4	2.0	15.2	9.1	2.3	1.4	6.5	3.7
1978-79	147,480	97.6	68.0	26.6	18.5	8.9	6.2	9.6	6.7	.8	.6	4.0	2.7
1979-80	168,280	92.6	55.0	33.5	19.9	30.3	18.0	10.4	6.2	1.5	.9		
TOTAL													
FY 1977-78	1,002,710	512	51.1	137	13.7	183	18.3	91	9.1	33	3.3	45	4.5
1978-79	963,270	396	41.1	142	14.7	241	25.0	111	11.5	44	4.6	30	3.1
1979-80	1,069,810	453	42.3	164	15.3	259	24.2	123	11.5	51	4.8	19	1.8

Administration

There were three people who were involved in administering the support services. Two of those people had other responsibilities which pertained only to the museum. Thus the cost of administration was the full salary of one person and part of the salary of two others, together with some secretarial expenses.

BUDGET

The budgets of the five institutions were on a fiscal year ending August 31. Hence in the early spring of each year a budget for the various support services was prepared as well as a set of allocation percentages. By March the amounts in the next year's budget which were attributed to each institution were made known to them so that they in turn could include these amounts in their own budgets which were usually prepared in late spring.

The support services were actually funded by the museum. As the year progressed each institution was billed monthly for its share (based on the budget percentages) of the previous month's actual expenses. Thus if the budget showed that the drama school was to pay 14% of heating costs, the drama school would be billed in November for 14% of the total heating costs incurred in October. Though the August bill was rendered in September, the institutions would include it as part of their actual expenses for the year ending August 31.

Distribution of Support Expenses

In 1979 the eight categories of support services were being distributed on the following bases:

Accounting: about 16% of total.

Basis: Computer line entries were counted and the number pertaining to each user was noted. Allocation of cost was based on the user's line entries as a percent of total line entries. Some 30,000-40,000 line entries were generated each year.

Timing: Counting was done once a year in January for the year ending the previous August 31.

Switchboard: about 4% of total.

Basis: The number of telephone numbers (or extensions) each user had listed, as a percent of total numbers listed.

Timing: Counted in March when the next year's budget was being prepared. The dollars charged covered labor and equipment.

Purchasing, Supply and Printing: about 7% of total.

Basis: About 85% of this category was salaries. Bob Rust (the manager) estimated the percentage of time each of the four people spent on activities devoted to each user. The four percentages applying to each user were added and divided by four.

Timing: This was done once a year in March when the budget for the next year was being prepared.

Grounds Maintenance: about 23% of the total.

Basis: Total cost to be allocated was first reduced by the amount of labor cost for special work orders chargeable to those who made specific requests for work to be done. The time spent on special work orders represented from 2% to 20% of the total but averaged around 5%. The remainder was allocatable cost and included the cost of routine maintenance for specific institutions and the cost of general or common maintenance activities, plus the cost of equipment and supplies. The basis for allocation was the record kept of where the grounds people spent their time when working on routine maintenace at a specific institution.

Timing: When the budget was prepared in March, the previous twelve months record of hours spent was used to develop allocation percentages.

Heating Plant: about 27% of total.

Basis: The basis was the amount of steam metered into the various buildings. In this case there were some users who were not among the five. These other users paid their share.

Timing: Steam usage was measured to as near the end of the heating season as the budget process would allow, usually March. Thus the 1978-79 heating season was the basis for the 1979-80 budget allocation.

Service Building: about 4% of total.

Basis: The operating costs of the building were combined with depreciation charges. Depreciation on the building was set at 2% of its cost (50 year life) and the total cost allocated according to a formula determined shortly after the building was completed, the basis of which no one could quite remember.

Security: about 16% of total.

Basis: About 60% of the total patrol hours were directly related to a user. In the past, the total cost of security had been allocated on the basis of proportional usage of that 60% of the total time.

Timing: Once a year Captain Mark estimated the time spent providing security services to each of the users, on both regular patrols and on special occasions.

Administration: about 7% of total.

Basis: The last category allocated, the amount charged each user was based on each user's total as a percent of total support services cost before administration was allocated.

THE FIRST COMMITTEE MEETING

Mr. Davis appointed eight people to the committee whose charge was to recommend a procedure for distributing the support costs. Five members, including the chairman, were treasurers of the boards of the five institutions. The other three were paid staff; one was Jill Gray, the Financial Officer in charge of accounting; another was Bill Calder who was the full time operations manager for the support services; and the third was Tilford Burke who was recently hired as special assistant to the museum director and whose time would be partly devoted to administration of the support services.

Prior to the committee's first meeting on August 16, 1979 Mr. Davis asked Mr. Burke to review the situation, by talking with the five institute business managers and to present to the the committee what he discovered to be their complaints about the present system.

At the meeting Mr. Burke reported the following comments:

• Derivation of the distribution percentages was hard to understand. The Research Center business manager, for example, had seen his total charges go from $33,000 to $51,000, and increase of 60% while the total costs of support services had risen only about 6%. The previous summer, in an effort to reduce costs, the center had undertaken to mow its own grass but had seen no reduction in the amount it was charged.

• One business manager had complained that another business manager had managed to get large amounts of grounds work charged on special work orders rather than as routine work. Mr. Burke was not quite sure why that was a complaint but he reported it anyway.

- Three business managers thought the allocation of purchasing and printing costs seemed a bit arbitrary, though two said they had no reason to believe it was not fair. The third, the drama school manager, said they rarely used the printing services because they had bought their own duplicating machine and thought they were charged too much.
- The elementary school business manager said that $30,000 for security was far more than they needed. They had their own janitorial service (as did all the institutions) and beyond that a night watchman, if needed at all, would cost less than half that amount.
- The drama school business manager said they didn't need the switchboard service.
- The elementary school business manager said they had installed storm windows and turned down thermostats in the winter of 77-78 but saw no effect on heating costs.
- Several business managers complained that they were being charged for the space used by the electrical and carpentry shops in the service building, but used those services only in emergencies.
- One business manager noted that since most of the service costs seemed pretty well fixed, a reduction in usage by one user meant higher costs for the others even though they did not increase their usage.

The committee discussed these complaints at length. There was some agreement that they should investigate the separation of fixed costs, or "capacity costs" as one member called them, from variable costs. It was not entirely clear, however, how the two types of costs should be defined and identified. Furthermore, such a separation would not solve the problem of cost allocation, though if variable costs could be attributable to users, the amount to be allocated would be reduced.

Several members of the committee expressed concern that, while the proportions might or might not be equitable, there was no clear rationale, no basis on which the percentages could be defended. After some discussion of the need to have a defensible basis for allocating the capacity costs, the committee returned to a discussion of individual items.

At this first meeting of the committee there was no agreement on the most appropriate method of distribution. However, committee members did agree that they had gained a better understanding of the nature and extent of the problem.

At the end of the meeting the chairman asked Mr. Burke and Ms.

Gray to prepare a summary of what seemed to be the most appropriate
bases for the allocation percentages and to prepare a breakdown between
fixed and variable costs.

BACKGROUND FOR THE SECOND
COMMITTEE MEETING

Mr. Burke and Ms. Gray prepared a number of tables for use by the
committee at its next meeting. They were as follows:

Accounting.   Exhibit 2 shows a summary of accounting costs and
three bases for allocation: the present method of line postings, by payroll population and by checks issued. Ms. Gray favored one of the latter
two over the present method because, she said, the present method was
affected too much by the structure of accounts. The museum's fund accounting system had many interfund transfers, she said, which involved
no actual transfer of cash. The museum's treasurer had even thought of
combining funds to avoid the transfers and perhaps save $15,000.

Switchboard.   Since the switchboard had caused some controversy a
count was made of the volume of calls handled by the operators during
a four week period from August 20 to September 14. It revealed the
following distribution, shown alongside the allocation made during the
past two years:

	% Calls	Budget 78-79 Allocation	Budget 79-80 Allocation
Museum	38.8%	26.1%	24.2%
Elementary School	27.0	26.6	21.3
Art School	24.6	29.1	28.7
Drama School	8.4	11.1	8.6
Research Center	1.3	3.5	4.1

An analysis of FY 1979 showed that switchboard costs totalled
$45,732, a bit higher than the amount budgeted, and that $31,430 represented personnel and basic equipment costs and $14,302 represented
the telephone company's charge based on the number of line numbers
provided.

EXHIBIT 2

Measures of Accounting Activity

Function	Museum	Elementary School	Art School	Drama School	Research Center	Total
Accounts Payable						
June 1-Nov. 30						
Checks Issued	1,556	1,285	1,906	611	282	5,640
Monthly Average	259	214	318	102	47	940
Percentage	17.55	22.77	33.83	10.85	5.00	100%
Payroll						
Nov. 30						
Population	124	101	137	60	14	436
Percentage	28.44	23.17	31.42	13.76	3.21	100%
Variables not included: Schools closing for Summer Schools' Summer Programs Christmas Card Seasonal Staff						
Machine Postings						
(Based on FY 1978 Data, support services only)	50.05	13.70	20.27	10.06	5.92	100%
Posting percentages used in 1978-80 budget, recognizing 2.5% other	49.5	13.2	19.8	9.6	5.4	97.5%

Purchasing and Printing. The purchasing and printing department employees spent about 75% of their time on printing work, about 15% on purchasing and about 10% on mail distribution. The materials used in printing work done for the several institutions were charged to them at cost, just as with other purchased supplies. The cost of running the department was allocated on the basis of the department manager's estimate of time spent in behalf of each institution.

Grounds Maintenance. Exhibit 3 shows a report giving the number of grounds work hours used by the various institutions and the percentage distribution, by four-week period, over two years. Following these is a one-page report comparing previous allocations with the average distribution with and without inclusion of special work-order hours.

An alternative to the present system of allocation would be to eliminate separate charges for special work-orders and charge a flat rate for all institution work, allocating the general maintenance costs according to the average institutional usage.

Another alternative would be to add the cost of the general maintenance to the hourly charge.

The general maintenance costs could also be divided according to population, area, or some other reasonable measure.

Bill Calder said the recording and distribution of grounds work hours to the three categories and five institutions consumed a good deal of time on his part as well as that of his groundsmen. The data were not useful to him in managing the grounds crew—there was too much delay— and he would be delighted if the data were found to be unnecessary.

Heating. The following table shows the percentage of actual steam consumption during the last three years, 1977 and 1978 for the full year, and 1979 through February:

	FY 1977	FY 1978	FY 1979
Museum	47.2%	39.2%	41.1%
Elementary School	9.5	8.3	9.2
Art School	19.0	28.0	25.3
Drama School	14.2	13.8	14.0
Research Center	7.1	7.3	7.2
Other	3.0	3.3	3.2

The total pounds of steam used was much the same (within 5%) in all three years. Consumption at the art school was unusually high in FY

1978 because a broken steam line went undetected for over a month. Also in that year the museum's use of steam decreased significantly as a result of changed thermostats, reduced hours of opening and energy saving weatherproofing. In FY 1979 the art school had mended the steam pipe but also added a new building. The elementary school also added a building in 1979.

Of the $283,304 total costs of heating, $125,159 or 44.2% was for fuel costs; the rest was for labor and equipment maintenance costs.

Service Building. The cost of the service building, other than that part which housed the heating plant, was $26,719 in FY 1979. Of this space 3.5% was used by the art school and .7% by the drama school for storage areas; 35.7% was used by the carpentry and electrical shops and 60.1% was used for storage and repair of equipment used in grounds maintenance. The following table summarizes this.

	Space	Dollars
Grounds	60.1%	$16,058
Carpentry and Electrical	35.7	9,539
Art School	3.5	935
Drama School	.7	187
Total	100.0%	$26,719

Security. There were about a dozen security officers who provided various kinds of services, including patrols 24 hours a day, museum duty and traffic control. The grounds of the five institutions were surrounded by a fence and access was limited to four gates. Over the years the city had grown around and beyond the grounds and for many of the students and employees at the five institutions the fence and security force were a distinct benefit.

The costs represented in the security category were about 94% personnel, 3% vehicles and 3% for other equipment and supplies.

THE BUSINESS MANAGERS' PROPOSAL

Before the second meeting of Mr. Davis's committee on October 16, the business managers of the four non-museum institutions met and prepared a proposal. This was that fixed or capacity charges be separated from variable or direct charges and that each institution's share of the total of capacity charges be determined by dividing its total operating

Exhibit 3

Grounds Work Hours October 1977-July 1979

Four Weeks Ending	General Maintenance Hours	Museum	Elementary School	Art School	Drama School	Research Center	Total Paid Hours	Total Work Hours	Work Order Hours
1977									
10/24	403	687	127	397	104	35	2170	1753	277
11/21	773	403	163	318	143	20	2080	1820	32
12/19	726	350	171	294	161	34	2136	1736	51
1978									
1/16	779	329	153	217	141	10	2247	1629	99
2/13	886	530	211	325	173	24	2285	2149	86
3/13	810	451	166	286	148	21	2185	1883	83
4/10	709	392	151	343	192	9	2011	1796	73
5/08	1055	424	146	445	109	30	2369	2209	222
6/05	396	947	205	300	123	48	2275	2019	569
7/03	1269	437	170	319	135	40	2558	2370	93
7/31	760	699	150	380	134	56	2712	2185	129
8/28	894	482	158	429	108	16	2679	2087	97
9/24	880	312	186	376	182	44	2320	1980	23
10/23	701	444	180	228	166	10	1992	1723	123
11/20	819	327	169	282	153	24	2022	1774	40
12/18	844	304	180	245	149	23	1945	1745	36
1979									
1/15	644	225	173	198	141	20	2013	1401	36
2/12	808	343	190	168	195	9	1966	1713	9
3/12	858	271	174	169	150	18	1968	1640	20
4/09	819	378	198	242	191	0	1948	1828	125
5/07	1221	378	182	296	189	28	2480	2294	105
6/04	457	826	168	302	164	12	2157	1929	528
7/02	1121	517	194	320	188	40	2516	2380	40
7/30	990	452	194	358	182	24	2504	2200	35
Maximum	1269	947	211	445	195	56	2712	2380	
Median	833	609	169	307	150	28	2339	2010	
Mean	818	455	166	304	163	25	2231	1927	
Minimum	396	271	127	168	104	0	1966	1640	
Percentage of the Mean TWH	42.3	23.5	9.1	15.6	8.2	1.3	Total 100%, 1927 hours		

Grounds

Previous Allocations

Fiscal Year	Museum	Elementary School	Art School	Drama School	Research Center
1978	45.7	18.1	26.0	8.9	1.2
1979	38.7	13.4	31.4	13.0	3.4
1980	37.0	16.8	29.6	14.0	2.5

2 Year Average, Including Work Orders

General

42.3	23.5	9.1	15.6	8.2	1.3

2 Year Average, Routine Hours Plus Work-Orders

	40.9	14.9	27.3	14.7	2.3

2 Year Average, Routine Hours Only (Present Method)

	36.4	17.3	28.8	15.2	2.4

1979 Cost $222,982 (not including service building)

General Maintenance Hours

Includes the Following:

Daily Trash Pick-Up and Disposal
Leaf Pick-Up and Disposal
Snow and Ice Removal
Pick-Up and Delivery for Purchasing
Maintenance of Equipment
Gas Service
Maintenance Building Custodial, Grounds
Street Cleaning and Repair
Street Sign Maintenance
Street Drain Cleaning and Maintenance
Special Truck Runs for Support Services

221

Exhibit 4
Measures of Relative Demand

	Total	Museum	%	Elementary School	%	Art School	%	Drama School	%	Research Center	%
Population Served (hours of attendance)	2,786,732	495,844	18.8	652,800	23.4	831,000	29	705,320	25.3	101,468	3.6
Payroll-People	412	119	28.9	97	23.5	127	30	56	13.6	13	3.2
Payroll-$	331,129	88,072	23.1	100,977	26.5	121,547	31	58,268	15.3	12,265	3.2
Building Area	431,037	116,037	26.9	95,000	22.0	146,600	34	40,900	9.5	32,500	7.5
Expenses	8,210,987	1,801,877	22.0	1,867,474	22.7	2,906,549	35	1,356,534	16.5	278,553	3.4
Assets	13,676,459	5,939,519	43.4	2,450,295	17.9	3,109,810	22	401,795	2.9	1,775,040	13.0
Fund Balance	13,291,897	6,031,526	45.4	2,793,320	21.0	2,413,525	18	357,349	2.7	1,696,177	12.8

Notes:

1. Population Served: Schools—No. of students, parents, other clients times hours. Museum—Visitors times average of 2 hours per visit.
2. Payroll: A typical monthly payroll, Fall 1979. Seasonal variation: Museum up in Fall, Schools down in summer, etc. Source: SS Accounts.
3. Building Area: From Business Managers and Insurance Records.
4. Expenses: 1978 Statement of Revenues; Total General Expenses.
5. Assets: 1978 Balance Sheet; Total Assets less Land and Buildings.
6. Fund Balances: Total Fund Balances less net investment in Land and Buildings.

expenses (less interest and transfers to reserves) by the sum of these expenses for all institutions. Thus they said, "capacity costs would be divided among users according to their economic size. Each institution would have an equal stake in the management of capacity and these costs would be the same proportion of each institution's budget." The business managers figured that capacity costs would amount to about 60% of the total service costs and that this would be about 7.5% of total expenses. Each institution would therefore budget 7.5% of its total expenses for the capacity cost of support services.

THE SECOND COMMITTEE MEETING

After reviewing the data which had been made available for the meeting, a number of alternative distribution methods were proposed and discussed.

One committee member thought the easiest way to proceed would be to use the present method and refine the percentages so that they did a better job in reflecting actual usage.

Two others argued in favor of the separation of fixed capacity costs from variable costs. There was some question whether "variable" should mean ultimately variable or costs which were traceable to the user.

Handling of the capacity costs proved to be another bone of contention. One person said he thought the simplest way would be not to try to use a confusing multiplicity of percentages but to find one basis for distributing all capacity costs, more or less as proposed by the business managers. This idea stimulated extensive discussion of what that base should be. At this point Ms. Gray produced a chart showing several possible bases which might be considered. (Exhibit 4)

After the committee had studied this chart for several minutes, one senior member who had said rather little up to this point said he thought the whole confusing process could be greatly simplified because there wasn't very much difference between the various bases. He proposed that the committee approve a division as follows: Museum 30%, elementary school 20%, art school 30%, drama school 16% and research center 4%.

Spirited discussion followed with no sign of agreement as the time for adjournment approached. Recognizing that another meeting would be required, the chairman asked Mr. Burke to draw up a specific proposal, consulting whomever he wished, and using the actual FY 1979 figures noted in the following table.

	Actual FY 1979
Accounting	$ 174,051
Switchboard	45,732
Purchasing and Printing	56,044
Grounds Maintenance	236,491
Heating (including its share of the service building)	283,304
Service Building	26,719
Security	162,435
Administration	56,607
	$1,041,383

Case 11

Children's Rehabilitation Center*

On June 30, 1972, Mr. George Phillips, Administrator of the Children's Rehabilitation Center, was working late to complete the financial statements for the Center's past fiscal year. As he completed the last report he was reminded of a matter which had troubled him more and more in recent months. "If only I had a better idea of how our costs should be allocated," he thought. "I feel that we are charging our patients fairly but I'm just not sure."

Mr. Phillips was concerned with cost allocation for other reasons as well as for pricing. The public and private agencies upon which the Center depended for much of its support paid the Center according to a cost reimbursement formula. He knew that more representative cost information would place him in a better position to deal with these agencies. If he could show that there was a wide gap between reimbursed and incurred expenses, he intended to make an appeal to the agencies for additional help in offsetting costs. He thought additional cost information might also provide a valuable management tool for budgeting and control.

*Case prepared by William Rotch, Professor of Business Administration, based on a report written by Kyle T. Lynn in 1973 under the supervision of Associate Professor C.J. Tompkins. Copyright © 1974 by the University of Virginia Graduate Business School Sponsors.

CHILDREN'S REHABILITATION CENTER

The Children's Rehabilitation Center was a part of the University of Virginia Medical Center. It had been established and facilities built in 1957 by endowments and gifts to help handicapped children realize their potentials to become useful and productive adults. Additional gifts had enabled the Center to be enlarged in 1972. Children eighteen and under with motor, coordination, perceptual learning, orthopedic, or psychiatric disabilities were eligible for the Center's programs regardless of their economic circumstances. The Center's primary goal was quality patient care. As a part of the University of Virginia Medical Center, the Rehabilitation Center also had the responsibility to participate in University teaching and research.

The Center was located about two miles from the University of Virginia in a building with thirty inpatient beds. Comprehensive extended care (that level of care between acute care provided by traditional hospital wards and long-term custodial care) was offered to both inpatients and outpatients. Between July 1, 1971 and June 30, 1972 (fiscal year 1972), the Center provided 7,373 days of inpatient care and 4,667 outpatient visits.[1]

The programs of the Children's Rehabilitation Center were unique in their multidisciplinary approach. This approach attempted to restore the "whole child" by involving him with a team of specialists. This team made it possible to follow each patient's social, physical, and psychological development as a unit rather than treat each problem separately. While not the first facility to use this approach, the Center had been most successful in implementing it. Regular staff meetings as well as informal conferences ensured communications and cooperation among staff members. Conferences and follow-up with parents and local health agencies were also stressed to aid families in adjusting to a child's handicaps and to assure continuity of treatment. Appendix A describes the Center's programs in more detail.

Children could be admitted to the Center in several ways. They could be transferred from the University Hospital, admitted through one of the several clinics held at the Center, or directly upon the request of the patient's physician to the Medical Director. Children could be admitted either for evaluation of development or for an inpatient or outpatient therapeutic program with definite goals and duration.

---

[1] In fiscal 1971 there had been 6,243 days of inpatient care and 2,994 outpatient visits.

The Center's primary concern was not so much the parent's ability to pay but rather the patient's potential for a meaningful life. Approximately 80 percent of the patients at the Center were covered by public or private (third party) agencies (e.g., Blue Cross) which paid all or a large portion of billed expenses. Indigent patients' bills were carried for a short period of time and then written off. Unrecovered expenses were made up from the yield of the endowment fund (approximate yield = $150,000/year). The current collection rate was about 83 percent.

ORGANIZATION

The Children's Rehabilitation Center was run jointly by a Medical Director and an Administrator as shown in Exhibit 1. The Medical Director was a member of the Medical School faculty and was responsible to the Dean. He had responsibility for medical care, professional aspects of staff activities, and research. The administrator was responsible to the Director of the Medical Center through the Director of the Hospital. He had responsibility for the physical plant and assets, personnel policy, and financial matters. Both the Medical Director and Administrator were responsible to the Children's Rehabilitation Center Advisory Committee of the Medical Affairs Policy Board regarding long-range planning and policy.

People in charge of the various departments of the Center reported to the Administrator or Medical Director in their respective areas of authority. The Orthopedic Surgeon, Neurologist, and Pediatricians, as well as some other professional staff members were provided by the Hospital and Medical School. They reported to the Medical Director and their own superiors and utilized the Center to practice in their areas of specialization.

COST SYSTEMS IN HOSPITALS

Interest in cost systems for hospitals had increased in recent years, particularly as they might assist in pricing, financial planning and expense control. Several current trends lay behind the desire for better cost information. One was the increasing number of cost-based lawsuits dealing with discriminatory pricing of health services. Another was the growing recognition that hospitals' need for capital was outstripping their philanthropic sources. Many believed that in the future hospitals would have to depend upon operating revenues as the primary source of capital. Since most patient care would be under cost-based Medicare reimbursement formulas, close examination of the costs of rendering services was warranted. Finally, it was becoming increasingly important for hospitals to budget accurately in order to find out the level of internal funds that could be generated and thereby determine debt capacity. Accurate determination of debt capacity would allow a hospital to borrow a maximum amount of capital while retaining the ability to repay debts from operations. In summary, it was becoming clear that accurate cost information could help a hospital to maximize sources of capital, utilize available capital efficiently, and remain within legal constraints.

The changing hospital scene was discussed in an article "Prospects for Prospective Payment" by Elton Tekolste in the May 16, 1972 issue of *Hospitals*, the Journal of the American Hospital Association:

> ... For years hospitals have tried to operate under the burden of the bookkeeper's narrow definition of costs, which has dictated revenue requirements. . .
>
> A second burden on our industry has been the not-for-profit concept, which involves two distinct features. First, not-for-profit has been defined as a show of absolute zero on the bookkeeping ledger, in which bad debts, charity costs, and other non-cash items are not included as expenses. Second, hospitals have been expected to be charitable institutions. The result of these concepts has been that many hospitals are operating at a deficit.
>
> Finally, the inadequacies of cost allocation have hampered efforts to define departmental costs and have restricted our ability to adequately determine departmental revenue requirements.
>
> However, hospitals have survived these burdens for a variety of reasons. First, because they are charitable institutions, they are able to conduct fund-raising drives. For a long time, the monies raised in this way kept hospitals from recognizing depreciation as a recoverable cost. Second, they were able to continue paying inadequate wages to personnel because employees were indoctrinated with a philosophy of altruism and because hospitals often employed "supplemental income" earners.
>
> Last, to survive hospitals engaged in the "Robin Hood theory" of pricing, in which some patients were charged more to make up for losses incurred with other patients. It is hoped, however, that some of the current activities to discredit discriminatory pricing, such as lawsuits in the health care field and in air transportation, will help solve this problem.

EXHIBIT 1
Organizational Chart for Medical Center

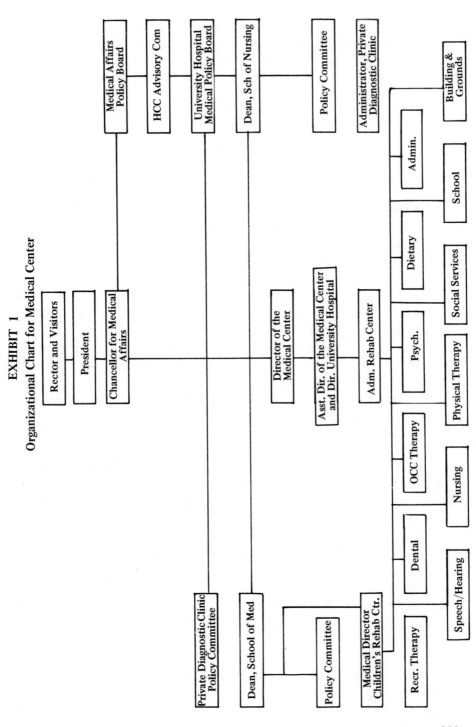

However, we can no longer accept the bookkeeping definition of not-for-profit. We must be alert to the possible decline of the fund raising drive and must recognize that the self-paying patient is disappearing, with increasing emphasis on Medicare, Medicaid, and other third party systems. If self-payers don't disappear totally, they at least will be so few that they will be unable to pay the astronomical premiums that will be needed to offset losses in hospital revenue.

The Rehabilitation Center's Present Cost System

The Rehabilitation Center's cost system was based upon the University of Virginia Medical Center's cost collection system. Mr. Phillips received a monthly report which presented monthly and fiscal year expenses for each of ten departments within CRC. An end-of-year summary of these reports is presented as Exhibit 2. From these reports and other data, Mr. Phillips assembled the information shown in Exhibit 3 and assigned costs to inpatients and outpatients according to a ratio determined by the number of inpatient days, the number of outpatient visits, and the assumption that one inpatient equalled three outpatients. Costs per outpatient or inpatient were then used as a basis for setting the next year's rate per inpatient day or outpatient visit. During fiscal 1972 the Center charged an all inclusive rate of $45 per day with special charges for only a few ancillary services, such as operating room, IV solution and x-ray. The outpatient rate was $15 per visit.

"I'm not at all pleased with our present costing methods," said Mr. Phillips. "Our rates are always a year behind the times and have formed the basis for the present cost reimbursement formula. Worst of all, I'm no longer confident that they reflect the present operations of the Center."

Developing Better Cost Information

As the first step in developing a new cost analysis Exhibits 4, 5 and 6 were assembled from CRC records and supervisors' estimates to give an indication of resource utilization and services provided by each department.

Exhibit 4 gives a statistical summary of patient activity.
Exhibit 5 gives an allocation of floorspace and building cost.
Exhibit 6 gives information on distribution of effort by each department.

EXHIBIT 2

Summary of Fiscal Year 1972 Expenses by Department

Medical and Surgical Services

Item	Expense	Detail
Salaries and insurance	$ 7,507	Administrative charge made by Medical Center for operating room nurse (not used at CRC)
General Repairs	71	$37 Dental equipment, $34 general
Direct Patient Services (X-Ray, Lab, Consultants)	13,603	Charged to individual patients
Travel w/normal duties	55	Nurses travel
Travel, educational	20	Nursing workshop
Laundry and Dry Cleaning	2,078	Linen for inpatients' wards
Office supplies	35	Publicity materials
Medical and lab supplies	12,521	General
Housekeeping materials	42	Curtains for O.T. Dept.
Educational supplies	7	Chalkboard for inpatients' wards
Wearing apparel for patients	68	Shoes (orthopedic) directly charged patient
Photographic supplies	39	General
Electronic supplies	4	General
Other supplies	120	General
Educational Assistance	105	Nursing Aide Course
Office equipment	87	General
Medical equipment	59	General
Books and periodicals	7	General Medical Reference
Dues and subscriptions	20	General Medical Reference
	$36,454	
Less direct charges	13,603	
	$22,851	

*Figures in this and other exhibits do not always add exactly because of rounding and dropping the cents.

EXHIBIT 2, CONTINUED

Nursing Department

Item	Expense
Salaries, wages, insurance*	$140,363
Supplies	11
Dues, subscriptions	6
	$140,380

*Salaries vary widely and all personnel are utilized by inpatients exclusively except:

1 R.N.	— Orthopedic Clinic	16 hrs./wk. Salary at $7,680 yr.
1 R.N.	— Neurology Clinic	8 hrs./wk. Salary at $7,680 yr.
1 Attendant	— Cystic Fibrosis Clinic	8 hrs./wk. Salary at $4,128 yr.
1 R.N.	— Dental Clinic	20 hrs./wk. Salary at $9,168 yr.

Social Services Department

Item	Expense
Salaries, wages, insurance	$3,241
Travel w/duties	28
Travel, professional education	135

Position	Annual Salary	Employment Dates
Case Worker	$5,160	1/1/72 — Current
Case Worker	Wages, part time = $827 in	FY 1972

Physical Therapy Department

Item	Expense
Salaries, wages and insurance	$25,000
General Repairs	2
Travel with normal duties	15
Educational travel, conventions, conferences	445
Medicine and lab chemicals	48
Medical appliances	331
Educational and recreational supplies	163
Photographic supplies	237
Other supplies	25
	$26,271

Position	Annual Salary
Supervisor	$10,992
Therapist	8,400
Aide	5,880

Occupational Therapy Department

Item	Expense
Salaries, wages and insurance	$27,552
Equipment repairs, phonograph	22
Professional travel	611
Medicine and lab supplies	140
Housekeeping supplies	38
Educational and recreational supplies	380
Professional educational movies	16
Chairs and desks	89
Professional magazine subscriptions	3
Other supplies	69
	$28,923

Position	Annual Salary
Supervisor	$10,032
Therapist	8,040
Aide	4,920

Dietary Department

Item	Expense
Salaries, wages and insurance (6 cooks and a supervisor)	$26,046
Food supplies	12,081
Towels, soap, utensils, tableware	938
Office, equipment, repairs	84
Household equipment, tables	80
	$39,230
Refund (receipts, pay cafeteria)	76
Net Expenses	$39,154

EXHIBIT 2, CONTINUED

Buildings and Grounds Department

Item	Expense
Salaries, wages, insurance, O.T.	$40,627
General repairs	276
Motor vehicle repairs, w/reimbursement from accident	(207)
Routine maintenance	10,444
Electricity and water	7,019
Freight	9
Entertainment	5
Heating oil	651
Housekeeping supplies	2,630
Small tools, hardware	10
Motor vehicle—fuel, oil, supplies	1,608
Employees apparel	73
Electronic supplies	67
Other supplies	619
Household equipment	73
Maintenance equipment	312
Other equipment	597
Rent, auto due to wreck	233
Fire insurance	1,364
Workman's compensation, treatment of finger	32
	$66,450

Position	Annual Salary
Supervisor	$8,040
Housekeeping Super	4,128
4 Housekeepers	3,432 to 4,128

Speech/Hearing, Psychology—Special Studies

Item	Expense	Detail
F. Wickers, Psychologist, salary (75%)	$9,162	CRC pays only .75 salary
Travel w/education or convention	375	
Education & recreation supplies	165	
Other supplies	54	
Books and periodicals	18	
	$9,777	

Recreational Therapy Department

Item	Expense
Salaries, wages, insurance*	$12,626
Travel and lodging for professors	878
Travel for professional education of employees	168
Travel to and from local recreational facilities	34
Xeroxing	17
Office supplies	10
Educational and recreational supplies	375
Photographs	13
Other supplies	42
	$14,166

*Supervisor $ 9,340
Aide 3,216
Usually 1 student assistant. CRC pays for
his supervisor to visit and check his progress. -0-

Administrative Department

Item	Expense	Detail
Salaries	$55,771	
Wages	6,232	
Federal O.A. Insurance	2,464	
Sub total	$64,468	
General repairs	8	Safe repair
Maintenance contracts, service	821	On office equipment
Lab and x-ray service	12	On job injury
Travel w/normal duties	112	Staff on business
Travel education or convention	553	Educational travel, administration
Travel aid to patients	16	Indigent inpatient parents
Freight	172	To transport employees to CRC
Telephone	5,817	
Printing	748	Publicity booklet
Advertising, radio, newspaper	17	Want ad for nurses
Xeroxing	22	

Administrative Department (*continued*)

Item	Expense	Detail
Other services	16	
Office supplies	2,517	
Housekeeping supplies	15	
Photographic supplies	10	
Electronic supplies	158	
Other supplies and cable	427	
Office equipment	1,789	
Household equipment	36	
Books and periodicals	153	
Rent	2,945	Xerox machine
Auto insurance	82	
Dues and subscriptions	92	Professional dues
Sub total	$16,546	
	$81,015	

Position	Annual Salary	
Administrator	$15,000	G. Phillips
Secretary	4,920	Lynch
Secretary	2,580	Taylor
Secretary	4,320	Abbott
Secretary	5,160	Clark
Secretary	5,160	L. Rowlett
Secretary	5,160	Kidd
Secretary	4,920	Dunlap
General Secretary	7,344	Rameriz
	4,320	Farley

EXHIBIT 3

Cost Reports Fiscal Year Ended June 30, 1972

Costs Attributable to:	Inpatients		Outpatients	
	Cost	Cost per Day	Cost	Cost per Visit
1. Medical-Surgical	$ 18,868	$ 2.56	$ 3,983	$ .85
2. Nursing	115,913	15.72	24,468	5.24
3. Social Service	2,812	.38	593	.13
4. Physical Therapy	21,692	2.94	4,579	.98
5. Occupational Therapy	23,882	3.24	5,041	1.08
6. Recreational Therapy	11,697	1.59	2,469	.53
7. Speech-Psychology	8,074	1.09	1,704	.37
8. Dietary	32,329	4.38	6,825	1.46
9. Buildings & Grounds	54,869	7.44	11,582	2.48
10. Administration	66,894	9.07	14,121	3.03
Totals	$357,093	$48.41	$75,365	$16.15

Based on: total cost per department (Exhibit 2)

7,373 inpatient days
4,667 outpatient visits

Assuming one inpatient day = three outpatient visits

Thus 82.57% of costs allocated to inpatients
17.42% of costs allocated to outpatients

EXHIBIT 4

Statistical Summary of Patients, Fiscal Year 1972

Inpatients			
Total days care rendered			7,373
Outpatient Visits			
Handicapped Children's Clinic (HCC)	459		
Learning Disabilities Clinic	23		
Cystic Fibrosis Clinic	208		
BCC Myelomeningocele Clinic	121		
Scoliosis Clinic	83		
Orthopedic Clinic	357		
Clinics Total		1,251	
Physical Therapy Service Visits	474		
Occupational Therapy Service Visits	675		
Recreational Therapy Service Visits	608		
Speech and Hearing Service Visits	473		
School Service Visits	492		
Psychology Service Visits	55		
Dental Service Visits	268		
Child Psychiatry Service Visits	38		
Service Visits Total		3,083	
Children and Youth Services Visits			
Audiology	212		
Speech and Hearing	121		
Children and Youth Total			333
Total Outpatient Visits			4,667

NOTE: These statistics were reproduced from CRC records and do not account for: Neurology Clinic; Neonatology Clinic; Juvenile Amputee Clinic; Respiratory Health Camp; Obesity Clinic; and Cleft Palate Camp. See Exhibit 6 for additional statistics on these programs.

EXHIBIT 5

Allocation of Floor Space to Departments

Department or Activity	Square Footage	
2. Nursing	628	2.2%
3. Social Services	600	2.1%
4. Physical Therapy	1,436	4.9%
5. Occupational Therapy	1,250	4.3%
6. Recreational Therapy	4,652	16.0%
7a Speech & Hearing	1,202	4.1%
7b Psychology	613	2.1%
8. Dietary	2,150	7.4%
9. Buildings and Grounds	5,031	17.3%
10. Administration	1,411	4.9%
11. Dental	135	.5%
12. School	1,025	3.5%
13. Inpatients and Wards	6,030	20.8%
14. Outpatients and Clinics	1,629	5.6%
15. General (all departments)	1,245	4.3%
	29,037	100.0%
Hallways, stairs and unused areas	8,363	
	37,400	

Original structure (1957)	21,400 Sq. ft.	Cost $	420,000
New addition (1972)	16,000 Sq. ft.	Cost	600,000
Total	37,400 Sq. ft.	Cost $1,020,000	

NOTE: Though it was known that equipment, furniture, tools, etc. originally cost $26,161, there were no records indicating in which department these assets were used.

EXHIBIT 6

Distribution of Efforts by Department

Developed from supervisor estimates and appointment records. There was no regular statistical report other than the summary of patients shown in Exhibit 4.

2. *Nursing*
All nursing service is directed toward care of inpatients on wards except:

A.	1 R.N.	Orthopedic Clinic	16 hours/week
B.	1 R.N.	Neurology Clinic	8 hours/week
C.	1 Attendant	Cystic Fibrosis Clinic	8 hours/week
D.	1 R.N.	Dental Department	20 hours/week

3. *Social Services*
   A. Although there are approximately 8 persons in the department, only 2 are paid by the Center:
      1 full time aide   Inpatients only
      1 part time aide (40 hrs/wk)   1 day/wk Cystic Fibrosis Clinic
                                     1 day/wk Myelomeningocele Clinic
                                     1 day/wk HCC Clinic
                                     2 days/wk inpatients
   B. All patients of the Center are covered by Social Services personnel either paid by the Center or the University Medical Center.

4. *Physical Therapy*
Taken from appointment records. Sessions were of various lengths from those who were mainly given apparatus to manipulate to those who required constant attention.
   A. *Inpatients* = 2,228 inpatient days (1 or more sessions)
   B. *Outpatients* = 648 patient days (1 or more sessions)
   C. *Clinics:*

Scoliosis (Supervisor)	12 hrs/mo (approx.)
Cystic Fibrosis (Therapist)	4 hrs/mo (approx.)
Myelomeningocele (Supervisor or Therapist)	6 hrs/mo (approx.)
HCC (entire staff)	16 hrs/mo (approx.)
Juvenile Amputee (Therapist done for Dept. of Pediatrics)	8 hrs/mo (approx.)

5. *Occupational Therapy*
   A. *Therapy and Evaluations:*
      Inpatients—3,300 visits, 5,227 sessions = 2,613.5 hours
      Service visits for outpatients—723 visits, 958 sessions = 479.0 hours.

B. *Clinics:*
Supervisor only, Learning Disabilities Clinic
   1 hour/week for 9 months
Supervisor only, Neonatology Clinic (Pediatrics Dept.)
   6 hours/month
Supervisor only, Juvenile Amputee Clinic (Pediatrics Dept.)
   3 hours/month
Entire staff, HCC Clinic
   3 hours/month
1 staff member (rotating) HCC Clinic Meeting
   4.5 hours/month (estimate)

C. *Inpatient Rounds:*
Supervisor and therapist
   3 hours/week (estimate)
Supervisor only
   2 hours/week (estimate)

6. *Recreational Therapy*
A. Standard departmental schedule FY 1972:
   6.5 hrs./day inpatients
   1.5 hrs./day outpatients
B. The Supervisor also participated in the following events:
   1.5 hrs/wk Obesity Clinic
   15 min/wk Scoliosis Clinic
   15 min/wk Cystic Fibrosis Clinic
   Both members of the staff participated in:
   Respiratory Health Camp   14 hrs/day × 14 days
   Cleft Palate Camp   2.5 days × 5 weeks

7a *Speech and Hearing*
Records were available for a 9 month period in FY 1972. During this 9
month interval the following was accomplished:

A. Inpatients:

	Visits
Therapy	117
Evaluations	172
Parent conferences	71

B. Outpatients:

Therapy	346
Evaluations	42

C. Handicapped Children's Clinic

Evaluations	306

D. C & Y

Evaluations and conferences	149
Other evaluations and conferences	21

Speech and Hearing (continued)

Evaluations   =   1 hour (estimate)
Therapy   =   .5 hours (estimate)
Conferences   =   .5 hours (estimate)

7b *Psychology*
The Psychologist (according to appointment records) sees about 4 in-patients/week and 1 outpatient/week. (Not all are reported on the Statistical Summary.)

8. *Dietary Department*
   A. The Dietary Department serves 3 meals/day to each inpatient. Additionally, 12-14 (estimated) staff members/day eat lunch in the cafeteria and pay a fee to offset the meal's cost. Part of these receipts are used to provide coffee for the staff, the rest is refunded to the Dietary Department.
   B. Approximately 2 outpatients/day are fed free of charge at lunch.
   C. The Supervisor does not attribute any significant additional time or cost to providing for the special dietary needs of some patients.

9. *Buildings and Grounds Department*
   A. *Housekeeping* – The Housekeeping staff cleans all Center spaces once a day except the kitchen and cafeteria (3 times) and the wards (2 times). (Estimated)
   B. *Vehicles and Shuttle Service* – Shuttle service and transportation is provided all departments to transport patients to the University Hospital for tests and pick up and deliver supplies, equipment, and personnel.
   C. *Maintenance and Repairs* – The Supervisor provides minor repairs for all departments. Special projects (bookcases, shelves, etc.) are also constructed upon request.

10. *Administration*
Assignments of personnel are as follows:
   A. George Phillips' secretary   Rowlett
   B. Nursing secretary   Lynch
   C. Medical Director's secretary   Kidd
   D. Outpatient Coordinator-PT, OT, RT, Dental Section   Taylor
   E. Social Services, Education, Psychology secretary   Clark
   F. Admissions secretary   Dunlap
   G. Coordinator for volunteer workers, secretary   Schlamb

H. Personnel, purchasing, records,
   head secretary   Rameriz
I. Assistant to Rameriz, secretary   Farley

11. *Dental*
All patients receive a dental examiniation (with rare exceptions) and necessary treatment.

12. *Education (School)*
Average enrollment FY 1972:
   25 inpatients
    2 outpatients

The services of several members of the professional staff were not charged to the CRC budget but were carried by the Medical School, Pediatrics Department, or the Medical Center in their various programs. For example, the only charges against the Dental Department were for 50 percent of the medical supplies utilized by that facility (estimated by the Dentist at $900/2 = $450) because of a grant to offset costs of giving dental treatment to handicapped children.

In order to organize cost information in a more useful format, several levels of cost centers had been recognized. The present system gathered costs into ten cost centers, some of which performed functions supporting the activities of other centers.

1. Medical-Surgical Supplies and Services
2. Nursing
3. Social Services
4. Physical Therapy
5. Occupational Therapy
6. Recreational Therapy
7. Speech and Hearing/Psychology
8. Dietary (Support)
9. Buildings and Grounds (Support)
10. Administration (Support)

Further refinement was also recognized, in that these cost centers provided a variety of programs and clinical services and it seemed likely that some programs were more costly than others. There were twenty-one identifiable clinics and programs which were provided for outpatients in addition to the treatment and services provided the inpatients. Counting inpatients, the 22 programs were as follows:

1. Inpatients
2. Handicapped Children Clinic
3. Learning Disabilities Clinic
4. Cystic Fibrosis Clinic
5. BCC Myelomeningocele Clinic
6. Scoliosis Clinic
7. Orthopedic Clinic
8. Neurology Clinic
9. Neonatology Clinic
10. Juvenile Amputee Clinic
11. Resp. Health Camp
12. Obesity Clinic
13. Cleft Palate Camp
14. Children & Youth Service
15. Physical Therapy Service Visits
16. Occupational Therapy Service Visits
17. Recreational Therapy Service Visits
18. Speech & Hearing Service Visits
19. Psychology Service Visits
20. School Service Visits
21. Dental Service Visits
22. Psychiatry Service Visits

The information given in Exhibit 6 on the distribution of effort by the various departments was intended to try to measure how much professional time was spent on these 22 programs. Exhibit 7 summarizes the results of this analysis in both dollars and hours.

LOOKING TO THE FUTURE

"We are trying now to do more of what we are capable of doing, filling a void in pediatric care," said Mr. Phillips. "There are not enough comprehensive pediatric facilities to go around. There are facilities which specialize in orthopedic, psychiatric, and other handicaps, but they cater to both adults and children with little recognition given to the special needs of children. All told, there are probably no more than three good, comprehensive centers for handicapped children on the East Coast.

"The Governor's Commission on Handicapped Children has recognized that we can be a tremendous resource for Virginia's children but has given little in the way of direction. The state is still primarily rural and our main problems lie in taking the medicine and treatment to the people. If we are really going to take care of the children, we are going to have to set up satellite facilities around the state and publicize the fact that these services are available to everyone.

"All of our future programs need direction and money. The Center has changed dramatically from its inception as a custodial care facility in 1957. Today we handle more and more acute cases and provide a variety of programs. I imagine that we will eventually grow into a 100-120 bed children's hospital. The difficulties to be overcome in growing that big are substantial and cover not only financial and control problems but the very spirit of the Center. The team approach has been facilitated somewhat by our small size; maintaining it throughout the next period of growth could be one of the most difficult problems we will face."

EXHIBIT 7

Final Cost Centers Utilizing Professional Time		HCC	Learning Disabilities Clinic	Cystic Fibrosis Clinic	Myelomeningocele Clinic BCC	Scoliosis Clinic	Orthopedic Clinic	Obesity Clinic	Neurology Clinic	Neonatology Clinic	Juvenile Amputee Clinic
Occupational	$	1017	265							533	265
Therapy	hrs	137	36							72	36
Recreational	$							164			
Therapy	hrs							78			
Psychology	$										
	hrs										
Physical	$	3947		272	369	491					657
Therapy	hrs	576		40	54	72					96
Speech &	$	108									
Hearing (S/HO)	hrs	306									
Nursing	$			716			5990		1598		
	hrs			347			629		416		
TOTALS	$	5072	265	988	369	491	5990	164	1598	533	922
	hrs	1019	36	387	54	72	629	78	416	72	132

Note: Final totals subject to slight rounding error, 1%.

Summary of Costs of Professional Time

Occupational Therapy $28,183 ÷ 3,790 = $7.44
   3,790 = productive hours; 3 to 4 staff members

Recreational Therapy $13,672 ÷ 6,494 = $2.11
   6,494 = productive hours; 2 to 3 staff members

Psychology $9,162 ÷ 1,560 = $5.87 per hour
   1,560 = productive hours of one psychologist, 75% of his time

Physical Therapy $25,462 ÷ 3,714 = $6.86 per patient day
   3,714 inpatient days + outpatient days + clinic hours
      Three staff members

Professional Time and Expense Allocation

Respiratory Health Camp	Cleft Palate Camp	Physical Therapy Service Visits	Occupational Therapy Service Visits	Recreational Therapy Service Visits	Speech & Hearing Service Visits	Psychology Service Visits	School Service Visits	Dental Exams and Service Visits	Psychiatry Service Visits	Children & Youth Services (S/H)	INPATIENTS	TOTALS
			3560								22,529	28,183
			479								3,030	3,790
824	420			2298							9,962	13,673
392	200			1092							4,732	6,494
						1832					7,330	9,162
						312					1,248	1,560
		4441									15,272	25,462
		648									2,228	3,714
					130					54	84	376
					367					153	239	1,065
								4768			127,308	140,314
								1082			8,736	11,210
824	420	4441	3560	2298	130	1832	-0-	4768	-0-	54	182,486	217,200
392	200	648	479	1092	367	312	-0-	1082	-0-	153	20,213	27,833*

Speech and Hearing $376 ÷ 1,065 hrs = $.35 per hour
   Therapy visits = 1 hour; evaluations and conferences = ½ hour
   Salaries paid by the hospital; $376 is for supplies and travel

Nursing $140,380 ÷ 11,210 = $12.52 per nursing hour supplied
   Clinics—nursing hours supplied (one nurse at a time)   2,474
   Inpatient—nursing hours supplied, 24 hours a day, seven days a week.
   (Nursing staff 12.7 nurses)   8,736
                                        Total nursing hours   11,210

APPENDIX A

Children's Rehabilitation Center
Description of Departments

Taken from CRC publicity materials.

2. *Nursing*

The Nursing Service Department provides round-the-clock care. Nurses provide support for therapy and act as *locus parentis* to the child.

3. *Social Service*

Social Service functions as a liason between the staff, the child's family, and any public or private agency which may be involved. Recommendations of the staff are interpreted to the family in light of their home situation and appropriate counseling is given to help them adjust to the child's limitations.

4. *Physical Therapy*

The Physical Therapy Department works to enable the child to function at his maximum motor potential. Development of gross motor development and neuromuscular-skeletal system. Skills taught include locomotion using aids such as braces, artificial limbs, crutches and wheelchairs.

5. *Occupational Therapy*

The Occupational Therapy Department develops a child's ability to perform the skills of daily living. Treatment objectives are stimulation of motor development, developing strength and range of motion in upper limbs, teaching fine coordination, and developing functional prehension as necessary for feeding, dressing and writing skills. Therapists also train children with upper extremity orthotics and prostheses. The program attempts to enhance a child's self-confidence and esteem by giving him as much independence as possible.

6. *Recreational Therapy*

The Recreational Therapy Department is involved with efforts in two main areas: adaptive physical education and therapeutic recreation. The adapted physical education program consists of active sports, games, and exercises modified to fit the child's abilities and physical limitations.

Therapeutic recreation is a broad spectrum of physical and social activities ranging from camping to dramatics which develop the ability to be active, to learn leisure time skills, and undergo social experiences.

7a Speech and Hearing

The Speech and Hearing Department works with a child's hearing, and language development. As specific difficulties are diagnosed and evaluated, a therapy program is initiated to enable the patient to increase his level of language understanding and lingual expression.

7b Psychology

Psychological assessment including intellectual capacity and development and personality and behavioral dynamics is provided to any child referred specifically or in conjunction with other therapy as needed.

8. Dietary

The Dietary Department offers the patient a well-rounded nutritional program as well as special dietary requirements as prescribed by the physician.

9. Building and Grounds

The Buildings and Grounds Department provides housekeeping, minor repair, and plant maintenance services. The department also operates the Center's vehicles and provides shuttle service between the Center and the University Hospital. Major repairs as well as most external maintenance are subcontracted.

10. Administration

The Administration Department handles the myriad paperwork involved in dealing with public and private agencies as well as purchasing, personnel management, and utilization of facilities. Finance and bookkeeping are shared with the University Medical Center.

11. Dental

The Dental Department performs an evaluation of each child participating in Center programs as well as therapy or surgery when possible. This care has been necessary because the special needs of handicapped children often make it impossible for them to obtain dental care through normal channels.

12. *Education (School)*

The School is under the auspices of the State Department of Education and the local public school system. The Education Department cooperates with the child's home school to maintain and continue his academic status. Diagnostic testing and teaching is tailored to the individual child and periodic follow-ups are made to ensure the local school is providing for the child's special needs.

16. *Non-Departmentalized Services and Personnel*

In fulfilling its educational and research responsibilities to the University, the Center receives the services of many University medical personnel. Orthopedic surgeons, child psychiatrists, neurologists, pediatricians, as well as their residents are carried by their respective departments and not charged to the CRC budget.

Case 12

California County Public Facilities Corporation*

In late 1973, the six directors of the Public Facilities Corporation of a northern California county were meeting to determine the financing for a number of construction projects in their county.

The Corporation, a nonprofit organization, had recently been formed under the laws of the State of California to finance public buildings and facilities for the entire county. The County Board of Supervisors had recognized the need for several new public buildings to serve adequately the county's rapidly expanding constituency. However, the cost of borrowing for long-term capital expenditures had become almost prohibitive in the 1971 bond market. Subsequently, the following year, the Supervisors decided to find new and innovative means of providing necessary financing for facilities. The Public Facilities Corporation was thus formed and its directors charged with devising a plan to provide funds for the needed public improvements.

THE PROJECTS

The Board of Supervisors had identified seven construction projects which they considered of highest priority. They had requested bids

*This case was prepared by Alexander A. Robichek and Arthur Segal, Stanford University, Graduate School of Business. Reprinted from Stanford Business Cases 1977 with the permission of the publishers, Stanford University Graduate School of Business, © 1977 by the Board of Trustees of the Leland Stanford Junior University.

from contractors to determine construction costs. After negotiations, the Board members reached agreements on the amount of funds required and the number of days needed for construction of each of the projects. The final approval for each project was, of course, subject to the County's ability to obtain the financing.

Two of the projects were new buildings, one was the rehabilitation of an existing structure, and four were additions to existing structures. The addition to the Main County Jail consisted of work to be completed on the unfinished top floor of the building. The remaining three projects were extensions of existing structures.

Project Description	Agreed Cost	Days Allowed
Children's Shelter: an addition to the Children's Shelter, including dining facilities, nursery, dormitory areas, activity rooms, and offices.	$ 168,000	240
Animal Shelter: a south county animal shelter, containing offices, kennels, space for small animal cages, examination rooms, quarantine facilities and related facilities.	189,800	180
Communications Center: an addition to the County Communications Center.	222,600	180
Main County Jail: an addition to the Main County Jail consisting of cells, security facilities, and related facilities.	604,400	270
Women's Felony Cells: an addition to the Elmwood Rehabilitation Center women's felony cells.	148,391	240
Superior Court Building: the reconstruction of the Old County Superior Court Building, to provide five courtrooms and ancillary facilities.	691,777	240
Men's Barracks: a men's barracks at Elmwood Rehabilitation Center.	393,800	240
Prepaid Rentals	617,500	
Legal fees and other services	63,432	
Total Construction Fund	$3,099,700	

THE DIRECTORS

The Directors had been chosen by the Board of Supervisors on the basis of their experience and expertise in private and public finance, as well as their interest in civic affairs:

Dorothy L. Bates—Manager of Public Affairs, Lockland Missiles and Space Company, Inc.; member of the Board of Directors of the County Chamber of Commerce and various other civic groups.

Christopher J. Harbach—Chairman of the Board of Directors; Retired automobile agency owner; Past President of the County Chamber of Commerce; and Past Foreman of the County Grand Jury.

A.W. Lieu—Independent insurance agency owner; President of the County Fire Commission.

Charles E. McGowan—Investment banker and senior partner, Smith, Dean and Company; Past President of the American Bankers Association; member of various civic organizations.

Merrill L. Pierce—Vice President of Safeland Stores; member of the Board of Smith, Fenner and Peabody, brokerage firm; member of Boards of Directors of three health agencies.

R. Carlton Seever—Attorney and senior partner of Barnard, Bates and Seever; founder of Triton Civic Opera Society; and member of various service organizations.

THE PROPOSAL

At a subsequent meeting, Charles McGowan presented his views on an optimal financing plan to the Board members. Because McGowan had the greatest amount of expertise in real estate financing, the other members had requested him to draw up a plan from which they could begin to work. The plan which McGowan described was based upon financing through lease rental and revenue bonds.

According to McGowan, the Public Facilities Corporation would finance the acquisition, construction, and improvement of public buildings by leasing property from the County, constructing the improvements, and leasing the improved property back to the County. Financing for construction and other improvement costs would be provided by the proceeds of a sale of bonds secured by a lien on the interest of the Corporation in real property and on rental income and other revenues of the Corporation. Upon sale of the bonds, the Corporation would begin construction of the various improvements and additions on the sites and lease them back to the County for a term longer than the maturity of the bonds. The interests of the Corporation in the properties and all rentals and other revenues of the corporation would be pledged to secure payment of the bonds under an Indenture of Trust. McGowan then explained the details of his proposal.

THE DETAILS

The Leases: Through a "Site Lease," the County would lease seven sites to the Corporation and the Corporation would agree to construct the designated improvements for a leaseback to the County. Although the County would call for public bills for the site leases and their leasebacks, it was anticipated that the Corporation would be the only bidder for the leases, and that the County would then award the leases to the Corporation.

The leased sites consisted of six separate parcels of land and one parcel of air space, namely, the third floor space within the existing Main County Jail. The Site Lease would provide that the Corporation receive from the County prepaid rental amounting to $617,500 and any taxes and assessments.

The "Facility Lease" would provide for the construction of various buildings and improvements by the Corporation for their leaseback to the County. Annual rentals would be required to cover annual debt service and other expenses of the Corporation. A uniform annual rental of approximately $312,000 would be payable by the County to the Corporation for its use and occupancy of the properties. It was anticipated that the County would raise rental funds from available sales tax monies which would be sufficient to pay all of the bond service as it was due plus an additional rental of up to $10,000 annually. Under the Facility lease, the County would assume full responsibility for maintenance and repair of the site and improvements in its possession, arrange for and pay for all utility services, and reimburse the Corporation for any taxes and assessments. The Corporation's obligations would be to execute contracts for constructing the project, and to lease the improved premises back to the county.

The Bonds: A serial bond issue would be sold for the amount of $3,700,000 in principal, with interest payable semi-annually, commenc-

EXHIBIT 1

Proposed Bond Issue

Year Ending August 1	Interest at 6%	Principal Maturing	Total Bond Service
1972	92,500	—	92,500
1973	222,000	—	222,000
1974	222,000	90,000	312,000
1975	216,600	100,000	316,600
1976	210,600	100,000	310,600
1977	204,600	110,000	314,600
1978	198,000	120,000	318,000
1979	190,800	120,000	310,800
1980	183,600	130,000	313,600
1981	175,800	140,000	315,800
1982	167,400	150,000	317,400
1983	158,400	160,000	318,400
1984	148,800	170,000	318,800
1985	138,600	180,000	318,600
1986	127,800	190,000	317,800
1987	116,400	200,000	316,400
1988	104,400	210,000	314,400
1989	91,800	220,000	311,800
1990	78,600	230,000	308,600
1991	64,800	250,000	314,800
1992	49,800	260,000	309,800
1993	34,200	280,000	314,200
1994	17,400	290,000	307,400
Total	3,214,900	3,700,000	6,914,900

ing August 1, 1972. Principal would mature serially beginning August 1, 1974 through to 1994, as shown in the accompanying table (see Exhibit 1). It was anticipated that interest would be at the rate of 6%. Bonds would be issued as coupon bonds in denominations of $5,000.

The bonds, as noted earlier, were secured by the Corporation's pledge of its gross revenues and its interests in the sites and improvements under the leases. The County would use an "Accumulative Sales Tax Revenue Fund" to pay the bond service on the bonds issued by the Public Facilities Corporation. Future sales tax receipts were projected on an historic basis (Exhibit 3).

EXHIBIT 2
Assessed Valuation and Tax Rates

	Assessed Valuation	Basic County Tax Rate per $100
1961/62	$1,416,867,070	$1.772
1966/67	2,091,477,200	2.065
1967/68	2,227,760,860	2.133
1968/69	2,432,737,380	2.052
1969/70	2,723,475,400	2.059
1970/71	3,095,299,540	2.441
1971/72	3,333,093,850	2.627

Note: The ratio of county assessed value to market value, as reported by the State Board of Equalization, ranges from 22.7 percent to 24.5 percent for 1966/67 to 1971/72 inclusive. The 1971/72 ratio is 24.5 percent. Assessed valuations for 1969/70 through 1971/72 include Homeowner's and Business Inventory exemptions as authorized.

Exhibit 3
Projected Use of Sales Tax Receipts

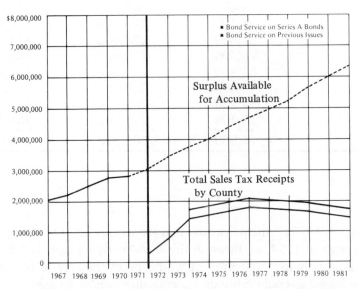

The chart above shows sales tax receipts by the county, historically for the past five years and as projected by the county finance officer through 1981-82. These revenues are used by the county to support several building projects, including those of the Public Facilities Corporation. The chart also shows the amounts required to support existing bond issues and the remaining amounts available to support the current and future bond issues of the Public Facilities Corporation. The sales tax receipts have increased both with the increase in total retail sales and with the increase in the number of items subject to sales tax. In 1971 the California Legislature approved extension of sales tax to gasoline sales.

The Indenture: The Indenture is an agreement between the Corporation and the Trustee, normally a commercial bank, for the benefit of the bondholders. The Indenture

- states the terms and conditions of the bonds
- provides for the disposition of bond proceeds and the allocation of revenues to funds
- sets forth the covenants of the Corporation and the duties of the Trustee, and
- describes the remedies available to the Trustee and the bondholders.

The Indenture would provide that proceeds from the sale of bonds and all subsequent Corporate revenues be deposited with the Trustee for allocation among specified funds:

1. Construction Fund—used to pay prepaid rental under the Site Lease, construction costs and expenses, and costs incidental to the sale of the bonds.
2. Revenue Fund—used to receive surplus construction monies and earnings, if any, base rental payable by the County under the Facility Lease, and any other Corporate Revenues not otherwise allocated by the Indenture.
3. Interest and Redemption Fund—used to pay interest or principal on the bonds when due.
4. Operation and Maintenance Fund—used to pay costs of project operation, if its possession by the County is interrupted.
5. Reserve Fund—used to further ensure timely payment of bond interest and principal, and for funding necessary repairs excluded from insurance recovery through deductible amount or coinsurance provisions.
6. Corporate Operation Fund—a separate fund used to receive amounts termed additional rental under the Facility Lease for paying the Corporation's administrative expense, including compensation and reimbursement due to the Trustee and other administrative personnel.

Proceeds from the sale of the bonds would be applied by the Trustee first to make the initial deposits in the Interest and Redemption, Corporate Operation and Reserve Funds. The remaining balance would be deposited in the Construction Fund. (The estimated use of bond proceeds is shown in Exhibit 6).

EXHIBIT 4

Direct and Overlapping Debt (February 23, 1972)

	Percent Applicable	Debt February 23, 1972
County, Building Authorities, and Public Facilities Corporation	100.	$119,050,000[1]
Unified school districts	100.	67,394,045
Community college districts	Various	21,384,071
High school districts	Various	62,275,125
School districts	Various	62,038,979
City Building Authorities	100.	102,532,667
Other cities	100.	79,811,000
City special districts and special assessments and authorities	100.	43,548,447
County special districts and special assessments	100.	76,327,101
Total Gross Direct and Overlapping Bonded Debt		$634,361,435[2]
Less: City and city special districts bonds supported by revenues and Redevelopment bonds not on regular tax rolls		$ 49,746,489
Flood Control and Water District, Zone W-1 (100% self-supporting, pump tax and water sales)		39,960,000
Total Net Direct and Overlapping Bonded Debt		$544,654,996

Ratios to County Assessed Valuation ($3,333,093,850)   Ratios to Population (1971 estimate 1,088,000)[3]

Direct debt	2.31%	Direct debt	$ 70.73
Total gross debt	19.03%	Total gross debt	$583.17
Total net debt	16.34%	Total net debt	$500.60

[1] Includes County Public Facilities Corporation Bonds.
[2] Except as noted, sales between February 2 and February 23 are excluded.
[3] From State Department of Finance.

Source: California Municipal Statistics, Inc.

EXHIBIT 5

County Revenues and Expenditures by Source and Purpose

	1968-69	1969-70	1970-71	1971-72
Revenues				
Property taxes				
Secured	46,425,633	49,522,480	64,581,298	75,219,408
Unsecured	5,201,215	5,505,476	5,925,616	7,614,127
Sales tax	2,486,655	2,711,634	2,826,265	3,052,000
Other taxes	1,455,877	1,230,360	1,883,713	1,197,711
Licenses and permits	335,049	412,975	486,992	497,590
Fines and penalties	1,564,178	1,787,652	1,804,375	1,861,943
Revenue from money & property	4,807,911	4,456,821	6,146,422	4,061,340
State sources				
Motor vehicle in-lieu	5,842,373	5,964,130	6,490,490	6,743,540
Highway users tax	6,602,615	7,272,568	7,643,880	8,249,100
Other	24,466,146	33,414,612	40,702,588	51,878,737
Federal sources	29,620,657	37,070,293	46,955,334	61,311,415
Other revenue	9,575,849	11,686,021	12,636,419	11,998,646
TOTAL REVENUES	138,024,158	161,035,022	198,083,392	233,685,557
Expenditures				
General government	20,873,905	22,690,688	24,715,559	26,348,319
Protection to persons & property	20,306,318	24,024,717	28,352,931	31,576,058
Roads	12,063,315	12,448,290	14,733,870	13,552,775
Health & sanitation	8,409,702	10,345,478	12,064,711	13,860,806
Public assistance	66,958,362	82,276,759	106,936,121	136,612,339
Education	2,649,173	2,949,373	3,344,803	3,755,667
Recreation	1,021,964	1,181,159	1,380,789	1,440,689
Debt service	8,592,346	8,360,559	8,149,971	7,940,192
TOTAL EXPENDITURES	140,875,085	164,277,023	199,678,755	235,086,845

EXHIBIT 6

Use of Bond Proceeds

Interest and Redemption Fund	
Interest during construction[1] ....$	203,500
Corporate Operations Fund	
The sum of	4,000
Reserve Fund	
Maximum annual debt service......................	318,800
Construction Fund	
Estimated balance of proceeds[2]	3,099,700
Bond Discount	
Estimated amount included........................	74,000
Principal Amount of Bonds............................	**$3,700,000**

[1] Interest at 6.0 percent from March 1, 1972 through February 1, 1973.

[2] Any interest accrued on delivery of the bonds will be placed in the Interest and Redemption Fund and increase the balance available for the Construction Fund.

Mr. McGowan ended his presentation with a request that Mr. Seever help in the preparation of the legal aspects of the indenture agreement. Mr. McGowan felt that through the bond issue, the lease and the lease-back arrangements, and the indenture arrangements, the County's Public Facilities Corporation could proceed with the capital projects outlined by the Board of Supervisors. He then looked around the room for a reaction to his proposal among the other members of the Board.

THE RESPONSE

Ms. Bates opened the discussion by stating that it had been her impression that the great advantage of lease financing was the balance sheet accounting. She felt that since long-term net leases did not have to appear on a firm's balance sheet, the cost of the debt would be lower due to the more favorable perceptions of investors and lenders regarding financial risk. However, since this was a public agency, she wondered what advantage lease financing provided? Furthermore, she claimed that she was not really sure how to evaluate the proposal, what criteria should be used and what alternative financing forms might be considered. Finally Ms. Bates asked what objectives the Board was trying to achieve.

Mr. Seever's comments were much more specific. He expressed concern that Mr. McGowan had assumed an interest rate that was far too high. He wanted to see numbers, specifically a cash flow analysis for both the County and the Corporation, before he felt he could judge the plan.

Mr. Pierce agreed that they needed more data, but he also felt it unfortunate that Mr. McGowan had not analyzed the numbers adequately. He wanted to know the rate of return implicit in the basic lease term rental stream, i.e., the rate which caused fixed basic term rents to be just sufficient to completely amortize the acquisition cost during the basic term. Also, Mr. Pierce asked what would happen if the basic lease term, the periodicity, or the timing of basic term rentals changed? He disagreed with Mr. Seever's contention that Mr. McGowan had overestimated the interest rate, but rather he believed he had underestimated it. He was concerned that continued high interest rates were making bonding schemes too expensive to service. Mr. Pierce wanted to see a sensitivity analysis of the effects of changes in the cost of debt as well as the effects of varying sales tax revenue receipts. Furthermore, in evaluating the proposal, Mr. Pierce wondered what discount rate Mr. McGowan would recommend?

At this point, Mr. Lieu candidly expressed his lack of understanding about the entire proposal. Why, he wondered, were they considering lease-rental arrangements when they were going to have to issue bonds anyway? Before Mr. McGowan had the opportunity to answer any questions or comments, however, Mr. Harback, the Chairman, announced that the meeting would have to adjourn. Although Mr. McGowan would be able to answer some questions at the next session, the Chairman stated that each member should try to analyze the proposal to the best of his or her ability, since the County Board of Supervisors was anxiously awaiting a financing plan.

APPENDIX

The California County Public Facilities Corporation
County Population

		10-Year Increase	Rank Among California Counties
1920	100,700		
1930	145,118	44.1%	5
1940	174,949	20.6	6
1950	290,547	66.1	6
1960	642,315	121.1	6
1970	1,066,421	66.0	5

Source: 1920-1970 U.S. Census. 1971 estimates rank the County fourth.

Population Projections

	1975	1980	1985	1990
County Planning Department				
High	1,250,000	1,420,000	1,600,000	1,780,000
Low	1,200,000	1,320,000	1,440,000	1,570,000
California	25,585,000	26,406,000	29,475,000	

APPENDIX (CONTINUED)

Employment by Industry Group 1950-1971 (in thousands)

	1950	1960	1967	1968	1969	1970	Nov. 1971*
Agriculture	16.2	11.1	7.3	7.3	7.2	6.7	5.1
Contract construction	9.4	17.8	18.1	19.9	21.5	20.2	17.8
Manufacturing							
Electrical machinery	2.5	16.8	40.2	43.0	47.6	47.8	42.4
Other durable	6.5	34.8	55.5	57.4	55.5	53.2	48.1
Food products	10.9	12.7	14.3	15.8	15.7	14.9	12.3
Other non-durable	2.2	6.0	9.7	10.8	11.8	12.1	11.0
	22.1	70.3	119.7	127.0	130.6	128.0	113.8
Transportation, communications and utilities	6.1	9.6	14.7	15.1	16.7	17.6	18.0
Trade	22.6	40.7	65.9	72.0	76.7	80.9	73.2
Finance, insurance and real estate	3.2	7.9	13.2	14.1	15.3	16.0	14.0
Services	18.3	43.2	82.5	87.0	93.0	97.2	75.8
Federal government	3.8	5.2	9.1	9.1	9.4	9.5	9.3
State and local government	7.9	21.6	41.5	44.4	47.2	50.7	53.2
All others	0.3	0.6	0.9	1.1	1.1	1.4	41.4
ALL INDUSTRIES	109.9	228.0	372.9	397.0	418.6	428.3	421.6
Unemployment							
Total	14.1	14.4	17.7	17.3	18.1	25.7	24.1
Percent of Labor Force	11.4%	5.9%	4.5%	4.2%	4.1%	5.7%	5.4%
Seasonally Adjusted							5.7%

Source: State of California Department of Human Resources Development.
*Preliminary figures. Methods of classification have been changed, accounting for change in service and other employment.

APPENDIX (CONTINUED)

Summary of County Building Activity (1963-1970)

	No. of Dwelling Units Authorized	Percent Single Family	Value of Non-residential Permits (1,000s)			
			Industrial	Office	Store	Total
1963	21,372	42.1%	$19,337	$14,880	$12,779	$46,996
1964	14,729	51.2	14,322	18,180	16,110	48,612
1965	10,416	65.5	19,554	11,741	20,345	51,641
1966	6,707	77.3	41,444	20,967	13,661	76,072
1967	10,235	73.4	44,924	5,881	25,407	76,212
1968	17,561	53.5	41,525	15,215	21,420	78,160
1969	18,771	36.1	53,912	18,455	24,451	96,818
1970	17,618	35.9	50,624	38,319	44,831	133,774
1971 (11 mos)	18,311	48.2	n.a.	n.a.	n.a.	n.a.

County Public School Enrollment

	Elementary	Secondary	Total
1950	36,381	10,126	46,507
1960	115,393	30,354	145,747
1969	197,895	70,249	268,144
1970	201,057	73,163	274,220
1971	201,324	80,489	281,813

APPENDIX (CONTINUED)

Taxable Sales in the County (000)

	1965/66	1966/67	1967/68	1968/69	1969/70	1970/71
Apparel	$ 86,997	$ 94,099	$ 100,408	$ 107,378	$ 114,113	$ 111,421
General merchandise	247,880	267,139	292,900	320,043	342,290	370,995
Specialty stores	96,696	110,372	121,975	132,001	141,888	164,348
Food stores	90,574	99,754	119,649	139,058	156,080	166,848
Packaged liquors	32,926	34,807	38,390	40,896	46,077	50,198
Eating and drinking places	97,858	110,637	121,720	137,175	152,029	161,420
Home furnishings and appliances	77,791	79,802	85,855	97,674	101,372	100,178
Building materials and farm implements	88,517	82,654	96,787	107,907	112,537	112,386
Motor vehicle dealers and auto supplies	237,538	252,440	280,055	317,094	324,184	346,678
Service stations	21,339	23,339	25,077	26,369	27,336	27,426
Retail Stores Total	$1,078,116	$1,155,043	$1,282,816	$1,425,595	$1,517,906	$1,611,898
Business and personal services	$ 44,441	$ 45,436	$ 50,103	$ 55,564	$ 60,477	$ 65,715
Manufacturing, wholesaling, etc.	346,662	397,206	469,246	536,651	579,586	581,656
Total All Outlets	$1,469,219	$1,597,685	$1,802,165	$2,017,810	$2,157,969	$2,259,269

Case 13

Creditworthiness of the Commonwealth of Massachusetts*

When the new Governor of Massachusetts, Michael Dukakis, assumed office in January 1975, he was dismayed to learn that the projections of the State deficit were $150-$200 million. This was almost four times the $50-$60 million deficit forecast by his predecessor during the gubernatorial campaign. Furthermore, the general reserve fund, which had been substantial in previous years, had been all but exhausted by the end of 1974.

After only a month in office, Governor Dukakis found that the State's economic situation was swiftly deteriorating. New projections indicated that Massachusetts was facing a $450 million deficit on a budget of $3.5 billion. (This $3.5 billion budget included $900,000 in Federal contributions, about 26%.) Also, it was expected that the Commonwealth of Massachusetts would be among those hardest hit by the national recession and that 1976 revenues would reflect an even more serious financial predicament.

Unlike the Federal government, state and local governments cannot legally go into debt. Their budgets, no matter how painful the effort, must be balanced.

*This case was prepared by Alexander A. Robichek and Arthur Segal, Stanford University, as the basis for class discussion. Reprinted from *Stanford Business Cases 1976* with the permission of the publishers, Stanford University Graduate School of Business, ©1976 by the Board of Trustees of the Leland Stanford Junior University.

Dukakis had few options. He could raise taxes at a time of severe economic crunch; he could fire vast numbers of State employees at a time when the State was leading most of the nation in unemployment; he could convert a part of the State budget to bonded indebtedness. In early January, Dukakis had immediately frozen all State hiring to reduce the number of State employees by attrition. He requested each of the members of his cabinet to scrutinize every penny of their expenditures. Dukakis emphasized the crisis confronting the Commonwealth by halving his own executive staff, selling most of the State's limousines, and even taking the train to work each day. But such attempts to cut the amount of State expenses were limited and Dukakis had to consider new tax measures and bonding more of the State's budget.

The economic health of most states was on the wain at the start of 1975. Increasingly, large industrial states had been bonding more and more of their state budgets. For example, the State of New York included its Manpower affairs expenses in its capital budget since manpower expenditures were "investments of human capital over time." Other states had attempted similar conversions of operating items to capital ones, the idea being that state and local governments can leverage themselves more than they have in the past. Almost universally, however, these so-called "conversion items" met with a large degree of resistance. In 1975, bonding larger portions of state budgets seemed inevitable as several states realized the extent of their economic plight and their dependence on falling individual taxes and corporate State tax revenues. Their only other alternatives were:

1. Drastic cuts in State expenditures thus reducing welfare payments, which in Massachusetts comprised one-third of all expenditures, during an economic recession, and/or cutting sorely needed State aid to cities and towns, which comprised one-quarter of all State expenditures (see Exhibit 1—Charts C-D);
2. New tax sources which (as will be discussed later) seemed virtually impossible in Massachusetts, particularly during a major economic recession (see Exhibit 1—Charts A-B);
3. Federal relief funds to states and localities in the form of expanded revenue sharing programs.

Governor Dukakis asked his economic aides for a breakdown of Massachusetts' position relative to other states of similar populations—to ascertain the State's future debt requirements. They provided the following facts.

Exhibit I

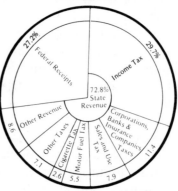

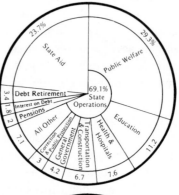

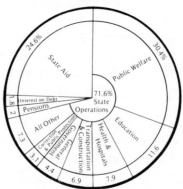

Chart A
How the State Revenue Was Obtained
(Including Bond Issues)
Fiscal Year Ended June 30, 1974
$3,379,820,140

Chart B
How the State Revenue Was Obtained
(Excluding Bond Issues)
Fiscal Year Ended June 30, 1974
$3,275,520,140

Chart C
Direct Expenditures—State Funds
(Including Debt Retirement)
Fiscal Year ended June 30, 1974
$3,603,549,779

Chart D
Direct Expenditures—State Funds
(Excluding Debt Retirement)
Fiscal Year Ended June 30, 1974
$3,479,052,779

268

ECONOMIC CHARACTERISTICS

The Commonwealth of Massachusetts' unemployment figure for January was near 10 percent, while the nation had a national average of around 8 percent. Pockets of unemployment in major blue-collar industrial cities such as New Bedford, Fall River, Lowell, Lawrence and Haverhill (old textile mill and shoe towns) were over 15 percent.

Massachusetts' low and declining manufacturing sector (measured against other industrial states, Exhibit 2) was a trend that had continued since the early Depression years, although the pace slowed during the late 1950s and 1960s with the introduction of a highly sophisticated electronics industry. The amount of manufacturing wages paid, and manufacturing wages per capita, demonstrate the State's low manufacturing dependence (Exhibit 3). Even neighboring Connecticut earned 36% more in per capita manufacturing wages. In just 20 years (1947-67), the number of manufacturing establishments in Massachusetts fell 42%. The continued exodus of manufacturing firms in recent years was attributed to high property tax rates and the high cost for utilities, heating fuels, and telephones. From 1969 to 1990, labor earnings in New England were expected to increase only 56% as against 80% nationally.

Increasingly, Massachusetts, like the rest of the nation, was becoming more service oriented, i.e., toward utilities and education. Largely due to the State's high number of educational institutions, Massachusetts in 1975 was ahead of most states in the service sector of her economy.

Other relevant economic characteristics include:

- the State, until the recent recession, was relatively strong in the valuation of new private housing units under construction; and
- the State was not particularly strong in the amount of commercial bank time deposits (Exhibit 4).

This latter point may be due to Massachusetts' proximity to the New York banking community.

Population Characteristics

Population projection forecasts to 1990 suggested that Massachusetts would grow from almost 6 to 6½ million people (roughly the same rate as Connecticut) and that the northern migrations of blacks and Spanish-speaking peoples of the 1950s and 1960s would all but end.

EXHIBIT 2
Economic Characteristics
Employment Composition by Percent of Dollars Earned for 1971 and (1980) for 5 States
(in 1967 Thousands of Dollars)

	Massachusetts	Connecticut	Wisconsin	Indiana	New Jersey
Agriculture, forestry, fisheries	.1	.1	4.9	4.0	.6
Contract construction	7.0	6.9	5.8	5.8	6.3
Manufacturing	27.5 (25.1)	35.8 (33.6)	34.9 (33.6)	41.1 (40.0)	32.6 (30.4)
Transportation, communication, public utilities	6.0	5.0	6.0	6.3	8.2
Wholesale and retail	17.1 (16.3)	14.8 (14.2)	16.0 (15.5)	14.7 (14.4)	16.7 (16.2)
Finance, insurance, real estate	6.4	6.7	4.2	4.0	4.9
Services	19.9 (23.7)	16.7 (19.7)	13.1 (15.5)	11.1 (13.2)	16.0 (19.2)
Government (all)	15.1 (14.9)	12.6 (12.6)	14.6 (14.9)	12.3 (12.6)	14.5 (13.9)
State and local	10.2 (10.7)	9.5 (9.9)	9.2 (9.7)	9.0 (9.6)	9.7 (9.7)

Source: Adapted from "Survey of Current Business," Vol. 54, No. 4 (April, 1974), pp. 16-45.
Example: Government earnings in 1971 in Massachusetts are $2,583,722 out of a total of $17,102,509 in all earnings or 15.1%.

EXHIBIT 3

Economic Characteristics

| | Manufacturing Wages Paid | |
	In millions of dollars	Dollars per Capita
Massachusetts	5,445	$ 955
Connecticut	3,949	1,299
Wisconsin	4,675	1,054
Indiana	13,633	2,617
New Jersey	8,121	1,287

Source: Adapted from *The 1974 U.S. Statistical Abstract* Nos. 1235, p. 731, Date—
1972 and "The Survey of Current Business," *Ibid.*, p. 31. Also "The Survey of Current
Business," October, 1974, p. 17-18.

The median age in Massachusetts was higher than the midwestern states
but the same as Connecticut, and its citizens had a level of education
that was significantly higher statistically than the other states studied.
This characteristic suggested a highly educated populace that was usually
more "willing to pay" under economic duress than a less educated population. Although unemployment in the State was higher than the nation as a whole at that time, the ratio of people working as a part of the

EXHIBIT 4

Other Economic Characteristics

New Private Housing Units Authorized by Building
Permits for 1973 (in millions of dollars)

Massachusetts	801.2
Connecticut	422.3
Wisconsin	596.8
Indiana	666.7
New Jersey	993.6

Commercial Banks: Assets and Time Deposits for 1973
(in millions of dollars)

	Total Assets	Time Deposits
Massachusetts	17,550	6,085
Connecticut	7,966	3,175
Wisconsin	15,250	8,342
Indiana	18,261	8,974
New Jersey	23,304	11,873

Sources: Adapted from *Statistical Abstract, Ibid.*, No. 729, pp. 454, 858.

EXHIBIT 5

Population Characteristics

Number (in millions)	Change 1970-1990	1970	1980	1990
Massachusetts	22%	5,699	6,267	6,876
Connecticut	24%	3,039	3,358	3,710
Wisconsin	15%	4,433	4,737	5,013
Indiana	24%	5,208	5,784	6,364
New Jersey	26%	7,195	8,080	8,923

Age	Median Age	% Below Age 21	% Below Age 45	% Over 45
Massachusetts	29.5	37	68	32
Connecticut	29.5	37	68	32
Wisconsin	27.4	39	69	31
Indiana	27.3	39	71	21
New Jersey	30.5	37	67	33

Education	% 4 years High School or more	% 1 year college or more
Massachusetts	58.5	24
Connecticut	56.0	24
Wisconsin	54.5	20
Indiana	52.9	17
New Jersey	52.5	21

Employment (1000s) and (Employment Population Ratio)

	1969		1980		1990	
Massachusetts	2,351	(.41)	2,857	(.46)	3,143	(.46)
Connecticut	1,278	(.42)	1,555	(.46)	1,720	(.46)
Wisconsin	1,730	(.39)	2,067	(.44)	2,195	(.44)
Indiana	2,059	(.39)	2,549	(.44)	2,826	(.44)
New Jersey	2,931	(.41)	3,659	(.45)	4,071	(.46)

Source: Adapted from "Survey of Current Business," op. cit., p. 31 and Statistical Abstract, op. cit., p. 32.

population was higher than the midwestern states studied. The size of the population per household was roughly the same for all five states studied at 3.2 people per household.

Property Value

The assessed valuation of Massachusetts' property was fairly high vis-a-vis other states considering its small geographic size. However, this was a characteristic susceptible to the idiosyncrasies of the laws of each state (see Exhibit 6).

Incomes

There were problems with looking at per capita incomes in that present income levels do not explain future income levels. Massachusetts had a fairly high per capita income in 1975 but the severity of the prevailing economic recession might alter these figures and relationships in future years (see Exhibit 7).

Savings

Savings and Loans and life insurance were popular saving vehicles for Massachusetts citizens, although the State ranked fourth in savings of the five states studied. New Jersey had a significantly higher savings rate over the other states although it also had a higher percentage of older population and a higher median age. Business savings were relatively low (see Exhibit 8).

Retail Sales

Massachusetts had a significant retail trade that was larger than any of the other states studied except New Jersey. Retail sales were gener-

EXHIBIT 6
Assessed Value of Property—1973

	Gross (millions of dollars)
Massachusetts	23,732
Connecticut	19,003
Wisconsin	21,862
Indiana	13,112
New Jersey	42,074

Source: Adapted from *Statistical Abstract, Ibid.,* No. 421, p. 264. Moody's *Municipals and Government Securities* has a different set of figures for this year although the relationship between the states is the same. On December 31, 1974 the value of Massachusetts' taxable property totalled 29,858 million dollars.

EXHIBIT 7

Income Characteristics

	Personal Income (Millions 1967 $) % Change 1969-1990	1970	1980	1990
Massachusetts	120%	21,780	33,024	46,443
Connecticut	112%	12,413	18,720	26,255
Wisconsin	109%	14,666	21,899	29,921
Indiana	117%	14,281	26,577	38,027
New Jersey	122%	28,245	43,212	60,788

	Per Capita Income ($) % Change 1969-1990	1970	1980	1990
Massachusetts	81%	3,822	5,269	6,755
Connecticut	72%	4,111	5,575	7,077
Wisconsin	83%	3,308	4,623	5,969
Indiana	75%	3,318	4,595	5,975
New Jersey	77%	3,926	5,348	6,812

Source: Adapted from "Survey of Current Business," *op. cit.*, p. 31. Also, "Survey of Current Business," October 1974, pp. 17-18.

EXHIBIT 8

Savings (millions of dollars except per capita)

	Commercial Bank Time Deposits	Savings & Loans Assets (per capita)	Life Insurance (per capita)
Massachusetts	6,085	4,548 (798)	49,844 (8,746)
Connecticut	3,175	1,840 (605)	32,718 (10,766)
Wisconsin	8,342	4,558 (1,028)	36,028 (8,127)
Indiana	8,974	4,321 (829)	45,545 (8,745)
New Jersey	11,873	8,119 (1,128)	74,685 (10,380)

Source: Adapted from *Statistical Abstract*, ibid., No. 729, 736, 764, pp. 454, 457, 469. Commercial bank and life insurance figures from 1973; Savings and Loan figures from 1971.

ally a function of the degree of urbanization of a particular area, and Massachusetts was more urbanized than the Midwestern states or Connecticut (see Exhibit 9).

Amount of Total Debt

Massachusetts had a large amount of debt outstanding, although smaller on a per capita basis than Connecticut by nearly 40%. Total

EXHIBIT 9
Retail Sales 1967
(millions of dollars)

Massachusetts	9,167
Connecticut	5,043
Wisconsin	6,634
Indiana	8,329
New Jersey	11,362

State and local debt in 1972 for Massachusetts was 5.5 billion dollars, of which 4.9 billion or 89% was long term. State debt alone on February 1, 1975 totalled 1.7 billion dollars, or about $280 per capita. This compared favorably for other urban, industrial states (see Exhibits 10,15).

Level and Trend of Tax Rates

This was a particularly acute area of the Massachusetts economy, since Massachusetts' taxes were the highest of any state in the nation at this period. Tax revenues per capita in 1972 were $639 in Massachusetts, as opposed to $522 for the country as a whole. This relationship remained true in 1975.

Unlike some states that rely on sales or gross receipt taxes, Massachusetts had increasingly relied on individual income taxes at a 5% rate of taxation. From 1972 to 1974, individual income taxes grew from 30% to 41% of all State revenues collected, while the corporate tax grew from 13% to 16%, and the sales tax grew from 8% to 11%. In 1972, in-

EXHIBIT 10
Amount of Total Debt
General Debt Outstanding for State and Local
Governments—1972

	Amount in Millions	% U.S.	Per Capita	Long Term Amount in Millions
United States	174,502	—	888	158,781
Massachusetts	5,533	3	956	4,917
Connecticut	4,097	2	1,329	3,306
Wisconsin	2,805	1	620	2,756
Indiana	2,466	1	466	2,327
New Jersey	6,490	4	881	5,685

EXHIBIT 11
The Level and Trend of Tax Rates

1972 Tax Revenues Per Capita ($)	
United States	522
Massachusetts	639
Connecticut	631
Wisconsin	602
Indiana	444
New Jersey	554

State Tax Collections—1972 (millions $)

	Total	Individual	Corporate	Rate Individual
Massachusetts	2,052	876	259	5%
Connecticut	1,122	51	139	6%*
Wisconsin	1,868	728	136	3.1%—11.4%
Indiana	1,190	285	10	2%
New Jersey	1,919	26	171	2—15%**

Sources of Massachusetts Revenues—Trends by %

	1972	1973	1974
Individual income	30%	39%	41%
Corporate	13	15	16
Sales and use	8	10	11
Total of three types of taxes:	51%	64%	68%

*Tax on capital gains.

**2.5% NY commuter tax plus 2.5% surcharge; 2.3% Pennsylvania commuter tax also.

Source: Adapted from (1) *1974 Financial Report of the Comptroller*, Commonwealth of Massachusetts, (2) Moody's, *Ibid.*, and (3) *Statistical Abstract, Ibid.*, No. 411, 412, 418, pp. 253, 254, 260.

dividual income taxes nationally accounted for 22% of all State revenues, while sales, gross receipts, and custom taxes accounted for 56% of all State revenues across the country.

State Expense Breakdowns

Welfare expenses comprised the bulk of Massachusetts' expenses over one-third of the State budget. While this amount had increased recently, the percentage of the total budget had decreased slightly since 1972. Massachusetts' welfare payments per capita exceeded all of the other states studied, and the national average by 65%.

Another expense that increased sizably over a few years included

EXHIBIT 12

State Expense Breakdowns

Massachusetts State Expenses in Millions of $ and (% of Budget)

	1972	1973	1974
Health & Welfare	1,187 (41)	1,326 (39)	1,331 (37)
State Aid to Cities and Towns	588 (20)	873 (26)	854 (24)
Education	371 (13)	405 (12)	404 (11)
Transportation and Construction	260 (9)	191 (6)	241 (7)
Debt Servicing	96 (3)	114 (3)	104 (3)
Other	405 (13)	493 (14)	669 (18)
	2,907 (100)	3,402 (100)	3,603 (100)

Per Capita Expenditures (1972) on Public Welfare
by State and Local Governments

United States	101
Massachusetts	165
Connecticut	90
Wisconsin	83
Indiana	50
New Jersey	98

Sources: See Exhibit 11 sources.

State aid to cities and towns, while educational expenditures and transportation expenses stayed roughly the same. Debt servicing remained fairly constant at about 3% of the budget (see Exhibit 12).

Size of the State Government

For a population of its size, Massachusetts had a large number of State employees. Furthermore, the earnings of State and local employees exceeded the earnings of State and local employees for any other state studies (see Exhibit 13).

The Structure of the State Debt

In 1976, the debt of 1.7 billion dollars and .6 billion dollars in interest was comprised of 50% General Fund loans for capital outlays, 20%

EXHIBIT 13

State Government Employees 1973

	Number of Employees	Number per 10,000 Population
Massachusetts	75	118
Connecticut	45	124
Wisconsin	65	113
Indiana	72	104
New Jersey	78	93

State and Local Government Employees
Percent of all Earnings in State

	1971	1980
Massachusetts	10.2	10.7
Connecticut	9.5	9.9
Wisconsin	9.7	9.7
Indiana	9.0	9.6
New Jersey	9.7	9.7

Source: "Survey . . .," *ibid.*, pp. 16-45 and *Statistical Abstract, ibid.*, No. 426, p. 266.

Highway Fund loans, and 9% Metropolitan Water District loans. The vast bulk of the bonds (78%) had one- to 20-year maturities, with 36% due over the next decade. The per capita debt was $287. While local government debt increased dramatically in Massachusetts as elsewhere in the early 1970s, the State debt had grown at only a moderate pace. In fact, the debt burden was actually reduced from 1973 to 1974.

Since there was no constitutional or statutory debt limit and no requirement for general voter approval of State debt, debt capacity could only be measured by the willingness of the legislature to approve the recommendations of the Governor by a two-thirds vote and the willingness of the market to absorb the bonds. There was a constitutional provision for a referendum by the voters after action by the legislature, but it was seldom, if ever, used on debt matters.

On February 19, 1975, $125 million in bonds were issued at a winning bid of 5.6%. Municipal rates ranged from a low of near 3.5% in 1967 to nearly 7% in 1970 and again in mid-1974. Although figures for ownership of individual State bonds were not easily available, overall commercial banks owned 60% of all State and locals. This had fallen from 74% in 1968. Households and Fire and Casualty companies owned the remaining balance (see Exhibit 14).

The last four characteristics indicated that in 1975 Massachusetts was:

- A heavily taxed state;
- Dependent on the individual income tax for its revenues;
- Spending one of the highest per capita amounts on public welfare in the country—comprising over one-third of its budget;
- Maintaining a large and probably well-paid bureaucracy vis-a-vis the other states studied;
- Holding the debt service requirement each year at 3% of the total budget; and
- Supporting a moderate debt load of $287 per capita evenly dispersed mostly on one- to 20-year maturities.

Massachusetts' debt strengths and/or weaknesses at this time are indicated by Exhibit 15, a ratio analysis describing her debt capacity vis-a-vis other industrial states. Exhibit 15 illustrates that Massachusetts' current debt burden was fairly modest, somewhere between that of New Jersey's and Connecticut's. The two midwestern states either didn't have any debt (Indiana) or had just begun to issue debt (Wisconsin).

However, with the depressed economic situation cutting severely into expected tax revenues, and with public welfare expenditures expected to increase dramatically as State unemployment worsened, Governor Dukakis was facing an increasingly bleak economic picture.

SOLUTION?

Governor Dukakis was told by his economic advisors that if Massachusetts were to bond some of its expected present deficit by capitalizing more expenditure items, the effects on its per capita debt and on the 1976 debt service requirement would be as follows:

Debt Expansion (in millions of dollars)

Expanded Debt Amount	Total Debt	Per Capita Pop. 5,800 M
400	2,061	355
300	1,961	338
200	1,861	321
100	1,761	304
Present	1,661	287

EXHIBIT 14

CREDITWORTHINESS OF THE COMMONWEALTH OF MASSACHUSETTS

Treasury Department

Boston, February 5, 1975

PROPOSAL FOR BONDS

($125,000,000)

Exempt from All Present Federal and Massachusetts Income Taxes

Sealed proposals for the following issues of Serial Bonds of the Commonwealth of Massachusetts amounting to $125,000,000 will be received at the office of the Treasurer and Receiver-General up to 12 o'clock noon Eastern Standard Saving Time on February 19, 1975.

The bonds are duly authorized by Acts of the Massachusetts Legislature on account of the following loans:

LOT A–$4,250,000

ITEM 1. $2,000,000 Department of Natural Resources Recreational Facilities Capital Outlay Loan, Act of 1971.
Section 6 of Chapter 954, Acts of 1971.
Payable $200,000 each year, March 1, 1976-March 1, 1985, inclusive.
Interest payable March 1 and September 1 of each year, accruing from date of the bonds, March 1, 1975.

ITEM 2. $500,000 Vietnam Conflict Loan, Act of 1973.
Chapter 646, Acts of 1968, as amended by Chapter 325, Acts of 1969, and further amended by Section 3 of Chapter 692, Acts of 1973.
Payable $50,000 each year, March 1, 1976-March 1, 1985, inclusive.
Interest payable March 1 and September 1 of each year, accruing from date of the bonds, March 1, 1975.

ITEM 3. $500,000 City of Chelsea, Disaster Relief Loan, Act of 1973.
Section 3 of Chapter 1206, Acts of 1973.
Payable $50,000 each year, March 1, 1976-March 1, 1985, inclusive.
Interest payable March 1 and September 1 of each year, accruing from date of the bonds, March 1. 1975.

ITEM 4. $500,000 Coastal Wetlands and Inland Wetlands Capital Outlay Loan, Act of 1971.
Section 9 of Chapter 839, Acts of 1971.
Payable $50,000 each year, March 1, 1976-March 1, 1985, inclusive.
Interest payable March 1 and September 1 of each year, accruing from date of the bonds, March 1, 1975.

ITEM 5. $500,000 SuAsCo Watershed Project Plan, Act of 1970.
Chapter 723, Acts of 1970.
Payable $50,000 each year, March 1, 1976-March 1, 1985, inclusive.
Interest payable March 1 and September 1 of each year, accruing from date of the
bonds, March 1, 1975.

ITEM 6. $250,000 Clam River Watershed Improvement Project Loan, Act of 1968.
Section 1 of Chapter 680, Acts of 1968.
Payable $35,000 each year, March 1, 1976-March 1, 1977, and $30,000 each year,
March 1, 1978-March 1, 1983, inclusive.
Interest payable March 1 and September 1 of each year, accruing from date of the
bonds, March 1, 1975.

LOT B–$108,050,000

ITEM 7. $24,000,000 Capital Outlay Loan, Act of 1971.
Section 7 of Chapter 976, Acts of 1971.
Payable $1,200,000 each year, March 1, 1976-March 1, 1995, inclusive.
Interest payable March 1 and September 1 of each year, accruing from date of the
bonds, March 1, 1975.

ITEM 8. $18,000,000 Capital Outlay Loan, Act of 1969.
Section 7 of Chapter 767, Acts of 1969.
Payable $900,000 each year, March 1, 1976-March 1, 1995, inclusive.
Interest payable March 1 and September 1 of each year, accruing from date of the
bonds, March 1, 1975.

ITEM 9. $14,000,000 Capital Outlay Loan, Act of 1970.
Section 7 of Chapter 633, Acts of 1970, as amended by Section 7A of Chapter 976,
Acts of 1971.
Payable $700,000 each year, March 1, 1976-March 1, 1995, inclusive.
Interest payable March 1 and September 1 of each year, accruing from date of the
bonds, March 1, 1975.

ITEM 10. $13,000,000 Water Pollution Control Loan, Act of 1970.
Section 3 of Chapter 747, Acts of 1970.
Payable $650,000 each year, March 1, 1976-March 1, 1995, inclusive.
Interest payable March 1 and September 1 of each year, accruing from date of the
bonds, March 1, 1975.

ITEM 11. $9,050,000 State Government Center Loan, Act of 1971.
Section 9 of Chapter 976, Acts of 1971, as amended by Sections 1 and 2 of Chapter
566, Acts of 1972.
Payable $455,000 each year, March 1, 1976-March 1, 1985, and $150,000 each year,
March 1, 1986-March 1, 1995, inclusive.
Interest payable March 1 and September 1 of each year, accruing from date of the
bonds, March 1, 1975.

EXHIBIT 14(*continued*)

ITEM 12. $8,600,000 Highway Improvement Loan, Act of 1972.
Section 9 of Chapter 765, Acts of 1972.
Pursuant to Section 1.
Payable $430,000 each year, March 1, 1976-March 1, 1995, inclusive.
Interest payable March 1 and September 1 of each year, accruing from date of the
bonds, March 1, 1975.

ITEM 13. $7,500,000 Public Housing Modernization and Renovation Loan,
Act of 1970.
Section 4 of Chapter 694, Acts of 1970, as amended by Sections 6A, 6B and 6C of
Chapter 884, Acts of 1973, and further amended by Sections 6 and 8 of
Chapter 853, Acts of 1974.
Payable $375,000 each year, March 1, 1976-March 1, 1995, inclusive.
Interest payable March 1 and September 1 of each year, accruing from date of the
bonds, March 1, 1975.

ITEM 14. $5,700,000 Metropolitan Recreation and Environmental Loan, Act of 1972.
Section 8 of Chapter 803, Acts of 1972.
Payable $285,000 each year, March 1, 1976-March 1, 1995, inclusive.
Interest payable March 1 and September 1 of each year, accruing from date of the
bonds, March 1, 1975.

ITEM 15. $2,500,000 University of Massachusetts Medical School Loan, Act of 1967.
Section 7 of Chapter 276, Acts of 1967.
Payable $115,000 each year, March 1, 1976-March 1, 1991, and $110,000 each year,
March 1, 1992-March 1, 1997, inclusive.
Interest payable March 1 and September 1 of each year, accruing from date of the
bonds, March 1, 1975.

ITEM 16. $2,100,000 University of Massachusetts Boston Campus Loan, Act of 1969.
Section 11 of Chapter 898, Acts of 1969.
Payable $105,000 each year, March 1, 1976-March 1, 1995, inclusive.
Interest payable March 1 and September 1 of each year, accruing from date of the
bonds, March 1, 1975.

ITEM 17. $1,500,000 Shore Protection and River and Harbor Loan, Act of 1970.
Section 3 of Chapter 727, Acts of 1970.
Payable $75,000 each year, March 1, 1976-March 1, 1995, inclusive.
Interest payable March 1 and September 1 of each year, accruing from date of the
bonds, March 1, 1975.

ITEM 18. $1,000,000 Metropolitan Flood Control Loan, Act of 1972.
Section 20 of Chapter 803, Acts of 1972.
Payable $50,000 each year, March 1, 1976-March 1, 1995, inclusive.
Interest payable March 1 and September 1 of each year, accruing from date of the
bonds, March 1, 1975.

EXHIBIT 14 *(continued)*

ITEM 19. $600,000 Airport Capital Outlay Loan, Act of 1973.
Section 28 of Chapter 1140, Acts of 1973.
Payable $30,000 each year, March 1, 1976-March 1, 1995, inclusive.
Interest payable March 1 and September 1 of each year, accruing from date of the
bonds, March 1, 1975.

ITEM 20. $500,000 Charles River Flood Control, Act of 1961.
Section 3 of Chapter 520, Acts of 1961.
Payable $50,000 March 1, 1976, and $45,000 each year, March 1, 1977-
March 1, 1986, inclusive.
Interest payable March 1 and September 1 of each year, accruing from date of the
bonds, March 1, 1975.

LOT C–$10,485,000

ITEM 21. $7,785,000 Metropolitan Water District-Water Use Development Loan.
Section 26A of Chapter 92 of the General Laws.
Payable $260,000 each year, March 1, 1976-March 1, 2002, and $255,000 each year,
March 1, 2003-March 1, 2005, inclusive.
Interest payable March 1 and September 1 of each year, accruing from data of the
bonds, March 1, 1975.

ITEM 22. $2,700,000 Metropolitan Sewerage Loan, Act of 1972.
Section 6 of Chapter 803, Acts of 1972.
Payable $90,000 each year, March 1, 1976-March 1, 2005, inclusive.
Interest payable March 1 and September 1 of each year, accruing from date of the
bonds, March 1, 1975.

LOT D–$2,215,000

ITEM 23. $1,000,000 Metropolitan District Commission, Charles River Marginal
Conduit Loan, Act of 1971.
Section 2 of Chapter 881, Acts of 1971.
Payable $25,000 each year, March 1, 1976-March 1, 2015, inclusive.
Interest payable March 1 and September 1 of each year, accruing from date of the
bonds, March 1, 1975.

ITEM 24. $1,215,000 Metropolitan Water District Additional Loan, Act of 1971.
Section 3 of Chapter 982, Acts of 1971.
Payable $25,000 each year, March 1, 1976-March 1, 2018, and $20,000 each year,
March 1, 2019-March 1, 2025, inclusive.
Interest payable March 1 and September 1 of each year, accruing from date of the
bonds, March 1, 1975.

The bonds will be issued in coupon form of a denomination of $1,000 each, except that if requested by the purchaser within forty-eight hours of the award, all the bonds referred to in the proposal will be issued in coupon form of a denomination of $5,000 each. Coupon bonds may be exchanged for fully registered bonds in multiples of $1,000. The bonds when put into registered form cannot be reissued as coupon bonds.

Bids must be submitted for the entire list of $125,000,000 of bonds and the bonds will be awarded as a whole. Name only one rate of interest (which must be a multiple of 1/8 or 1/20 of 1%), for each lot, Each bid should state the unit price per bond for each lot. The rate bid for the bonds in Lot A cannot exceed the rate bid in Lot B, Lot C or D. Bids will be compared on the basis of the lowest net interest cost to the Commonwealth (total interest for the duration of the loans less the amount of the premium bid) for the entire $125,000,000 and the bid selected shall be the one which in the opinion of the Treasurer is in the best interest of the Commonwealth.

Each proposal must be accompanied by a certified check or cashier's check for $2,500,000 drawn to the order of the State Treasurer of the Commonwealth of Massachusetts, on a national bank or trust company doing business in the Commonweatlh or in the City of New York. Interest will not be allowed upon deposit of a successful bidder to the date of delivery of the bonds. Each proposal is to be enclosed in a sealed envelope addressed to Robert Q. Crane, Treasurer and Receiver-General, and designated "Proposal for the purchase of bonds."

All bids will include accrued interest.

Any award by the Treasurer to a successful bidder is subject to the approval of the Governor on all items.

The Treasurer reserves the right to reject any or all bids which are not in his opinion advantageious to the interest of the Commonwealth.

All Metropolitan District bonds, although they are direct obligations, are assessed against the cities and towns in the Metropolitan District.

Date and Place of Payment: Principal and interest on the coupon bonds will be payable at the State Treasury in Boston, or at: Bankers Trust Company, New York; or The First National Bank of Chicago, Chicago, Illinois.

Date and Place of Delivery: It is expected that the coupon bonds in permanent form will be delivered at the Bankers Trust Company, 1 Battery Park Plaza, New York City, New York, in approximately five weeks after the award of the issues.

Legal Opinions: The purchasers of the bonds will be furnished with an opinion of the Attorney General affirming the legality of each issue. A legal opinion will be printed on each bond.

CUSIP numbers will be imprinted on the bonds.

Statement of Public Debt, Sinking Funds and Taxable Property of The Commonwealth of Massachusetts

Funded Debt—February 1, 1975

	Gross Debt	*Sinking Funds*	*Net Debt*
Direct Debt . . .	$1,406,495,000.00	$6,219,400.00	$1,400,275,600.00[1]
Contingent. . . .	260,488,000.00	–	260,488,000.00
	$1,666,983,000.00	$6,219,400.00	$1,660,763,600.00

Water Debt (included in above Contingent Debt)

Water Debt. . . . $ 131,069,000.00 $ 131,069,000.00

Contingent Liability: Under Chapter 200 of the Acts of 1948, Chapter 667 of the Acts of 1953 and Chapter 705 of the Acts of 1966, the Housing Authority Law, the Commonwealth of Massachusetts has guaranteed City and Town Housing Authority notes and bonds. The amount outstanding December 31, 1974 was $558,185,000, represented by notes $496,871,000, by bonds $61,314,000. (These figures compiled from information supplied by the Department of Community Affairs.)

There are also Temporary Notes outstanding for funds advanced for the following purposes:

Massachusetts Bay Transportation Authority . . . . $100,000,000.00[2]

Regional Transit Authority . . . . $ 487,000.00[2]

[1] Highway Debt (included in above Direct Debt) $336,279,000.

[2] Notes due November 20, 1975 from assessments against cities and towns in the district served.

TAXABLE PROPERTY

The amounts of taxable property and taxable income of the Commonwealth of Massachusetts, as furnished by the Commissioner of Corporations and Taxation for the calendar year ended December 31, 1974, as follow:

Local Taxation

Value of assessed real estate $27,805,251,540.00

Value of assessed personal estate 2,053,374,963.00

State Taxation

Sales and Use Tax. . . . . $ 257,072,968.00

Taxable deposits in savings banks. 5,138,418,890.00

Taxable income; savings banks 853,016,468.00

Taxable income; individuals, etc. (after all exemptions,

    deductions and credits) 18,400,000,000.00*

Taxable income; National Banks and Trust Companies. . .   137,299,985.00

Insurance companies, value of taxable premiums and

    reserves 4,092,606,244.00

*Estimated.

ROBERT Q. CRANE,
Treasurer and Receiver-General

% Increase Over Present	Debt Service at 5.6%	Debt Service per capita	% Increase Over Present
23.7	132	23	20.0
17.8	127	22	15.4
11.8	121	21	10.0
5.9	116	20	5.4
0.0	110	19	0.0

Was this the way to go? And how far? Given these figures and all the other data, Governor Dukakis prepared to make his decision. Considering that a bond's quality is a function of the current outstanding debt, the ability of the State to withstand more debt, and the competition in the marketplace among other municipals, would Massachusetts' bond quality be weakened by an increased debt load?

EXHIBIT 15

State Debts Alone (Excluding Cities and Towns)
(in millions of dollars except where specified)

State	Total Debt	Debt per capita[a]	Debt Service	Service per capita	Debt per total Expenditures	Service per total Expenditures	Debt[a] per total Income
Massachusetts	1,661[b]	$291	$110	$19	45%	3.0%	7.6%
Connecticut	1,857	607	140	46	149%	11.3%	15.0%
Wisconsin[c]	536	121	N/A	N/A	23%	—	3.6%
Indiana	None	—	—	—	—	—	—
New Jersey	1,148	160	88	12	32%	2.5%	4.1%

[a]Per capita and state income figures from 1970 census of population.
[b]Debt and debt service figures are all for 1973 except Massachusetts which is for 1974.
[c]Wisconsin began issuing debt in 1969.

287

SIX

BUDGETING

Budgeting in Nonprofit Organizations*

Budgeting is that function of management which makes certain that the organization will have the financial resources to carry out its programs and plans. Budgeting is part of planning and strategy formulation (the subject of the preceding chapter). It involves estimations of revenues and costs, and tradeoffs and decisions as to the allocation of resources among competing claims—claims for which there are often inadequate funds. Finally, budgeting provides the framework for reporting and control.

In setting up a budget for a nonprofit organization, the first step is to define the mission objectives (or, more likely, the objectives of multiple missions) of the organization as precisely as possible. Each mission should be budgeted; that is, the relevant revenues and expenditures should be associated with each mission. Such budgeting allows the examination of alternate uses of funds—getting the "biggest bang for the buck" among the various missions. Financial effectiveness is not necessarily the sole or major determinant of which mission should be favored or abandoned in a nonprofit organization. Nonetheless, without information on revenues and expenditures broken down by missions, it is impossible to discuss tradeoffs between the various missions or how to discharge the package of missions most efficiently.

*This note was written by Professor Leslie E. Grayson, The Colgate Darden Graduate School of Business Administration, University of Virginia. Copyright ©1981 by the University of Virginia Graduate Business School Sponsors.

Annual budgeting should begin with a realistic estimate of revenues, and—as a second step—a projection of expenditures based on available revenues. Many nonprofit organizations start the budgeting process with the expenditures, however, and then attempt to match revenues to them. The result of this reverse process is either a budget that is based on wishful thinking or one which sends the administration scampering for funds, or both.

All too often, nonprofit organizations begin budgeting with an annual estimate of incremental increases in expenses. (For instance, a 10% increase in salaries and a 20% increase in fuel bills.) Once this estimate of increases in major expenses is completed, limited attempts are made to guess at revenues. Administrators appear to assume that they will come up with the revenues to balance the budget. Once the budget appears to be in balance, the trustees have little reason not to approve it. What they approve, however, may be a fiction.

Not only does the emphasis on expenditures reverse the logical budgetary sequence, but even in estimating expenditures, a better method could be used than incremental budgeting. If mistakes exist in the present budgeting system—and none is ever without fault—incremental budgeting simply continues these past mistakes. Moreover, incremental budgeting takes into account only one reason why next year's budget may be different from this year's—inflation. It allows no examination of the other two causes of a change in expenses—change in the quantity or quality of the organization's missions. Inflation is, of course, determined by forces outside the institutions, but the quantity and quality of the institution's programs are determined by the institution itself, and the changes must be thought through as carefully as the original definitions of missions.

ALLOCATING COSTS

In a graduate business school, professors and staff often participate in a number of the programs of the school. A professor may teach master and doctoral students, also teach in executive programs, supervise doctoral and master's theses, do research and course development, consult, administer, and perform other academic activities. How does an administrator allocate salaries among the various missions? "Unbundling" such joint costs has never been easy, even in profit-making enterprises. (For instance, oil companies have difficulty in separating their refining and marketing costs.) Nonetheless, if the missions are defined well, the costs associated with each activity can be approximately defined also by, for example, assigning the time spent by each faculty member on the activities to the appropriate program.

The federal government's Office of Management and the Budget has proved to be an accomplished practitioner of aligning costs with specific programs, and its methods are well worth studying.

EFFICIENCY AND EFFECTIVENESS

Armed with cost data and some measures of performance for the missions, one may examine the efficiency of each program. Consideration of efficiency or cost effectiveness must carefully reflect the mission of the program. Size of enrollment in a class, for example, should not be used as a measure of effectiveness of the class if, in fact, the class was offered with a different mission in mind. In an MBA program, to offer an elective with very small enrollment cannot be justified on efficiency grounds; financial resources might be employed more efficiently in some other activity, but not necessarily more effectively. The course might be offered to meet the needs of faculty development or to round out the elective offerings.

One "myth" that should not put off the administrator is that quality and efficiency are mutually exclusive. They are multi-dimensional and may require definite tradeoffs, but they are not necessarily mutually exclusive. It is quite possible to deliver a quality mission that is also efficient. The opposite myth is certainly not true; namely, that large amounts of resources will necessarily guarantee quality activity.

Quality is frequently tied to some quantitative determinant. Again, taking an MBA program as an example, it is fairly obvious that a course with an enrollment of 3 is not cost effective and a classroom containing more than 200 students will probably not deliver a quality educational experience. But what is the "ideal" average class size—55, 65 students? If so, why 55 or 65, and why not some other number between 3 and 200? In discussing allocation of resources in such a situation, the point is to present both the people in the program and the administrators with the relevant cost data associated with each level of program quality (to the extent that it can be defined) so that alternative uses of resources may be rationally discussed.

One ideal technique of determining the quality and efficiency trade-off is a cost-benefit analysis. Such an analysis, however, depends on organizational agreement as to what the costs and benefits are. That is easier said than done. Moreover, under certain circumstances it may be appropriate to cross-subsidize among programs; for instance, the total mission of a graduate business school might justify the use of funds raised by the executive education programs to help defray the cost of the research program. Here again, however, the point is that both academicians and administrators should know the degree of cross-subsidization, and for that purpose, it is necessary to have separate budgets for all major activities.

BUDGETING IN THE PLANNING PROCESS

Budgeting assists administrators in evaluating the revenue and expenditure implications of expanding or contracting certain programs. If one desires to expand a program, one must estimate changes in income and costs: how much will it cost and where will the funds come from? Most nonprofit activities are highly labor-intensive, with salaries frequently accounting for as much as 80% of total costs in the fields of education, health care, and welfare. Thus, the allocation of costs in expanding a program is made easier because adjusting salaries will be the greatest expense; overhead and other direct and indirect costs are frequently allocated in proportion to the salaries.

Increased revenues also must be estimated for each activity for which expansion is being considered. In fact, these estimates should precede the cost forecast. If fees are charged to offset or partially offset the cost of services in the program, what kind of increase in fees can be realized from expansion, and when? Outside private or government funding may be involved. Expansion of a program may open up such possibilities or may require them if costs are to be covered. Again using a graduate business school as an example, generally the executive programs run by the schools produce their own revenue (and, in fact, surplus); the MBA programs earn about 65% of their expenditures, and the research programs have to be paid for from public and private sources outside the programs themselves. All these factors must be considered when the budgeting process includes possible expanded programs.

Estimates of costs and revenues can be done simultaneously so long as revenues are estimated realistically and are not simply used as a "plug" figure to cover costs. The danger of that approach was mentioned at the outset of this note.

REPORTING AND CONTROL

The final step in the budgeting process is establishing, executing, and monitoring a reporting and control system. The actual results need to be reported in a form that will allow their comparison with the budget. For control purposes, the system must allow the reporting of results to the "right" people at the "right" time. A performance audit on the budget can measure both to what extent the various missions of the nonprofit organization have been accomplished and also whether costs have been contained and expected revenues have been realized.

Case 14

Budgeting in
State Government*

INTRODUCTION

In late Spring 1974, Mr. Mark Davidson assumed the position of Secretary of Administration and Finance (A&F) for a medium-sized industrial state in the midwestern United States. Mr. Davidson was replacing Charles Williamson who had resigned to run for the office of State Attorney General. One of the principal problems facing Mr. Davidson concerned the State's budgeting system and the many changes which had taken place as a result of the recent reorganization of the Executive Branch into ten Secretariats (analogous to cabinet secretaries at the Federal Government level). There were essentially five participants in the budget preparation process—the Governor and his staff, A&F, the other Secretariats, the Bureau of the Budget (BOB), and the Legislature. The role of each participant had not been well-defined either with respect to the budget or in relation to the other participants. Mr. Davidson was concerned with developing procedures and systems which would assure the State of effective budgeting and control.

Olin Thomas, Assistant Secretary of Administration and Finance and Director of the Office of State Planning and Management, reflected on

*Copyright © 1975 by the President and Fellows of Harvard College. Reproduced by permission. This case was prepared by David W. Young under the supervision of Charles J. Christenson.

the nature of the changes which had taken place in the Executive Branch:

> State reorganization took place in 1971 and 1972. The basic intention was to increase the Governor's control by having him deal directly with fewer people. Prior to reorganization, there were several hundred agency heads reporting to him, creating a very unwieldy system.
>
> The agencies were organized into Secretariats (see Exhibit 1), and each Secretary was given the power of budget review; that is he was to review the budgets submitted to him from each agency within his Secretariat, assure himself that they were adequate and properly directed, and make whatever changes were necessary before submitting them to A&F for final review. Under reorganization, the Secretaries were also given the responsibility of program evaluation, resulting in the power to create, budget for, evaluate, and dispose of both programs and agencies within their Secretariats.
>
> At least that's how the process was supposed to work. I'm not clear as to exactly why it's not working that way, but it isn't. Yet, if I were a Secretary and could have just one power, I would choose the power of budget review, since theoretically it should give me all the clout I need. I just don't know what happened between theory and reality, but I do know that most of the Secretaries are not very happy with the system.

The system of preparing and implementing the state's annual operating budget was a long and complex process which had undergone a number of changes between 1972 and 1974. In order to understand these changes and their impact on the budget process, it is first necessary to review the budget cycle. Next, developments and changes which took place since FY 1973 are discussed. Finally, the various issues facing Mr. Davidson in mid-1974 are looked at from the points of view of several participants in the process.

THE BUDGET CYCLE

Budgeting in state government is a yearly process carried out in conjunction with the legislative program activity of the Executive Branch. The timing is such that both the budget and the Governor's proposed legislation are submitted to the Legislature in January, six months prior to the fiscal year to which they pertain. Exhibit 2 shows the timing of the various activities, which are discussed in detail below.

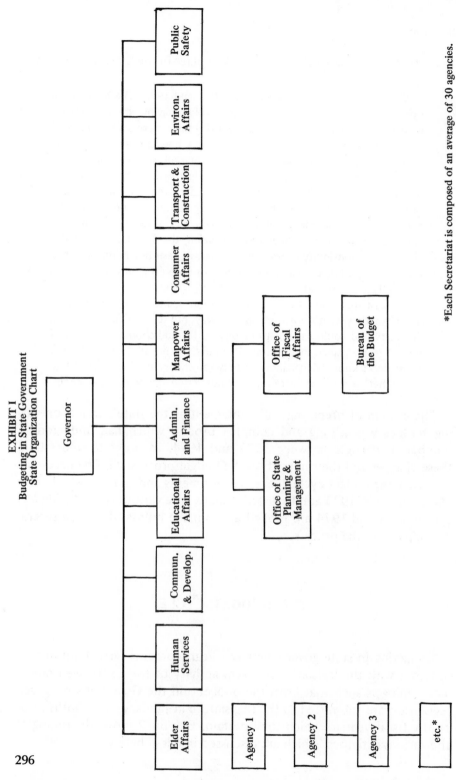

EXHIBIT I
Budgeting in State Government
State Organization Chart

Governor

Human Services

Commun. & Develop.

Educational Affairs

Admin. and Finance

Manpower Affairs

Consumer Affairs

Transport & Construction

Environ. Affairs

Public Safety

Office of State Planning & Management

Office of Fiscal Affairs

Bureau of the Budget

Elder Affairs

Agency 1

Agency 2

Agency 3

etc.*

*Each Secretariat is composed of an average of 30 agencies.

EXHIBIT 2

Legislative and Budget Cycles Compared

	1973 Legislative Session						1974 Legislative Session					
	FY 1973			Fiscal Year 1974								FY 1975
Months	Jan Feb Mar Apr May Jun July	August	September	October	November	December	January	Feb Mar Apr May Jun Jul

LEGISLATIVE PROGRAM ACTIVITY

- *Sept 1973* Governor's staff reviews agencies' suggested legislative programs
- *Oct 1973* Gubernatorial legislation for FY 1975 begun
- *Nov 1973* Agencies submit proposed FY 1975 legislation directly to the Legislature
- *Dec 1973* Gubernatorial legislation for FY 1975 completed
- *Jan 1974* Governor submits proposed FY 1975 legislation to Legislature

BUDGET ACTIVITY

- *July 1973* Agencies begin to prepare FY 1975 budget
- *Sept 1973* Budget reviewed by A&F and appeals instituted
- *Nov 1973* Appeals process taken to Governor where necessary
- *Jan 1974* FY 1975 budget submitted to Legislature

Exhibit 3
Budgeting in State Government
Responsibilities Within the Secretariat of Administration and Finance

Secretary of A&F	Deputy Secretary for Fiscal Affairs	Bureau of the Budget
The governor shall appoint a commissioner of administration, who ... shall be the executive and administrative head of the said office; and every division, bureau, section and other administrative unit and agency within the said office, other than the comptroller's division and the purchasing agent's division, shall be under his direction, control, and supervision. ... He shall act as the executive officer of the governor in all matters pertaining to the financial, administrative, planning and policy coordinating functions and affairs of the departments, commissions, offices, boards, divisions, institutions and other agencies within the executive department of the government. He shall inquire into the business affairs of the State and the laws governing them; shall supervise program planning and the coordination of the activities and programs of the State in its dealings with the federal government; shall review and report to the governor and the general court on all proposed legislation affecting the organization, structure, efficiency and administrative functions,	The executive officer for administration and finance shall include ... a fiscal affairs division, headed by a deputy commissioner for fiscal affairs ... The deputy commissioner ... for fiscal affairs ... shall be appointed by the prior written approval of the governor, and shall serve at the pleasure of the commissioner, shall be a person of ability and experience, shall devote his entire time to the duties of his office, and shall perform such functions as the commissioner shall from time to time assign to him. *Source:* General Laws Acts of 1974, Ch. 7, Sec. 4A.	There shall be within the fiscal affairs division a budget bureau, headed by a budget director. ... The said budget director ... shall be appointed by the commissioner, with the approval of the governor, and may be removed, for cause, in like manner; shall be a person of ability and experience, and shall devote his entire time to the duties of his office. *Source:* General Laws Acts of 1974, Ch. 7, Sec. 4A. The Bureau of the Budget has the following responsibilities: collection and review of agency budget requests; preparation of the budget document; review of allotments; review of accounting reports; verification of agency estimates for objects of expenditure such as food, fuel, and equipment; and

review of the accuracy of agency calculations.

Source: The State's Taxpayers Foundation, Inc.

services, procedures and practices of the departments, commissions, offices, boards, divisions, institutions and other agencies, or any of them, under the executive department of the government; shall conduct studies of the operations of the said agencies with a view to effecting improvements in administrative organization, procedures, practices and to promoting economy, efficiency, and avoiding of useless labor and expenses in the said agencies; shall from time to time recommend to the governor and the general court such changes as he shall deem desirable in the laws relating to the organization, structure, efficiency, or administrative functions, services, procedures and practices of any such agency or agencies; and shall have such other powers and duties as shall be assigned to him by statute and may from time to time be assigned to him by the governor in accordance with law.

Source: General Laws, Ch. 7, Sec. 3, p. 148.

In July of each year, the 300 or so state agencies begin to prepare their budgets for the next fiscal year. In late summer, the budgets are submitted by agencies to their Secretariats, where they are reviewed and modifications are made by each Secretary and his staff, usually in consultation with the appropriate agencies. They are then sent to A&F for final review.

A&F reviews the budgets, also making modifications.[1] Once the A&F review is complete, the Secretary of A&F notifies all other Secretaries of the changes he has made. If a Secretary wishes to appeal the A&F changes, he/she may do so, and A&F and the Secretary attempt to reach a compromise. Where a compromise cannot be achieved, the questions are taken to the Governor and his staff for final resolution. Once the differences have been resolved, the Governor submits the final budget to the Legislature as House Bill 1.

Revenue estimates are also included in House Bill 1, but receive minimal treatment. By law the Governor must submit a balanced budget, although to do so he may draw on the available balances of 17 different revenue funds, so that it is not necessary for revenue collections in a given year to equal expenditures for that year.[2] Of the 17 funds the two most significant (accounting for approximately 90 percent of total revenues) are the General Fund and the Highway Fund. The General Fund includes federal reimbursement, state income taxes, and other revenues not associated with one of the special purpose funds. The Highway Fund includes gasoline taxes, fees from the Registry of Motor Vehicles, and other highway-related revenue. Although most state expenditures are from the General Fund, many line items in House Bill 1 contain references to one or more special purpose funds, since by statute revenue from these funds is to be used for certain specified purposes.

House Bill 1 goes to the Ways and Means Committee of the House of Representatives where it is reviewed, and various officials of the Executive Branch are called on to testify. Every Secretary participates along with a representative of the Bureau of Fiscal Affairs. Frequently, agency heads and their staffs from within the Secretariats are also called on to testify.

---

[1] A&F review activities take place in the office of the Secretary of A&F, the office of the Deputy Secretary of A&F for Fiscal Affairs, and the Bureau of the Budget. The responsibilities of each are shown in Exhibit 3. Exhibit 4 contains information about personnel in the latter two organizational units.

[2] All funds have specific uses, and there is no transferability between funds. Therefore, if one fund has a large surplus, that surplus cannot be used to finance a deficit in another fund, unless there is a change in the law.

Exhibit 4
Personnel in the Office of Fiscal Affairs and the Bureau of the Budget

Name	Position	Years in Position	Years with State	Age	Education
Office of Fiscal Affairs					
1. Mike Edwards	Deputy Commissioner for Fiscal Affairs	2	2	34	Ph. D. Econ.
2. Stan Kurtzman	Program Management Specialist	2	2	33	MPA
3. Mark Roberts	Deputy Director for Program Evaluation	1	2	36	MBA
4. Steve Allen	Director of Program Evaluation	2	2	33	MPP
5. Lionel Lewis	Assistant Director for Program Evaluation	2	2	32	MPA
Bureau of Budget					
1. Harold Edmunson	Budget Director	11	31	68	
2. Kenneth Jackson	Deputy Budget Director	2½	24	57	
3. Milton Willard	Assistant to Budget Director	2½	28	53	

The Ways and Means Committee makes whatever modifications it deems necessary and then brings a full budget before the House for passage. This document contains the committee's total recommendations and a final figure. Debate takes place, amendments are frequently made from the floor, and ultimately the budget is passed.

The Senate Ways and Means Committee receives the budget after it has been passed by the House. This committee makes amendments to the bill, frequently of a fairly substantive nature, such as changes in appropriation levels, increases or decreases in personnel levels in programs, and occasionally the complete elimination of an expenditure item. Significant changes may also be made to the wording of the budget, such as the number of hours a teacher must work at a state-supported university, or specification that state funds cannot be spent until federal reimbursement is received.

The budget is sent by the Ways and Means Committee to the full Senate, which may also make changes, following essentially the same process as that in the House. Ultimately the Senate passes its version of the budget. When both houses have agreed and passed the budget, it is sent to the Governor for signature. He can line item veto or line item reduce whichever appropriation accounts[3] he wishes, as well as veto the budget in its entirety. Generally, he makes whatever line item changes he wishes and signs the budget into law.[4]

At this point the funds are appropriated to the Governor, and he in turn allots funds to the Secretariats through A&F. There are three allotments a year, each of which can contain whatever portion of the budget the Governor deems appropriate; generally, each allotment consists of about one-third of the budget. This process forces the Secretaries to conform to the cash flow schedule determined by A&F in that they are not allowed to spend more than their allotment for any four-month period. Additionally, with the exception of the state's public higher education institutions, which are fiscally autonomous agencies and must receive their entire appropriations, the Governor can refuse to allot the total amount appropriated if he deems it necessary to do so.[5]

If, as the fiscal year progresses, the Governor determines that it will be necessary to spend more than the Legislature has appropriated, he may prepare a Supplemental budget for the additional funds. This is submitted to the House, where it follows the same course as the original budget. There are two types of Supplemental budgets—Corrective and Deficiency. Essentially, the difference is that the Corrective budget anticipates shortfalls in funding and attempts to correct them before they

---

[3] See Exhibit 5 for the relationship between agencies, divisions, appropriation accounts, and subsidiary accounts. House Bill 1 does not contain subsidiary accounts. Changes to subsidiary accounts may be made by the Ways and Means Committee, and subsidiary account breakdowns are included in detailed schedules released after the budget has been signed into law. Essentially, then, appropriation accounts constitute budget line items.

[4] The Governor actually receives the Appropriations Act which consists of the budget plus a number of other sections related to the budget. These other sections place limitations on the way in which the Governor may implement the budget. For example, one section of the Act gives the Ways and Means Committee authority to regulate the number of personnel positions available to each agency as well as the pay grades of those positions. The Governor may not veto a section of the Appropriations Act without vetoing the entire Act.

[5] Higher Education expenditures constituted 7% of both total budgeted appropriations in FY 1974 and total budgetary recommendations in FY 1975.

EXHIBIT 5
Example of Budget Structure for a State Agency

Secretariat: Environmental Affairs
Agency: Department of Natural Resources
Divison: Forests and Parks
Appropriation Account: Maintenance of Sherwood Beach
Subsidiary Accounts:*   01 Salaries, permanent
                                   02 Salaries, other (temporary, overtime)
                                   03 Nonemployee Services (Consultants, etc.)
 04 Food
 05 Clothing
 06 Housekeeping, supplies
 07 Laboratory and medical supplies (including welfare subsidies)
 08 Heat and other plant operations
 09 Farm and grounds
 10 Travel and automotive expense
 11 Advertising and printing
 12 Maintenance and repairs
 13 Special supplies and expenses
 14 Office and administrative expenses
 15 Equipment
 16 Rentals
 17 State aid
 18 Capital outlays
 19 Debt service
 20 Pensions, retirement allowances, annuities, and benefits.

*The Maintenance of Sherwood Beach account would not necessarily have all subsidiary accounts.

occur; the Deficiency budget does not anticipate shortfalls, but attempts to correct them "after the bills have been received."

The Last Three Years

The budget preparation process for fiscal years 1973 through 1975[6]

[6] Fiscal years run from July to June. The FY 1974 budget, for example, was for the year beginning July 1, 1973 and ending June 30, 1974. See Exhibit 2.

was marked by a number of modifications, including the introduction of the Secretarial review procedure, which began in 1974 and the experiment with budget targets. The FY 1973 budget was the first one submitted after the establishment of the Secretariats. Since the budget was almost complete when most of the new Secretariats came into office, it went to the Legislature without their input. Generally, the Secretaries used the FY 1973 budget as a basis for gaining a better understanding of the agencies under their jurisdiction.

As mentioned, the FY 1974 budget was prepared with the Secretary in each case reviewing the budget for his agencies. The Secretaries were operating under two mandates from the Governor: (1) to organize budgets along the lines of proposed reorganization plans for each Secretariat, and (2) to maintain their budgets at specified target levels established by A&F. As a result, the Secretaries and their staffs modified many of the agencies' requests and rearranged the accounts (including subsidiary accounts in some instances) according to the proposed plans for full state reorganization. Additionally, in preparing the budget, the BOB omitted the column showing what each agency had requested, and included only the Secretaries' (Governor's) recommended figures. As a result of these actions two difficulties developed. In the first place many of the agencies whose budgets had been cut at the Secretariat level went directly to the House Ways and Means Committee saying that the budget recommended for them by the Governor was not enough. Secondly, the Legislature indicated that since full state reorganization had not been approved, the budget in the form submitted was not acceptable. Not only did the Legislature require the resubmission of the budget in the old format, but it also increased the appropriations for many agencies above the Governor's recommendation and indicated that in the future it would not consider a budget which did not contain both requested and recommended amounts.

The FY 1975 budget was prepared under the supervision of the Office of Fiscal Affairs, one of two major divisions of A&F (see Exhibit 1). The Deputy Secretary for Fiscal Affairs, Michael Edwards, and his staff worked closely with the Secretariats to define programs and priorities. No target figures were given to the Secretaries; instead the Secretaries were asked to rank their requests in discrete packages in priority order. Cuts were then made to Secretaries' budgets by eliminating whichever low priority programs were necessary to bring the total budget figure in line with what the Governor wished to submit. Two documents emerged: the program policy request, which was translated into a document called *The Budget in English*; and the standard line item request, sent to the Legislature as House Bill 1.

The appeals procedure discussed previously was instituted for the FY 1975 budget. Under this procedure the Secretary of A&F, Charles Williamson, reviewed the policy requests of the Secretariats and decided himself on a number of priorities. He then sent letters to both the agencies and the Secretariats outlining his decisions. The Secretaries and agency heads were allowed to appeal any decisions they did not like, and Williamson made some changes as a result of their appeals. He then prepared a formal letter outlining his final decisions and notifying the Secretaries that they could appeal his decisions to the Governor if they chose to do so. Several Secretariats—Education, Human Services, Elder Affairs, Manpower, and Community Development—appealed his decisions. Of the $125 million in dispute, some $80 million was conceded to the Secretariats by the Governor. Some $3.0 billion was requested by the Secretariats for FY 1975, of which about $2.8 billion was recommended by the Governor. The budget finally passed by the Legislature was about $61 million less than that recommended by the Governor. (See Exhibit 6 for a complete breakdown of the FY 1975 budget.)

Fiscal Year 1976

The FY 1975 budget went into effect in July 1974. As the Secretaries and agencies began to turn their attention toward preparation of the FY 1976 budget, they learned that a slightly different set of requirements was being established by A&F. The principal change was the return of target levels, but this time combined with the program policy request. Essentially, the Secretariats were being asked to specify which programs they would include if their total budget were ten percent below that for FY 1975, and what they would do with a variety of increments above the target should additional funds be available.

Effectively, since the base level was set at an amount below the FY 1975 level, the Secretariats were being forced to put some of their existing programs into the incremental levels. This change caused some concern on the part of some of the Secretaries and their staffs, particularly since many of them were not clear on the nature of the relationship between themselves, the Office of Fiscal Affairs, A&F, the BOB, and the Governor. In fact, a number of issues remained unresolved at this time which impaired the smooth functioning of the budget process. These issues are discussed next.

Exhibit 6
Summary of Fiscal Year 1975 Budget

	Requested Appropriation	Recommended Appropriation	Legislative Action
Legislature	$ 15,910,078	$ 15,910,078	$ 16,010,760
Judiciary	21,649,759	18,309,317	18,084,833
Executive	7,609,177	6,568,359	6,428,544
Secretary of the Commonwealth	4,582,339	3,406,114	3,965,557
Treasurer and Receiver General	63,563,394	63,397,105	63,424,820
Lottery Commission	9,655,866	9,655,866	9,655,866
Debt Service	201,833,840	201,833,840	201,833,840
Auditor	2,997,257	2,651,570	2,868,187
Attorney General	3,811,272	3,061,179	3,067,409

Secretariats			
Administration and Finance	175,896,369	143,057,823	118,559,931
Environmental Affairs	83,613,550	75,170,599	72,761,588
Community Development	51,946,255	49,526,185	50,240,270
Human Services	1,516,682,426	1,423,928,584	1,385,938,803
Transportation and Construction	117,007,556	575,195,431	113,182,632
Educational Affairs	622,915,859	575,195,431	588,408,119
Public Safety	57,389,366	43,587,219	42,347,348
Economic Development and Employment Services (Manpower)	16,009,867	15,290,274	13,640,066
Elder Affairs	6,177,407	5,055,010	3,378,007
Consumer Affairs	15,147,704	13,224,281	13,742,638
Special requests	12,955,718	—	—
Prior year deficiencies	5,000,000	5,000,000	—
Total State	$3,012,355,059	$2,788,435,367	$2,727,539,218

Source: State's Taxpayers' Foundation.

307

POLICY GUIDELINES

One of the principal issues was that of policy guidelines for use in budget preparation. Many of the Secretaries felt that they received no clear direction from the Governor as to his priorities. David Johnson, Assistant Secretary for Manpower Affairs, described the problem from his perspective:

> In the U.S. Government, the political priorities tend to get laid out early in the budget process; programs which are necessary for political reasons and must be included in the budget are specified. Then you send the troops out to prepare the budget. Here we don't know what the Governor's political priorities are in any detail until after we have put the budget together initially. Then we must begin the process of re-shuffling programs and the like.

Thomas Stevenson, Special Assistant to the Governor, commented on the problem the Governor faces in specifying his political priorities:

> I realize that the Secretaries may feel that they get no direction in the early stages of budget preparation, but I think they ignore the problem of the budget cycle in relation to the political cycle. (See Exhibit 2.) Currently (July 1974) the agencies are preparing their 1976 budgets, yet we're still in the middle of the 1974 legislative session. In the best of years we're three months behind the agencies.
>
> This is extremely important if you recognize that many of the legislative proposals prepared by the agencies have massive fiscal implications. For example, the Department of Public Welfare wants to file legislation increasing the cost of living allowance for all Family Assistance Programs; this implies several million dollars of increased expenditures. Since we simply cannot say what the Governor's legislative proposals will be prior to the time the agencies begin preparing their budgets, we tell them to plan to spend what they spent last year—we call this the zero-based budgeting approach. Effectively it deals with the problem of specifying priorities.

Harold Edmunson, the Director of the state's Bureau of the Budget added still another point of view:

> The Governor does not outline his objectives to the various state agencies, which means that they can request just about anything they want. Then the Governor can cut their requests and go to the Legislature saying that he has cut the budget.

Steven Charles, the state's first Secretary of Administration and Finance, currently a Senior Budget Analyst with the state's Taxpayers' Foundation, added his perspective:

> The Secretaries' role in the budget process is one of working with their agencies to assure appropriate discipline. As things stand now there is little discipline either among the Secretaries or between the Secretaries and their agencies. The Governor has got to make his priorities known to the Secretaries in order to resolve the first problem, and the Secretaries need to develop a system that will prevent their separate agencies from promoting their programs without consideration for the Governor's overall fiscal plan.
>
> As things stand now, the Executive Branch of government is not unified, and this lack of unity is best typified in the discrepancy between the two sets of figures in the budget—requested and recommended. The Legislature has required that two sets be submitted, but there is nothing to say that the two sets have to be different.

Mark Roberts, a staff assistant to Mike Edwards, commented further on the issues raised by Mr. Charles:

> You would think that the Executive Branch of government would be a team—a rather homogeneous group of individuals that works together for essentially the same ends. But that's not the case—many Secretaries, for example, are rather closely allied with the Legislature, which is like a sales manager going to the Board of Directors and saying "My boss says we don't need this money, but we really do." The situation is further complicated by the fact that the Governor is always in the position of trying to balance off conflicting demands of the electorate. His interest in fiscal matters consists of looking for ways to get the funds he needs to implement the programs he is interested in.

TARGET BUDGETING

Mike Edwards described his feelings about the target budgeting approach used in FY 1974:

> In general I don't believe in the target system, and it was used in FY 1974 only for the sake of expedience, since Chuck Williamson and I came to the state in October 1972 and budgets were due in January

1973. The target system limits the choices available to the Governor by eliminating competition among the Secretariats for funds. On the other hand, a target system has the distinct advantage of forcing a Secretary to eliminate some programs in favor of others; this in turn creates some interest in cutting old programs and developing new ones.

For FY 1976 we are adding an element to the target approach which helps the Governor make policy decisions that are consistent with his views and the Secretaries' priorities. Each Secretary has a base budget figure as well as a number of increments which are to contain programs in priority order with dollar amounts attached. If the Governor wishes to add programs he can pick them according to the Secretaries' priorities, knowing how much each discrete package will cost. Since the base figure is set at an amount below the current budget level, the Secretaries are forced to put some of their current programs into the increments. Thus, they are forced to be very careful in working out their priorities, and the Governor is not locked into all of the existing programs.

Of course, we have to make sure that the Secretaries don't "job" us; that is, that they don't put all the politically attractive programs into the increments so that the Governor has little choice but to accept increments.

David Johnson outlined the way in which he, as an Assistant Secretary, viewed budget targets:

> Budgeting is much easier with targets, but you must recognize that the Secretariats make most of the budget allocation decisions within the Secretariat-wide budget targets, and A&F only really reviews the budgets at the margins.
>
> Scale of operations is a very significant factor in this process, however. You cannot apply the same rules across the board—that's like saying that foot soldiers and fighter planes can be evaluated in the same way since they're both defense items. Our Secretariat has only about $12 million a year, while Human Services, for example, has over $1 billion, about one-third of the state's entire budget. It's relatively easy for me to say without consulting any of our agencies what the implications are of a 10 or 20 percent cut in funds. But in Human Services the same cut would require putting every agency through the exercise of making complex tradeoffs. In consequence, different sets of political "rules" for making budget decisions are applied to different areas of government.

Mark Roberts added some perspective to the question of making trade-offs within a target budget framework:

One problem with target budgeting, particularly when we talk about asking the Secretariats to come in with budgets below the level of the prior year, is that approximately two-thirds of the budget is nondiscretionary. It consists of pensions, retirement funds, certain welfare payments, and so forth, all of which must be included in the budget. In order to resolve this problem, we excluded these sorts of items when we calculated the targets. But there is an even more serious problem, and one for which we could not correct when we calculated targets: There are statutes on the books which require enforcement; that is, the Legislature has passed laws and expects us to enforce them. When we force agencies to come in at targets which are below their total budget levels of the prior year we are frequently putting them in a position of deciding which laws to emphasize enforcement for and which to not. A good example is the Department of Public Utilities (DPU). Laws have been passed that require the DPU to make a more careful analysis and review of the fuel adjustment clause. But the DPU is sorely understaffed, and if they are to meet the statutory intent of the Legislature they must have sufficient funds in their budget to carry a larger staff. By forcing them to meet targets, we make this very difficult.

The Role of A&F in the Budget Process

Owing to the changes that had taken place in the state over the past three years, the relationship between A&F (and its Office of Fiscal Affairs) and the other Secretariats was both a new and important one. Mr. Lionel Lewis, a staff assistant to Mike Edwards, commented on some of the directions being taken in that relationship:

It is paramount to understand what the Executive (i.e., the Governor and his staff) does—without this understanding it is difficult to comprehend the budget process. For example in some states, the Governor meets regularly with his fiscal advisors to review budget priorities and requests. Any proposed new programs affecting the budget are always cleared with the fiscal staff.

In this state, the Governor doesn't deal with all of his Secretaries directly, although he occasionally uses them as inputs to his speeches. Most of the direct contact with Secretaries is handled through the Governor's staff—people like Tom Stevenson. Chuck Williamson could always get to the Governor to contest a Stevenson decision, however, but he didn't always win. Win or lose, he was still responsible for balancing the budget.

In essence, then, the question is whether A&F should be a funnel for the budget or whether it should exist in a parallel relationship to other

Secretariats. Currently the funnel approach is theoretically used, but in fact the actual process is much more informal.

Mr. Charles put the situation in some historical perspective:

> Part of the problem with all of this, as I see it, is that reorganization is not fully understood. Governor Vickers (1967-1969), who had the original idea, conceived of the Secretaries as members of a cabinet who were to be the Governor's representatives. But, in fact, as each reorganization plan has been developed, the Secretaries have become advocates of the agencies under them, i.e., advocates of spending. As the reorganization plan has been operating there is really no strong central agency to draw things together, and the Secretaries have not yet learned to look at the total budget and recognize that there are priorities outside their own domains. To date, there has been too little emphasis placed on the *total* budgetary problems faced by the Governor.

Mike Edwards described the role of the Office of Fiscal Affairs as he saw it in relation to the Secretaries:

> Our major effort should be in defining what programs the state is spending its money on, and in determining how successful those programs are. We should identify major areas of possible cost savings, and I should help the Governor make major policy changes.
>
> I think it is important to underscore the basic philosophy which underlies this approach. The first and most important point is that ultimately all executive power is the Governor's; not the Secretariats and not ours. Clearly, though, A&F has a fair amount of influence in what he does.
>
> The second point to bear in mind is that the Secretariat should really not be a program advocate, but rather an extension of the Governor. Finally, the budgeting system should be one which focuses on discrete packages—i.e., programs—not on typewriters and pencils. We ought to be out of the day-to-day decisions of the Secretariats, and we shouldn't worry about whether the Department of Education, for example, monitors schools over the telephone or by actually driving out to the school.
>
> Once we have our base level or target system established and operating, I think we will be able to get out of day-to-day decisions. Since the Secretaries will have had to assign priorities and make the necessary tradeoffs in order to meet the base level target, I am willing to assume that they will have thought about what is important.

Frank Harris, Assistant Secretary for Environmental Affairs, in reacting to Mr. Edwards' ideas, emphasized his concern over the relationship between the Secretariats and the Office of Fiscal Affairs:

One of the major unresolved questions that faces us at the present is that of the role of the Secretary of A&F in relation to substantive program decisions within each of the Secretariats. Is it Mr. Edwards' business, for example, to tell me if I need more rinks and pools? Or should he make sure that I have assessed the need for rinks and pools adequately in light of other possible uses of funds? Or should he simply make sure that I know that the rinks and pools are well-managed and cost effective?

While I can't speak for all other Secretariats, I can assure you that most of us had a very difficult time with the 1975 budget. Without target figures or policy guidance we were forced to go it alone. Mr. Edwards' analysts tried to get into the substance of our programs instead of setting fiscally sound standards and norms, and they got into lots of trouble. Since I wouldn't develop a priority ranking of my programs, Edwards' analysts tried to do so, and failed miserably.

When we reached the negotiation stage we found that our budget was being reviewed by the Office of Fiscal Affairs for our program policy and by the BOB for technical soundness. A split developed between the two groups and we made maximum use of it. We first resolved the technical issues with the BOB, leaving only policy issues. Then, when I would negotiate a polciy issue with Edwards, I would tell my agency heads to work out the corresponding technical items with the BOB. Since communication was poor between the Office of Fiscal Affairs and the BOB, we were able to play one off against the other and generally I got everything I wanted.

William Burtons, Assistant Secretary in the Office of Educational Affairs, agreed with Mr. Harris' concerns, and added some of his own:

One of the most serious problems that we in the Secretariats must face is that we must deal with A&F, and they don't even know how to manage their own house. A&F has three layers in their budget review session—the Bureau of the Budget, Fiscal Affairs, and Personnel. With the exception of Fiscal Affairs, these are old bureaucracies with all sorts of traditional bureaucratic problems. The Bureau of the Budget does the routine green eyeshade work and has little power. Personnel counts noses and resists either cuts or increases in the number of employees. The Fiscal Affairs staff are all very competent, but they have been given the wrong assignments. They are trying to second-guess what I am doing rather than identifying policy issues in the relationships between the various Secretariats.

In a nutshell, then, reorganization has given increased power to the Secretaries, but it has not led to increased efficiency, since policy has not really been decentralized. I can create all sorts of techniques to evaluate and establish policy, but I can't implement them because A&F can't deal with the sorts of concepts I am employing.

In sum, I cannot even put my program priorities into the budget hopper. If I try to do so, I get caught in the establishment net: budget review by A&F, personnel review, or allotment procedures effectively prevent me from implementing any major changes in policy.

David Johnson commented on some of the politics involved in the relationship:

I think it is important to recognize that there are some internal politics involved. Mike Edwards has introduced some excellent techniques, but he is still not part of the Governor's political decision-making process. The political decisions get made in the Governor's Office by a relatively small group of people, and the Secretaries realize this. They will not take seriously anything Edwards says until the word comes from the Governor's Office. Finally, since there is no formal cabinet procedure, the Secretaries are really not part of the process either. All of this tends to inhibit the smooth operation of budgetary decision making.

Mr. Stan Kurtzman, a staff analyst in the Office of Fiscal Affairs, responded to some of the complaints of the Secretariats:

When those of us on Mike's staff start questioning specific policies, such as whether a Secretariat should increase a particular amount by 4% or 5%, that's wrong, unless we have clear criteria to judge against. But we *should* make judgments about whether an entity is efficient or not—that *is* our business. I should be asking the kinds of questions that will improve management and help me to understand if an agency is doing the right thing in the first place; that is, whether they have an established policy with performance measures established as well as workloads (i.e., efficiency and effectiveness measures). If they aren't doing the right thing, I should at least assure myself that they're doing the wrong thing well (i.e., efficient if not effective).

But my problem is how do I decide what's right and what's wrong? Without fully immersing myself in an agency's affairs, I don't have the ability to make this judgment, and I simply cannot answer Mike's questions about whether Agency A should have its budget increased at the expense of Agency B or C or whatever. Thus, I have taken the approach of insisting that the agencies for which I'm responsible establish measures of effectiveness and efficiency and routinely turn out reliable data which I can use to make judgments. So far I have seen little in the way of adequate information.

Objectivity is another issue that must be considered here. It's hard for a Secretariat staff person to be objective since he is competing for money. But we on Mike's staff are above that level, and can be much more objective in our inter-agency comparisons as well as inter-Secretariat comparisons. We can ask the right questions. We can insist that performance be measured so that we can determine if they are doing a good job. For a Secretary or his staff to answer questions of this sort is like trying to mix oil and water—they are in direct conflict. A Secretary is too often only an advocate or a spokesman for his agency and not a hard-nosed agency overseer, and in this role we really can't and shouldn't expect him to spend a lot of time worrying about the most cost-effective ways of doing things. It would be fine if the Secretariat would fulfill this role, but unfortunately it must be our concern.

Finally, Mr. Edwards added his point of view:

The Assistant Secretaries would like Fiscal Affairs to give them a target and let them make decisions within that target. But that begs the question of how the targets are decided—of how resources are allocated among Secretariats. Because resources are limited, the Governor cannot give each Secretary all he would like, and our job is to give him program data and staff backup to make these tradeoffs as rationally as possible. We pose the issue to the Governor as to whether he should have more rinks and pools or whatever in light of other possible uses of funds *both* within a given Secretariat or between that Secretariat and others. The problem is one of scarcity. Whenever we give one Secretariat some funds we are effectively taking them away from others.

ROLE OF THE BUREAU OF THE BUDGET

Under reorganization, particularly with the introduction of the Secretariats and the Office of Fiscal Affairs, the role of the Bureau of the Budget had changed considerably. The BOB had been placed under the Office of Fiscal Affairs (see Exhibit 1) in order to coordinate policy decision with budget preparation. Harold Edmunson, the Director of the BOB, commented on some of the changes:

The role of the Bureau of the Budget is in a state of flux with reorganization. In the first place, the Governor of this state, unlike many other Governors, is not particularly interested in the budget. I haven't talked to the Governor in the past five or six years, which is a very different situation than in most states. Here the power is distributed to the Secretariats, with A&F in charge of overall supervision of fiscal affairs under the Deputy Secretary of A&F for Fiscal Affairs. In the past few years the Office of Fiscal Affairs has taken away many of the functions of the BOB; in fact, Secretary Williamson saw the BOB as a group of technicians who simply assemble the budget rather than perform any control functions.

Another observer commented on the implications of the change in structure.

> Heretofore the Budget Bureau was not only the agency of the Executive to require program compliance, but was also the enforcement arm of the Executive and the Legislature to insist on compliance with the appropriation qualifications and amounts. Reorganization purposes to decentralize most of the budget preparation operations and practically all of the financial control procedures formerly under Budget Bureau jurisdiction. The so-called control features of the appropriation acts are to be made statutory and enforced by the various Secretaries. Thus, the Legislature would be required to deal with the ten Secretariats when the use of state funds is questioned, instead of a central bureau—at present the Budget Bureau.

THE ROLE OF THE LEGISLATURE

The role the Legislature plays in the budget cycle has been discussed previously. In fulfilling its constitutional requirements of reviewing and approving the budget, the Legislature was able to exert considerable influence over the way in which the Executive Branch was managed. One observer described the general situation:

> Our state is known as a strong legislative state, which is true. As a result, anything which tends to weaken the Legislature is opposed. The creation of the Secretariats was an attempt to put some additional strength in the Executive Branch of government; probably the only reason that reorganization even got through the Legislature was the fact that the President of the Senate thought he was going to be Governor, but that didn't happen. As a result of the new potentially stronger Executive Branch, the Legislature frequently attempts to emasculate the Secretariats.

Mr. Harris expressed his concurrence, and added some further dimensions to Mr. Edmunson's comments:

> When the Legislature finally enacts the budget, it delegates power to the Ways and Means Committee to schedule certain items, such as per-

sonnel positions. While the Governor can line-item veto a particular account, he cannot veto subsidiary accounts; so when he accepts an account he accepts it in whatever way the Ways and Means Committee establishes it. Further, nothing can happen until the Ways and Means Committee releases the schedules. Usually the budget is released in mid-June, but the schedules don't arrive until mid-August, after the Ways and Means Committee has decided which personnel positions to include. You can imagine the patronage which develops as a result of that process!

Mr. Johnson was also critical of the Legislature:

It's important to bear in mind that some 80 to 90 percent of the state's budget is committed by statutory legislation. Laws are on the books which require enforcement, and funds are necessary for that enforcement. This situation exists owing to the philosophy of our Legislature—they bite off more than they can chew and let the administration digest it. For example, we administer the minimum wage law. While you can argue that we shouldn't enforce the law since that is primarily the responsibility of the Federal Government, it is on the books here too, and we really don't have much of a choice except to enforce it.

Additionally, the minute restrictions put on budget management by the Legislature make our job difficult, and needlessly so. The Legislature, by delegation to the Ways and Means Committee, controls the minutest details of personnel manning, leasing, consultant contracting, and a number of other important areas. Many of the requirements have only nuisance value, since the Legislature takes no action. In other areas, such as changing or creating position titles or descriptions, the Legislature insists on substituting its judgment for that of the Executive. Aside from being bad management, this is a clear violation of the separation of powers spelled out in the state's Constitution.

Mr. Roberts expressed some disagreement:

In analyzing the contrasting roles of the Legislature and the Executive, it's important to understand how the budget really works. First, most accounts consist almost entirely of personnel expenditures, so the capability to move funds between subsidiary accounts is not really too important. Second, although you theoretically cannot move funds between accounts, people are frequently paid out of one account and work in another, which really amounts to the same thing. For example, the Division of Insurance has insurance inspectors, but about all they ever inspect is a typewriter, this is necessary if we are to pay an experienced clerk-typist appropriately. So even if the Legislature wants to set policy they really can't since they don't have the tools.

The Budget as a Management Tool

Mr. Roberts assessed the general way in which budgeting affects management in the state:

> In state governemnt, the thrust of budgeting is the preservation of a base and arguing at the margins. The statutory language distinguishes between maintenance and new programs, and it is new programs that both create the need for measures of effectiveness and occasionally lead to conflicts with existing programs. For example, deinstitutionalization has taken many mental health clients out of the large institutions and put them into smaller facilities in local communities. But, for political reasons, no employees have been fired from the institutions. A cost-effectiveness analysis would probably show that deinstitutionalization was highly desirable, but such an analysis does not include the cost of maintaining the institutions intact.
>
> So, the budget is really a management by exception approach, but in the most pejorative sense possible—old programs just keep going, new ones are analyzed. The result is a patchwork of programs. If we knew everything we need to know about all the programs in the budget, we would say, "My God, why are we spending money on that!" But basically we don't know what's going on.
>
> Probably the classic case of the control problem is the Welfare Administration account (Exhibit 7). This account consists of $56 million which is used to deliver services, administer payments, handle food stamps, and a variety of other activities. We don't know how much it's costing us to administer any of these programs individually, since all we know is position names, which doesn't really tell you what the person is doing. Nothing in the way of results is projected, so we really have no idea of effectiveness either.
>
> My personal feeling in response to this is that the Legislature doesn't really want to know about issues such as cost-effectiveness—it would be too much for them to deal with. Although they supposedly are the decision makers, they don't really have the time to dig into things. They focus on pet programs but don't see the big picture. The issue is visibility: convince the public that some sort of change is taking place by throwing dollars at a problem, regardless of how effective you are in actually dealing with the problem.

Mr. Edmunson added his comments:

> One of the fundamental problems with the current process is that budget hearings in the Legislature are not related to the big picture—the questions of expansion programs and how we're going to pay for them

Exhibit 7
Department of Public Welfare

440-1000   For the office of the commissioner; provided that the appropriations for the food commodity distribution program
shall not be expended for certain rentals of space; provided
further, that the commissioner shall report in writing to the
governor the total expenditures of his department for each
month within thirty days after the end of each month, and
said report shall be available to the public; provided further,
that the consolidation of welfare service offices shall be subject to prior approval of the house and senate committees
on ways and means; and provided further, that applications
for all federal subventions and grants shall be subject to prior
approval of the commissioner of administration and the
house and senate committees on ways and means; including
not more than five thousand and seventy-nine permanent
positions. $56,131,000

are really not adequately dealt with. For example, not one question was
raised in the House Ways and Means Committee in its FY 1975 hearings
about how the budget was going to be financed.

Mr. Burtons commented on the question of utilizing the budget for
planning and control:

Ther are two aspects to budgeting—planning and accounting. Accounting is essentially policing the level of expenditures after appropriation. But planning is far more important—it's the process of establishing
a program budget, assigning priorities, and making the necessary tradeoffs. For a number of reasons the current budgetary system does not allow for this. First of all, the Secretaries really don't have much power;
budgets we submit to A&F can be revised and cut at will. Secondly,
there is little planning competence in the civil service system, and while
a cabinet system presumably should counteract mediocrity, the existing
personnel policies do not allow us to weed out incompetent people.
Finally, and perhaps most importantly, if planning is to be at all effective a planner should be forced to make tradeoffs and live with his mistakes, but we are not forced to do this, Three budgetary bills are submitted a year—the appropriation, the corrective, and the deficiency. So,
if you make a mistake, you simply submit either a correction or a request for deficiency funding. Since the Legislature is always in session—

a highly unusual situation in state government—you can have immediate action on a bill and get the funds you need.

Mark Roberts substantiated Mr. Burtons' point, and added a further dimension:

> The process of developing a budget which contains accounts, subsidiary accounts, and personnel schedules effectively locks the Secretaries in. It amounts to making a person responsible for certain items but not giving him the tools to manage them effectively. In sum, the whole scheduling process greatly inhibits effective management of the budget.

One of the principal changes giving the Secretariats increased power over budgets was incorporated in Chapter 1230 of the Acts of 1973. Chapter 1230 gave the Secretariats the authority, "in cases of emergency," to approve transfers between all subsidiary accounts, except the 01 (direct hire personnel) subsidiary account. Mr. Harry James, Undersecretary for Administration and Finance, assessed the importance of Chapter 1230:

> The changes brought about by Chapter 1230 responded to the major complaint of the Secretaries. Effectively it made them into mini-A&Fs. They, of course, have no power to shift funds between accounts, and they shouldn't—after all, when the Legislature appropriates funds to an account it is effectively saying "this is where we want the taxpayers' dollars spent"; it wouldn't be right for a Secretary to have the power to change that. But at least now they have some flexibility within a given account.

Mr. Edmunson expressed a contrasting viewpoint:

> Chapter 1230, in my opinion, took away more than it gave. It gave the Secretaries the ability to transfer funds between all subsidiaries *except* the 01 subsidiary account. Since 65% of the total budget is in the 01 subsidiary, little flexibility was gained.

Thus, as work began on the FY 1976 budget, the five participants in the budget preparation process—the Governor and his staff, A&F, the other Secretariats, the Bureau of the Budget, and the Legislature—had not yet developed well-defined roles either with respect to the budget or among themselves. Indeed, many observers felt that until these roles were more adequately clarified and the budget preparation process itself more streamlined, the effectiveness of budgeting as a tool for managing the state's affairs would be severely impaired.

Case 15

Middlevale Health Center[*]

The Middlevale Health Center, a small community organization on Long Island, originated in 1966 as part of a Community Action Agency. It was funded by the Office of Economic Opportunity, a Federal agency, and at that time was solely a children's health clinic. Over the next two years its activity expanded to include drug and alcoholic rehabilitation and after care (counseling and support of the patients after release from a mental hospital). As activities expanded, funding shifted to city and state sources; in 1972 OEO funding ceased entirely.

As 1975 started, Joanna Knobler, director of the Middlevale Health Center, faced a decision. She had talked recently with Roger Rosenstein, an administrator in the State Health Department, who told her the State might be able to increase its support of the Center by $30,000. The additional funding could be used to increase the Center's activities in drug rehabilitation or alcoholic rehabilitation, but could not be split between the two. Ms. Knobler had to determine which of the two activities was more effective so she could write a proposal formally requesting the additional funds.

*This case was prepared by Charles T. Horngren and Paul E. Tebbets, Stanford University Graduate School of Business. Reprinted from Stanford Business Cases 1975 with the permission of the publishers, Stanford University Graduate School of Business, © 1975 by the Board of Trustees of the Leland Stanford Junior University.

The Center had recently hired a new controller, Paul Tebbets. Mr. Tebbets was familiar with program budgeting and financial reporting and had explained to Ms. Knobler some of the concepts behind it. It sounded like a useful tool and she hoped it would aid in analyzing which rehabilitation program produced the best results.

PROGRAM BUDGETING: PPBS

To learn how the Center might use program budgeting techniques, Ms. Knobler asked Mr. Tebbets to explain them in more detail. As an introduction, he told her that a program budgeting system appropriate for a small organization is actually a scaled down version of a concept known as Planning, Programming, and Budgeting System (PPBS) which had been experimented with extensively in the Federal government.

PPBS was first used in the Department of Defense in the early 1960s. It was instituted to allow the Secretary of Defense and others at a high level of command to analyze military activities in strategic terms. Questions could be asked such as how much of America's military resources should be devoted to defending the continental United States, achieving a first strike capability, etc. Previously, resource allocation questions had been approached in terms of division between the services: how much of the annual military budget should go to the Army, the Air Force, etc. Specific strategic questions were considered only within each of the services. As a result, a great deal of effort was duplicated and programs in one service often worked at cross purposes with programs in another.

PPBS worked well in the Defense Department for several reasons. First, outputs for DOD were definable and measurable: for instance, it was possible to calculate the likelihood of Russian weapons penetrating American defenses, or vice versa, under several policy alternatives. Second, there was commitment at the very top levels of DOD to use PPBS. Third, DOD had competent staff in an office close to the Secretariat level to perform the necessary analysis.

Recognizing the benefits of PPBS for DOD, President Johnson initiated implementation throughout the Federal government. Government agencies began defining programs and objectives, specifying quantitative output measures, and developing alternative methods for reaching each objective. Unfortunately, PPBS was unsuccessful in most agencies outside of DOD because the three factors mentioned in the preceding paragraph were usually missing. For example, the output of the Office of Education in HEW is to increase the educational level of the United States population. It was very difficult to relate it to a particular HEW program. In addition, top level bureaucrats in most agencies did not understand the potential usefulness of the PPBS; developing program budgets each year became for them merely an exercise in supplying the minimum amount of information required by the Office of Management and Budget.

In the early 1970s it was clear that PPBS had failed to gain widespread popularity in the Government. The principles behind it were still sound however, Mr. Tebbets told Ms. Knobler.

PROGRAM BUDGETING: FOR A
SMALL ORGANIZATION

Program budgeting is the term generally used for the more limited financial planning and analysis performed in smaller organizations using principles of PPBS. Neither PPBS nor program budgeting is a set prescription for setting up a financial system, but rather a philosophy or state of mind. In making plans for the future, an agency subscribing to the PPBS philosophy searches for plain statements of its purposes, alternative ways of achieving these purposes, and criteria for choosing between competing alternatives. One of the criteria usually considered is the cost of producing a unit amount of output. Not surprisingly, practical program budgeting systems borrow heavily from the concepts of cost accounting.

Mr. Tebbets explained to Ms. Knobler that in the past few years numerous nonprofit organizations have begun analyzing expenses by program. The American Institute of Certified Public Accountants has published an audit guide for voluntary health and welfare organizations requiring that financial statements be presented in terms of program activities or functions. However, many other types of organizations have also started using program concepts—whether simply for annual reporting or for more sophisticated budgeting, control or multi-year planning.

As with PPBS, program budgeting specifies no particular systems for analysis of accounting. Rather the director or controller subscribing to the program philosophy starts out by asking questions such as (1) What are the organization's objectives or goals? Program categories sometimes cut across organizational lines if two departments work together to reach the same goal. (2) How much does each program cost? Costs include identifiable direct labor and material, and an allocation of overhead using an appropriate method. (3) How is each program funded? The organization may receive funds earmarked specifically for one purpose. If other funds are used for the same purpose, it is helpful to know how much. Such knowledge can be useful in fund raising: a donor or funding source may donate money for a specific purpose even though he would not donate for general expenses. However, if an existing activity is paid for half with earmarked funds and half with general organizational funds, attracting a new chunk of money for the activity can free up the general funds for other purposes.

Whatever the specific system chosen, program budgeting in a small organization must be kept simple. A large government agency has staff to run a complex system but a small group does not. However, the net payoff from even a modest system can be great. In many groups the first reward is an understanding of the organization's goals. It is surprising how many nonprofit organizations have never clearly defined what they are set up to accomplish. A second reward is the ability to influence the course of future activity. Only after present goals are clarified can future goals be altered.

THE PROBLEM

Ms. Knobler was very interested in everything Mr. Tebbets had to say. She was surprised to find that accountants sometimes think in terms of philosophies and states of mind rather than just debits and credits. But perhaps more importantly, she felt that Mr. Tebbet's concepts would help the health center decide whether to seek increased funding for alcoholic or drug rehabilitation patients.

During the next two weeks Ms. Knobler and Mr. Tebbets outlined how they would develop a program budgeting system. First, for purposes of financial analysis they would divide the center's activities into four programs (1) Alcoholic Rehabilitation (counseling services); (2) Drug Rehabilitation (counseling present and former drug users) and clinical services for drug users; (3) Children's Clinical Services; and (4) After Care (counseling and support of patients after release from a mental hospital).

Ms. Knobler settled on "patients treated per year" as an output measure for the two rehabilitation programs. She would have preferred a more elegant measure to indicate long-run effectiveness, such as "patients cured" or "patients not requiring further treatment for two years," but the center did not have the resources to develop the necessary statistics. Ms. Knobler further decided "cost per patient per year" would be a helpful statistic in comparing the two rehabilitation programs. The Center's board and staff agreed that since the drug problem had become more acute in the past few years, if the "cost per patient per year" figures were equal, the drug program should receive any potential additional funding. However, if the cost per patient per year for the drug program was more than 20% higher than for the alcoholic program, the alcoholic program should receive the additional funding.

The Center's present line-item budget (simplified in Exhibit 1) showed total budgeted expenses but not how they related to the four activities of the Center. Ms. Knobler and Mr. Tebbets decided the costs by program could be determined only by asking each of the professional staff members (doctors, psychologists, nurses) the percentages of time he or she spent on each program. Costs for medical supplies would be allocated on the basis of physician's time per program: i.e., if 30% of total physician hours was spent in Children's Clinical Services, then 30% of medical supply expenses would be allocated to that program. General overhead (administrative expenses, rent, utilities, etc.) would be allocated on the basis of direct labor cost for each program (labor cost to include the time of doctors, psychologists, and nurses multiplied by the salary rate of each).

Mr. Tebbets had performed some quick calculations to obtain preliminary figures on cost per patient per year in each of the two rehabilita-

EXHIBIT 1
Summary of Budget for 1975
(all dollar figures in thousands)

Professional Salaries		
6 Physicians @ $37.5	$225	
19 Psychologists @ 25	475	
24 Nurses @ 12.5	300	$1,000
Medical Supplies		150
General Overhead		
Administrative salaries, rent, etc.		500
Total		$1,650

tion programs. He knew that on the average 30 patients were involved in the Alcoholic Rehabilitation program and that the average patient spent ½ year; thus he used 60 patients per year as the basis for calculation. The Drug Rehabilitation program saw an average of 40 patients at a time for an average of ½ year each so he used 80 patients per year as the basis for calculation. Each of these 80 received both counseling and clinical services. Based on the number of physicians, psychologists and nurses who were assigned to each program, the number of patients, and the medical supply and overhead allocation system described previously, cost per patient per year figures for the two rehabilitation programs were about equal. Mr. Tebbets knew, however, that more accurate figures required better estimates of staff time allocation, so he approached each of the doctors, psychologists, and nurses on the staff. Using the time allocation form shown in Exhibit 2, he gathered the statistics which are summarized in Exhibit 3.

Recalling some of his training in cost accounting, Mr. Tebbets set down on paper a summary of the procedures he planned to use in calculating the relative benefits of the two rehabilitaiton programs. The summary follows:

1. *Direct Labor Cost*—By program, list the number of professionals (physicians, psychologists, and nurses) as determined by the survey results in Exhibit 3. Multiply by the relevant salary of each. This yields direct cost. Treat Drug Rehabilitation Counseling and Drug Rehabilitation Clinical as separate programs until step 4.
2. *Allocation of Medical Supplies Cost*—Determine the percentage

EXHIBIT 2
Individual Time Allocation Form

1. Name of staff member

2. Occupation

3. Time spent in each program	Percentage
Alcoholic Rehabilitation	_____
Drug Rehabilitation	
Counseling	_____
Clinical	_____
Children's Clinical	_____
After Care	100%

EXHIBIT 3
Allocation of Professional Time between Programs
(compiled from individual time allocation forms)

Program	Number of Staff		
	Physicians	Psychologists	Nurses
1. Alcoholic Rehabilitation		6	4
2. Drug Rehabilitation			
a. Counseling		4	4
b. Clinical	2		2
3. Children's Clinical	4		4
4. After Care		9	10
Total	6	19	24

of total physician time dedicated to each program. Apply the percentage factor to the total cost of medical supplies for the Center. Add the appropriate dollar figure to each program.

3. *Allocation of Overhead Expenses*—For each program divide direct labor cost by the Center's total direct labor cost to find the percentage factors. Apply the percentage factor to the Center's total overhead expense to determine the amount allocated to each program.

4. *Unit Output Cost*—Add the costs of Counseling and Clinical to obtain total Drug Rehabilitation cost. Divide by patients treated per year to obtain cost per patient per year. Likewise divide cost for the Alcoholic Rehabilitation Program by patients treated per year.

5. *The Decision*—If the cost per patient per year for the Drug Rehabilitation program is more than 20% greater than for the Alcoholic Rehabilitation program, recommend to Ms. Knobler that she request additional funding for the Alcoholic Rehabilitation program; otherwise she should request funding for the Drug Rehabilitation program.

Note: Since the decision is not affected by Children's Clinic and After Care Program costs, it is unnecessary to determine their costs.

DISCUSSION QUESTIONS

1. Apply the Tebbets procedure in your analysis of the alternatives. What action should be recommended?
2. Would any other criterion for choice be more appealing to you if you were in Tebbet's position? In Knobler's position?

SEVEN

MARKETING*

All organizations engage in marketing whether they are aware of it or not. The difference between profit and nonprofit organizations is that the former know that they market and the latter—more often than not—do not know it. Yet consider the case of private universities: they search for prospective clients (students), develop their services and "products" (curricula, courses and faculty), distribute them (maintain facilities, let the clients know the time and place), promote the university (send out catalogues and other supporting literature), and announce the price (tuition, room, board, and fees). This example illustrates the four P's of marketing: develop the right *product*, provide the right *promotion*, and put it in the right *place*, at the right *price*. Similar examples could be drawn from the health care industry or any other nonprofit organization.

Although all such organizations do market, and always have, the concept of marketing frequently smacks to them of crass commercialism—pushing sales. Nonprofit organizations don't like to think of themselves as "pushing" their products or services and therefore their marketing efforts have generally been unsophisticated (lacking coordination, originality, and scope).

Marketing as a function took a back seat to other functions in nonprofit organizations until recently, because the major nonprofit sectors—

*This note was written by Professor Leslie E. Grayson, The Colgate Darden Graduate School of Business Administration, University of Virginia. Copyright © 1981 by the University of Virginia Graduate Business School Sponsors.

education and health care—were both in periods of rapid growth. As the 1980s arrived however, the growth rate in number of clients (students and patients) declined, particularly relative to the overbuilt facilities of the 1960s and 1970s, and funds also declined because of the sluggish economy. At that point, universities and hospitals began to try and develop more sophisticated marketing concepts and techniques than they had found necessary in the past. It should be noted that churches, museums, and orchestras, among others, had been feeling the client and financial pinch all along. Such organizations must contend with constantly changing attitudes and needs of society and continuing private (as well as growing public) competition for potential members', or audiences', energy, time, and funds.

Nonprofit organizations' search for appropriate marketing techniques could benefit from an understanding of certain useful marketing concepts. Marketing is not simply advertising, it is not public relations, and it is not selling bits and pieces of the organization or product. The purpose of marketing is to gain access to the various publics of the nonprofit institution. In the private university example, the purpose would be to attract students who will meet the university's criteria, on the one hand, and faculty to provide the services, and funds to finance the operation, on the other. These three groups are the university's principal markets. They are distinct markets and must be approached differently, but the total marketing effort must be coordinated among all of them.

A key to understanding marketing in nonprofit organizations is to view the markets in which the organizations operate as a competitive one. In that sense, little difference is found between the profit and nonprofit sectors. Many universities compete for bright students and many galleries and museums compete for funds. The first marketing step, therefore—as in the private sector—is an environmental analysis: discovering who the potential "consumers" are and what is the competition. For instance, in the case of a private university, such analysis would have to consider the number of high school graduates and the portion of them who are likely to attend four-year colleges. The private university is not competing for all these students, however. The total market must be segmented so that marketing efforts can focus on the most likely consumer. The environmental analysis must attempt to discover what portion of college-bound students might attend a private university (in the face of rising tuitions and, frequently, improved public higher education) and what the competition is for that segment.

Having identified potential consumers and competitors through market segmentation, the private university's next step is to create a strongly differentiated, if not unique, product to appeal to the chosen market segment. One nationally ranked private graduate business school, for example, decided to compete within its market segment by educating generalists for the world of practical affairs *via* the case method of instruction with heavy emphasis on required courses in a functionally integrated program. This focus allowed the school to differentiate its product from that of, say, a school emphasizing theory and quantitative methods.

It is, of course, not enough to describe the market segment and the strategy for competing within that segment. Marketing includes a concerted effort to design services so as to support the differentiated product. In the case-method school above, for example, the "right" kind of faculty must be assembled, which in turn requires a marketing effort. Projected demand for graduates of a case-method school must be forecast and publicized. The school must get the "right" kind of students to apply and, once admitted, matriculate. Price (i.e., tuition and fees) must be decided. The satisfaction of graduates (starting salaries and recruitment efforts) must be tailored to the market segment and made known to the potential students.

Market segmentation also needs to be done for the purpose of attracting resources. Fund-raising in nonprofit organizations has been approached with more sophistication in the past than has marketing to clients. A great deal of data is available on potential donors to nonprofit organizations; for instance, important segments of donors are single persons and people over 70. What is frequently missing from these data is an analysis of motivations for giving (and nongiving). The organization needs to discover who are its best potential donors—its market segment. For example, what kinds of people are likely to give to a case-method school? Once the segment is chosen, school services—regular curricula or executive education programs—can be designed to increase, not only revenues, but endowment. Marketing can assist in motivating donors within the market segment to give by informing them specifically as to how their funds are going to be used.

Attracting clients and resources in nonprofit organizations would be aided by answering the fundamental marketing question "What is our distinctive mission?" This question is no different from that commonly asked in the profit sector: "What business are we in?" As in the profit sector, the answers lie in environmental analysis, market segmentation, and a consistent, coordinated approach to promotion and pricing.

Case 16

Tuesday Evening Concert Series*

Because of the rapid increase in artists' fees, the Board of Directors of the Tuesday Evening Concert Series (TECS) was considering increasing the price of season memberships for the 1974-1975 season. Besides three pricing proposals before the Board, there were also three policy decisions under consideration:

1. What caliber of artist should TECS contract?
2. How can the Series best be promoted?
3. How often should ticket prices be raised?

BACKGROUND INFORMATION

The Tuesday Evening Concert Series was a nonprofit organization founded in 1948 and affiliated with the University of Virginia. According to its constitution, "The purpose of the Tuesday Evening Concert

*This case was prepared by Thomas A. Bubier and William P.H. Cary under the supervision of Professor Leslie E. Grayson of the University of Virginia. Copyright © 1973 by the Univeristy of Virginia Graduate Business School Sponsors.

Series is to make available to the general public, including students, faculty and local residents, a nonprofit series of musical events designed to enrich the cultural life of the community." The operating philosophy of the TECS was to provide a variety of chamber music (music for soloists or small ensembles), excellently performed at relatively inexpensive prices.

The Series itself consisted of eight concerts performed on Tuesday evenings in the period from October to April. The University provided the use of Cabell Hall (seating capacity 1,000) for the concerts at no charge. Admission to the concerts was, for the most part, restricted to season ticket holders of the TECS. Season memberships in the 1973-74 Series were priced at $9 for students and $12 for regular members and entitled the holder to a nonreserved seat in Cabell Hall.

The TECS was run by a volunteer Board of Directors consisting of ten student members and sixteen nonstudent members (mostly faculty and wives of faculty). Ernest Mead, Chairman of the Music Department, and Vincent Shea, the connoisseur Financial Vice President of the University, were *ex officio* members of the Board. According to the bylaws, the president of the Series must be a student. Although the Board had the final say in the selection of performers, Mrs. John Forbes had handled all the actual booking of the artists for the last 12 years, with the support of the Program Committee. The programs were presented to the TECS' Executive Committee and Messrs. Mead and Shea. Before the final program decision was made, the Board of Directors' approval was sought.

COST INFORMATION

The major operating expense of the Series was the cost of the artists who performed at the eight concerts. Historically, artists' fees accounted for approximately 87 percent of the Series' expenses; programs, advertising, printing and receptions comprised most of the remainder.

The artists were usually contracted a year or more in advance through their booking agencies which handled the transportation and negotiated the performance fees. The great majority of artists gave their agency an "asking price" which was then subject to negotiation with interested parties. The amount of flexibility in the asking price varied from artist to artist. In general, the greater the reputation of the performer, the firmer the asking price was likely to be.

Chapter 7

As Exhibit 1 illustrates, artists' fees for the eight concerts increased considerably in recent years. The overall increase from the 1966-1967 season to the 1973-1974 season was 54 percent. For the last four years, artists' fees increased at slightly less than 10 percent per year.

In the past seven years, nine artists or groups of artists appeared more than once. The prices for which they appeared are outlined in Exhibit 2. Since several of these performers continued to appear at considerably reduced fees, Exhibit 2 probably understates the degree to which artists' fees increased in recent years. For comparison purposes, Exhibit 3 provides some additional measures of general price trends in the 1966-1973 period.

A number of factors influenced the final price at which an artist or group of artists appeared for the TECS. The Tuesday restriction on performance dates tended to limit the negotiating position of the TECS vis-a-vis a booking agent who was trying to fit his client into a crowded schedule of concerts. Similarly, the proximity of Charlottesville to the artists' adjoining concerts had a bearing on the price charged. A pianist who was performing in Washington or Richmond on Wednesday would normally come at a lesser fee than if he were playing in St. Louis the next day.

Another factor which operated to reduce costs for the TECS was the booking of performers in a "package" from one agency. In past years the Series has dealt with two or three major New York agencies for the majority of its concerts. Thus, in the 1973-1974 season, for example, a package of four performers was bought for $7,000, a considerable saving over the sum of the artists' individual prices.

The nature of the Series itself enabled it to attract performers of outstanding ability within its limited budget. Because of the reputation of

EXHIBIT 1
Total Artists' Fees for Eight Programs

Season	Artists' Fees	% Change over Previous Season
1966-1967	$ 8,200	+ 30.2%
1967-1968	7,980	− 2.7%
1968-1969	8,175	+ 2.4%
1969-1970	8,954	+ 9.5%
1970-1971	9,800	+ 9.4%
1971-1972	10,700	+ 9.2%
1972-1973	11,600	+ 8.4%
1973-1974	12,600	+ 8.6%

EXHIBIT 2

Fees Paid to TECS Performers Who Appeared More Than One Time

	1966	1967	1968	1969	1970	1971	1972	1973
Rampal and Veyron-Lacroix[1]		$ 700		$ 700				$1500
Peter Frankel			$1500	1500				
Janos Starker		1100				$2000		
The Marlboro Trio					$ 800		$ 900	
Festival Winds[2]				1400				1350[3]
The Early Music Quartet			750			1100		
The New Cleveland Quartet[2]						950		1250
The Juilliard String Quartet	$1000		1700		2000			
The Hungarian String Quartet[2]					1100		1300	1250[3]

[1] Appeared in the 1972-73 season.
[2] Booked to appear in the 1973-74 season.
[3] Part of a four concert "package" from one agency.

335

EXHIBIT 3
Selected Price Trends, 1966-1973

	1966	1967	1968	1969	1970	1971	1972	1973	% Increase (1966-1973)
Consumer Price Index:									
All Items	97.2	100.0	104.2	109.8	116.3	121.3	125.3	132.7[1]	36.5%
All Services	95.8	100.0	105.2	112.5	121.6	128.4	133.3	138.4[1]	44.5%
Out-of-State Under-Graduate Tuition at UVA	$1037	$1037	$1042	$1057	$1214	$1217	$1374	$1447	39.5%
Regular Membership (TECS)	$ 10	$ 10	$ 10	$ 10	$ 10	$ 12	$ 12	$ 12	20.0%
Student Membership (TECS)	$ 7.50	$ 7.50	$ 7.50	$ 7.50	$ 7.50	$ 9	$ 9	$ 9	20.0%

[1] July

the TECS as a discerning and discriminating series, various artists had performed at reduced rates. Furthermore, many outstanding performers were so impressed by the hall's excellent acoustics, the audience, and University in general that they were willing to appear again at reduced fees. These good relations between agents, artists, and TECS were largely due to the efforts of Mrs. Forbes as Chairman of the Program Committee and the Committee itself.

REVENUE INFORMATION

Historically, season memberships accounted for about 83 percent of total revenue. Exhibit 4 illustrates the change in season memberships from 1966-1973, while Exhibit 5 provides total revenue figures over the same period. Although both the regular and student memberships fluctuated, the number of student memberships sold had been particularly volatile in recent years. Of the last five seasons, four were sellouts. A particularly successful season was often due—at least in part— to an active membership chairman.

In addition to the revenue derived from the sale of season memberships, the TECS also generated revenue from a number of other sources. In 1972-1973 eighteen sponsor memberships were sold at $36 each. These memberships consisted of two season tickets for the sponsor and a third which went into a pool of tickets available free to local high school students. Sponsor memberships were sold largely to local businesses.

A total of $598 was generated through the sale of memberships to the second half of the 1972-1973 Series. Other sources of revenue included ticket sales at the door (only when season tickets were sold out: $94 in 1972-1973), interest on savings deposits, and the McIntire Fund. After each season the McIntire Fund gave the TECS a subsidy according to the following formula: the difference between the regular membership price and student membership price ($3 in 1972-1973), multiplied by the number of student members, up to a maximum of $1,000.

TECS also received an indirect subsidy from Mrs. Forbes. The job of Program Committee Chairman was about half-time, and a person qualified to replace her could have expected anywhere from $5,000-$7,500. She also spent (without reimbursement) about $100/year on long distance phone calls and $250 for a once-a-year concert managers' convention in New York City. She had just been elected to another three year

EXHIBIT 4
Season Memberships (Capacity 1000)

Season	Regular	% Change over Previous Season	Student	% Change over Previous Season	Total	% Change over Previous Season
1966-1967	634	− 1.1%	328	+ 2.8%	962	+ 0.2%
1967-1968	561	− 11.5%	230	− 29.9%	791	− 17.8%
1968-1969	687	+ 22.5%	349	+ 51.7%	1036	+ 31.0%
1969-1970	725	+ 5.5%	320	− 8.3%	1045	+ 0.9%
1970-1971	628	− 13.4%	274	− 14.4%	902	+ 13.7%
1971-1972	731	+ 16.4%	335	+ 22.3%	1066	+ 18.2%
1972-1973	688	− 5.9%	349	+ 4.2%	1037	− 2.7%

EXHIBIT 5
Total Ticket Revenue

Season	Total Ticket Revenue[1]	% Change over Previous Season
1966-1967[2]	$ 9,916	+ 49.2%
1967-1968	8,162	−17.7%
1968-1969	11,072	+ 35.7%
1969-1970	11,499	+ 3.9%
1970-1971	9,782	− 17.6%
1971-1972[2]	13,562	+ 38.6%
1972-1973	13,815[3]	+ 1.9%

[1] Total income minus interest on savings deposits.
[2] Ticket prices increased.
[3] First year in which tickets were sold for the second half of the Series and individual tickets at the door.

term (1973-76) as Program Committee Chairman. Assuming that she might be reelected in 1976, she would be unable, for personal reasons, to continue to serve in this capacity beyond 1979.

MARKET

Exhibit 6 gives some indication of the market for TECS members in recent years. Clearly, the potential demand for Series tickets within the University community had increased very rapidly since 1966.

In addition to increasing ticket prices, the TECS took several other steps to increase total revenue. For instance, in recent years TECS oversold the concerts by about 100 seats. Because some members only attended a few of the eight concerts, there were always a certain number of empty seats at any given performance. A head count of empty seats conducted in the Fall of 1972 revealed that, on the average, about 125 seats were unoccupied during the first four concerts. Consequently, the Series now attempted to sell roughly 1,100 memberships and had increased the target to 1,200 for next year.

A second related course of action the TECS adopted in 1972-73 was the sale of memberships for the second half of the Series. After counting the average number of empty seats at the first four concerts, the Series then attempted to sell half season memberships at $8 for regular mem-

EXHIBIT 6
University Population

Year	UVA Student Body	UVA Faculty & Staff
1966	7,873	766
1967	8,597	867
1968	9,011	1,015
1969	9,735	1,155
1970	10,852	1,200
1971	12,351	1,260
1972	12,907	1,404
1973 estimate	13,500	1,524
% Change 1966-1973	+ 71.5%	+ 96.4%

SOURCE: Office of Institutional Analysis

bers and $6 for students. In other words, the Series was oversold twice: once at the beginning of the season and once midway through the season. In the event that more than 1,000 people appeared at Cabell Hall, approximately 40 folding chairs could be set up in the aisles to accomodate the overflow.

Finally, the Board of Directors recently passed a resolution allowing the solicitation of charitable contributions. Although the Board did not wish to actively promote contributions, there would be a notice on the 1973-74 ticket order form to the effect that tax-deductible contributions would be accepted.

POLICY AND PRICING DECISIONS

At recent Board meetings a number of policies central to the ticket pricing problem were discussed. There was some disagreement as to which policies TECS should adopt, and it was recognized that, at the next Board meeting, these differences would have to be settled before the pricing decision could be made.

First, there was the question of what caliber of artists TECS should bring to Charlottesville. While everyone agreed that the quality of the performances was good, some felt that it should be "great" ("it is great only ¼-½ of the time now"). Those who advocated upgrading the quality of the Series pointed out that the masters drew SRO crowds, while other performers did not fill the hall. In the Fall of 1973, the maximum fee for one artist or one group was $2,000; one proposal was to raise this to $3,500 for two of the eight concerts. Another proposal was to abandon the fixed maximum fee altogether and adopt a total fixed budget of $20,000, allowing TECS occasionally to present those elite artists who charged upwards of $5,000. Both proposals recognized that, since membership could not be increased significantly, a price increase would be necessary. Opponents of the proposals were skeptical that the Charlottesville audience would be willing to pay the price necessary to attract artists of substantially higher caliber than those presently available. They also argued that some members enjoyed the highly experimental nature of some of the programming, the ambience of the concerts, and that it was possible to enjoy an evening of fine music, competently—but not "greatly"—played, in an attractive setting.

Related to the issue of quality was the question of promotion. Some Board members felt that low prices arouse suspicion about the quality of the product, whereas high prices increase the perceived value. In fact, when prices were raised in 1966 and again in 1971, season memberships also increased (Exhibit 4). It was further argued that increased prices would enable TECS to book "big names," and that this would be a promotional benefit. Opponents of this strategy pointed out that, with the present level quality, the Series had sold out four of the last five years.

An important consideration in directing promotional efforts efficiently was the ratio of student memberships to regular memberships. With the present price differential of $3, the first 333 student memberships actually brought in the full $12 because of the McIntire Fund subsidy. Each student membership over 333, however, generated $3 less in revenue than a regular membership. Furthermore, if the differential between regular and student prices increased, it would become financially desirable to have fewer student members.

A final recommendation for promoting TECS involved establishing better communications between the Board and the members via meetings and/or newsletters. It was argued that increased communication would stimulate interest and involvement.

Many of these policy proposals entailed an increase in ticket prices, and the Board members recognized the necessity of occasionally raising prices. However, there was disagreement on how often prices should be raised. Frequent price increases may antagonize the membership, even though inflation of artist fees may justify it. Long periods without increases could be damaging in two ways: revenue is lost while costs are rising, and a momentum is established, making it even more difficult to raise prices later. One proposal offered to the Board advocated not increasing the price more frequently than every three years. Other members felt that prices should be raised whenever necessary to effect the Board's plans and policies for the coming season.

After the Board settled these matters of policy, a decision would have to be made concerning ticket prices for the 1974-1975 season (tickets for 1973-1974 were already on sale). There were three proposals before the Board:

	Student Membership	Regular Membership
Present prices	$ 9	$12
Proposal I	13	16
Proposal II	9	24
Proposal III	15	20

Proposal I was intended only to keep pace with inflation, and would not permit upgrading of the Series.

Proposal II was suggested specifically to allow for two "special" concerts per year, at which artists presently out of TECS's price range would appear.

Proposal III was advocated as a means of financing a significant increase in the quality of the Series.

Prices which are "comparable" to the TECS tickets are:

Present prices, regular membership	$1.50
Proposal I prices, regular membership[1]	2.00
Price of movie in Charlottesville	2.00
American Film Theater Series[2]	3.75
Carnegie Hall, cheapest ticket	3.00
Kennedy Center, cheapest ticket	3.00

The three proposals had unequal following among the Board members. The Board had to make a pricing decision in the early Fall of 1973 as the Program Committee needed to know what the budget would be for the 1974-1975 season. Artists were booked a year in advance.

---

[1] Same calculation can be made for Proposals II and III.
[2] Eight Enchanted Evenings, Series Cost—$30. Available in Charlottesville.

Case 17

University Arts Program*

In late March 1975, Andre Williams, Director of Mardi Gras University's Office of Public Events, was trying to determine the scope and policies of the University Arts Program for the next academic year (1975-76). He had just reviewed two persuasive reports. One, a consultant's report (Appendix 1), suggested reducing the number of performances by one-third and increasing the average ticket price by $1.00 in order to come closer to the Program's goal of breaking even. The other, prepared by a student intern (Appendix 2), advocated a policy of audience expansion, which would require Mr. Williams to develop special programs to achieve the desired increase in audience size. In designing the Program for 1975-76, Mr. Williams intended to consider carefully these two reports, which conflicted in a number of areas.

During the course of its 1974-75 season, the University Arts Program was scheduled to present 31 performers or groups in 42 performances

*This case was written by Patrick Hanemann and Professor Charles B. Weinberg, University of British Columbia, as the basis for class discussion. It is not intended to illustrate either effective or ineffective handling of an administrative situation. The assistance of Assistant Professor Christopher H. Lovelock, Harvard Business School, is gratefully acknowledged. Reprinted from *Stanford Business Cases 1975* with the permission of the publishers, Stanford University Graduate School of Business, © 1975 by the Board of Trustees of the Leland Stanford Junior University.

EXHIBIT 1
Ticket Sales by Category, First Six Months 1974-75

	Performing Group	Reserve	Student Discount	Student Rush	Group	Season	Special Series	Total Seats Sold
1	Inner City I	80	75	116	0	14	15	300
2	Inner City II	152	139	203	0	30	45	569
3	New York Chamber Soloists I	121	34	60	0	48	18	281
4	New York Chamber Soloists II	108	25	42	0	18	13	206
5	Gustav Leonhardl	81	44	84	0	20	15	244
6	Modern Jazz Quartet	393	380	202	0	54	30	1,059
7	Gary Graffman	208	75	172	0	40	16	511
8	Les Menstriers	243	158	168	0	62	63	694
9	Siobhan McKenna	473	167	0	0	72	22	734
10	Harkness Ballet	863	547	70	0	59	60	1,599
11	Emlyn Williams	187	54	72	0	68	22	403
12	Ely Ameling I	185	29	41	0	25	15	295
13	Ely Ameling II	312	60	90	0	50	19	531
14	Dorothy Stickney	199	18	49	0	36	23	325
15	Lotte Goslar Troupe I	70	25	27	0	18	12	152
16	Lotte Goslar Troupe II	109	121	106	0	59	49	444
17	Lotte Goslar Troupe III	210	305	9	0	—	—	524
18	Speculum Musicae	34	7	43	0	23	10	117
19	Anthony Newman	85	78	101	0	44	10	318
20	Secolo Baroco	148	58	69	25	64	62	426
21	I Musici	445	165	69	30	99	33	841
22	Jacob Lateiner	182	42	94	0	31	15	364
23	Repertory Dance Theatre I	98	81	89	0	40	37	345
24	Repertory Dance Theatre II	80	132	29	0	0	0	241
25	Repertory Dance Theatre III	112	38	78	0	39	23	290
26	P.D.Q. Bach	697	652	134	70	63	32	1,648
27	Music from Marlboro	97	14	14	0	56	27	208
	Totals	5,972	3,523	2,201	125	1,132	686	13,669
	Percent of Audience	44%	26%	16%	1%	8%	5%	100%
	Total Attendance	14,383						

EXHIBIT 2

Ticket Revenues by Category, First Six Months, 1974-75

	Performing Group	Reserve	Student Discount	Student Rush	Group	Season	Special Series
1	Inner City I	$ 319.00	211.00	232.75		49.84	49.80
2	Inner City II	619.00	421.00	408.25		107.37	141.40
3	New York Chamber Soloists I	544.50	127.50	120.00		162.24	56.70
4	New York Chamber Soloists II	486.00	93.75	84.00		60.84	40.95
5	Gustav Leonhardl	364.50	165.00	168.00		67.60	47.25
6	Modern Jazz Quartet	1,568.75	1,170.00	406.25		192.24	102.80
7	Gary Graffman	936.00	281.25	344.00		135.20	50.40
8	Les Menstriers	1,093.50	592.50	336.00		209.56	226.80
9	Siobhan McKenna	2,128.50	626.25	—		243.36	79.20
10	Harkness Ballet	3,486.25	1,479.00	140.00		211.94	192.00
11	Emlyn Williams	841.50	202.50	144.00		229.84	79.20
12	Ely Ameling I	832.50	108.75	82.00		84.50	47.25
13	Ely Ameling II	1,404.00	225.00	180.00		169.00	59.85
14	Dorothy Stickney	895.50	67.50	98.00		121.68	82.80
15	Lotte Goslar Troupe I	297.50	92.00	54.00		64.08	40.80
16	Lotte Goslar Troupe II	451.75	368.00	229.25		211.94	153.40
17	Lotte Goslar Troupe III	683.00	729.25	18.00		—	—
18	Speculum Musicae	153.00	26.25	86.00		77.74	31.50
19	Anthony Newman	382.50	292.50	202.00		148.72	31.50
20	Secolo Baroco	666.00	217.50	138.00	90.00	216.32	195.30
21	I Musici	1,844.75	484.00	144.75	90.00	352.44	103.95
22	Jacob Lateiner	819.00	157.50	188.00		104.78	47.25
23	Repertory Dance Theatre I	408.50	263.00	178.00		143.54	118.20
24	Repertory Dance Theatre II	236.00	224.00	58.00		—	—
25	Repertory Dance Theatre III	458.00	112.00	156.00		113.12	75.40
26	P.D.Q. Bach	2,667.75	1,811.00	268.00	266.00	224.28	110.40
27	Music from Marlboro	400.50	48.50	28.00		189.28	85.05
	Totals	24,987.75	10,596.50	4,491.25	446.00	3,891.45	2,249.15
	Percent of Revenue	53%	23%	10%	1%	8%	5%
	Total Receipts	$46,662.10					

of classical music, theatre and dance. Twenty-seven of these performances were given during the first six months of the season. Seating capacity for these performances was 32,783; total attendance was 14,383, or approximately 44 percent of capacity (see Exhibit 1). Expenses amounted to $84,000, while income on ticket sales totaled $46,700 (see Exhibit 2). Grants from the National Endowment for the Arts increased this figure to $52,500, leaving a net deficit of $31,500. Mr. Williams expected that the deficit for the entire season would approximate $50,000. Any losses incurred by the Program were underwritten by the University, which did not require the Program to make a profit. However, a deficit of this magnitude would not be tolerated on a continuing basis. (See Exhibit 3 for results of previous years.)

THE UNIVERSITY

Founded in 1885, Mardi Gras University was a private coeducational institution located in New Orleans, Louisiana. During the 1974-75 academic year, the University had enrolled approximately 6,500 undergraduates and 5,000 graduate students. There were 1,100 faculty members and 5,900 staff members. A high proportion of the students and faculty lived on campus. Most others lived in neighboring communities.

While Mardi Gras was a leading private university in the area, there were numerous other colleges and universities in this metropolitan region, which had a total population of approximately 1.5 million. Other private institutions included Tulane Univeristy, Sophie Newcomb College, Loyola University, and Holy Cross College. The University of New Orleans and Southern University of New Orleans were also located in town. There were also two so-called "black" colleges, Xavier and Dillard.

Mardi Gras University was located on an attractively landscaped, 700-acre campus in Chartrain, a suburb of New Orleans some ten miles from the city center. The University was quite well served by major highways but public transportation services to the campus ceased at 7 p.m. on weekdays.

THE PERFORMING ARTS IN NEW ORLEANS

Cultural offerings in the New Orleans area took several forms. The New Orleans Opera House Association had a six-week season each year

EXHIBIT 3
Results of Previous Years

	Number of Performances	Capacity	Audience	Audience as % of Capacity	Students as % of Audience
1972-1973 Season	20	25,972	14,726	56.7%	36.8%
1973-1974 Season	26	39,602	20,133	50.8%	39.1%
Fall 1974	10	16,132	8,492	52.6%	39.3%
Fall 1974[1]	9	10,132	7,448	73.5%	36.2%
Winter 1974	8	16,132	8,542	53.0%	NA
Spring 1974[2]	8	7,338	3,099	42.2%	35.6%
1974-1975 Season					
First 27 Performances	27	32,783	14,383	44.0%	42.0%

[1] The first performance of the year was the Utah Symphony in the 6,000 seat Amphitheater which was attended by 1,044. This row excludes that performance.

[2] There was considerable student unrest on campus during the spring concerning the denial of tenure to three popular faculty members.

at the 2300-seat New Orleans Theatre of the Performing Arts, while the New Orleans Philharmonic Symphony Orchestra performed during a 38-week season at the same location. Other permanent offerings included a year-round season at the 350-seat Beverly Dinner Playhouse and Black drama at the 120-seat Free Southern Theatre. Visiting performing arts companies often used the facilities at New Orleans' Municipal Auditorium and Rivergate Convention Center. Additional cultural events included those sponsored by other colleges and universities in the New Orleans area, although none of these institutions offered as extensive an arts program as that of Mardi Gras University.

THE PROGRAM

As Director of Mardi Gras's Office of Public Events, Andre Williams was responsible for administration of the University Arts Program. He had set a number of objectives for the Program, although he had not weighted them in terms of importance. Among these, Mr. Williams included the following:

- Present a self-supporting series of top-quality professional performing events.
- Keep prices as low as possible in order to make performances widely accessible.
- Augment academic offerings in the theory and practice of the arts.
- Contribute positively to the extracurricular educational experience of the Mardi Gras students.
- Contribute to the University's position within the New Orleans community as a cultural and intellectual resource.
- Contribute to Mardi Gras's national and international prestige by presenting a program qualitatively commensurate with other offerings of the University.
- Help solidify the importance of the arts in social development and, hopefully, to thereby insure the future of the arts.

In addition, Mr. Williams had exclusive responsibility for artist selection and scheduling. Of the first 27 performances offered during 1974-75, there were 13 performances of instrumental music, 9 of dance, 3 of drama, and 2 of vocal music.

Offerings covered a broad spectrum of the classical repertoire and featured some of the finest touring artists of the United States and Europe. Fourteen performances were held in Lafitte Auditorium, an 820-seat concert hall at the center of campus. Twelve performances were given in Memorial Hall, a 1,694-seat multi-purpose facility which also served the University as a lecture hall and convocation center. The remaining performance was presented off-campus in the 975-seat auditorium of a high school.

Other facilities on campus which were often used for theatrical and musical performances included the University Church (1,000 seats), Rittle Theater (192 seats), and the Amphitheater (capacity 6,000 persons).

PROMOTIONAL ACTIVITIES

The Program was advertised in three major ways: (1) direct mailing, (2) newspaper advertising, and (3) posters and flyers.

The direct mailing consisted of the University Arts brochure, a 32-page booklet featuring pictures and brief descriptions of the season's offerings, together with ticket information and a presentation of the programs scheduled by the Music and Theatre Departments of the University. Thirty thousand copies of the brochure were produced. Of these, 20,000 were distributed at the beginning of the fall quarter according to a mailing list, with additional copies available upon request. The 20,000 figure included 12,000 locally-based supporters of the Program and 8,000 Mardi Gras alumni who were selected on the basis of their proximity to the University. This alumni mailing excluded those living in New Orleans, however, because it was felt that interested alumni in the immediate vicinity of the University would learn of the Program through local newspaper advertising. The list had been compiled from a number of different sources over the past several years, and efforts had been made during the summer of 1974 to eliminate duplications. Mr. Williams conceded, however, that he had no way of determining the impact of the brochure on Program attendance levels, nor indeed any way of knowing what percentage of names on the list were still in the area or had any interest in receiving the brochure. In addition to this mailing, which generally went to nonstudents, there was an on-campus distrubution of "The Season," a listing of the year's performance schedule.

Over the first six months of the season, costs for the brochure amounted to $2,200 (allocated on a performance basis for twenty-seven of the scheduled forty-two performances), with The Season and the Winter Almanac accounting for an additional $213. Including mailing expenses (approximately $540), the costs of the direct mail promotion for the six-month period totaled $2,950, or 24 percent of the total promotional budget for this period.

A second element of promotional activity, newspaper and publication advertising, accounted for 62 percent of the period's advertising budget, and was distributed as follows:

The Times Picayune	$2,460
New Orleans States-Item	2,420
Mardi Gras Daily	1,028
Clarion Herald	814
Alumni Almanac	728
Student Life	54
Total	$7,504

With the exception of the Student Life, where advertising appeared only quarterly in the form of a listing of the quarter's events, newspaper advertising copy was fairly uniform, consisting of the University Arts logo and a brief description of each of the events scheduled over the next few days, together with relevant information regarding time, place and ticket prices (see Exhibit 4).

The third area of promotional activity, constituting 14 percent of the period budget, was devoted to posters, flyers and "table tents." Posters were used both on-campus (on kiosks, bulletin boards and at the Jackson box office) and off-campus (at remote Ticketron outlets and in heavily-traveled, consumer-oriented areas such as the shopping center). Flyers were generally used for student distribution, and "table tents" were displayed on tables in the Jackson Union and in the dining rooms of campus housing facilities.

PRICING

Standard prices for reserved seating generally were $4.75, $3.75 and $2.75 in Memorial Hall, and $4.50 in Lafitte Auditorium. A discount of $.75 per reserved ticket was offered to all under 18 years of age and to

EXHIBIT 4
Sample Newspaper Advertising, Spring 1975

THE ARTS AT MARDI GRAS UNIVERSITY

TONIGHT	THE	*EARLY MUSIC SERIES*
8:00 p.m.	NEW	The liturgical drama
University	YORK	of the Spanish Ren-
Church	PRO	aissance Mass "Missa
	MUSICA	Ave, Maris Stella"

by Cristobal de Morales will be magically recreated *in Mardi Gra's University Church as* part of the Pro Musica's last concert. *TICKETS: $4.75, 3.75, 2.75/students $4, 3, 2 (Student Rush, if available, $2).*

TONIGHT	THE	*DRAMA DEPART-*
8:00 p.m.	ARCHI-	*MENT PRODUC-*
MAY 8-12	TECT &	*TIONS*
& 15-19	THE	A brilliant, inventive
6 midnight	EMPEROR	and exhilarating ex-
perfs. Rittle	OF	perience in "the the-
Theater	ASSYRIA	atre of panic."
	by	**EXTRA MIDNIGHT**
	ARRABAL	**PERFORMANCES:**

May 10, 11, 12 and 17, 18, 19. *TICKETS: AT DOOR ONLY 7:30 p.m. & 11:30 p.m.* PRICES: $2/students $1.00. TIME: 8:00 p.m. and midnight.

8:00 p.m.	THE	*MUSIC DEPART-*
Saturday	Mardi Gras	*MENT SERIES*
MAY 12	GLEE	A happy musical
Lafitte	CLUB	revue of show tunes,
Auditorium	Robert	popular songs, and
	MacKinnon	folk music, featur-
	Director	ing the Axidentals.

TICKETS: $2.00/students $1.00.

Tickets at Jackson Box Office, Maison Blanche Box Office and all area TICKETRON agencies. By mail send s.a. envelope with check or money order payable to Jackson Box Office, Mardi Gras University. Phone 321-2300, X4317. Discount tickets available at Jackson Box Office only.

THE ARTS AT MARDI GRAS UNIVERSITY

LAST WEEK	THE	*DRAMA DE-*
8:00 p.m.	ARCHI-	*PARTMENT PRO-*
MAY 15-19	AND THE	*DUCTIONS*
3 Midnight	EMPEROR	A brilliant, inventive
perfs.	OF	and exhilarating ex-
Rittle	ASSYRIA	perience in "the
Theater	*by*	theater of panic."
	ARRABAL	**EXTRA MID-**

NIGHT PERFORM-ANCES: May 17, 18 & 19. *TICKETS: AT DOOR ONLY 7:30 p.m. 11:30 p.m.* PRICES: $2/students $1. TIME: 8 p.m. and midnight.

8:00 p.m.	THE	"Bouyant ensemble
Saturday	NEW	playing and vibrant
MAY 19	YORK	solo work" by Paula
Lafitte	CAMER-	Hatcher, Charles
Auditorium	ATA	Forbes and Glenn

Jacobson of the New York Camerata will ensure an evening of artistic excellence. Program: Boismorter. Trio Sonata in E minor. Op. 37, No. 2, for flute, viola da gamba and contindo: Bach. Suite in G for solo cello. Handel, Flute Sonata; Scarlatti, Music of the English Renaissance for recorders and harpsichord. Two Sonatas for harpsichord: Rameau. *TICKETS: $4.50/students $3.75. (Student Rush, if available, $2).*

Tickets at Jackson Box Office, Maison Blanche Box Office and all area TICKETRON agencies. By mail send s.a. envelope with check or money order payable to Jackson Box Office, Mardi Gras University. Phone 321-2300, X4317. Discount tickets available at Jackson Box Office only.

anyone who held a current student body card. Student rush tickets were sold, at a price of $2.00 per ticket, for all seats which were still available fifteen minutes prior to scheduled curtain time. A discount of 20 percent was offered to groups of twenty or more people attending the same performance. In addition, there were seven separate series ticket plans. The "Choose Your Own" plan enabled the patron to select any ten performances during the year at a savings of 23 percent to 28 percent off the individual ticket prices. The remaining six series—Dance, Theatre, Keyboard, Early Music, Connoisseur and Celebrity—provided discounts ranging from 20 percent to 30 percent on particular groupings of performances.

CONSULTANT REPORT

In response to the increasing deficit which developed during the course of the year, Mr. Williams requested in February of 1975 that the Management Studies Office, an in-house Mardi Gras consulting group, examine the Program's operations and make recommendations for improvement. After conducting a breakeven analysis on the Program's revenue and expense data for the first six months of the 1975-76 season, Mr. James Finster of the Management Studies Office proposed two basic modifications for the 1975-76 season:

1. Reducing the number of performances from 42 to 25;
2. Increasing the average regular (reserved) ticket prices by $.75 for all seats in Memorial Hall, and by $1.00 for all seats in Lafitte Auditorium. (See Appendix 1 for full report.)

NEXT YEAR

Mr. Williams had to submit a plan for 1975-76 by the end of March. By then he had to decide how many performances the University Arts Program would have next year in order to finalize contractual arrangements with the artists. To make that decision, he would have to evaluate both Mr. Finster's report and one prepared by Mr. Seth Granger, an MBA student from the Tulane Graduate School of Business, who had been working as an intern in the Public Events Office (Appendix 2). In conversations with Mr. Granger, Mr. Williams had heard repeated arguments showing a need for an aggressive policy of audience expansion. On the other hand, the low attendance for the current year, less than 50 percent of capacity, was a major problem. Any audience expansion plan must first be able to explain these low attendance levels.

Mr. Williams turned his attention to the following questions:

1. Why was attendance averaging less than 50 percent of capacity? What could be done to increase audience size?
2. What would be the advantages and disadvantages of having 25 performances as Mr. Finster suggested? Of raising prices?
3. What plan should he develop? Why?

APPENDIX 1
MANAGEMENT STUDIES OFFICE REPORT

Date: March 14, 1975

To: Andre Williams
From: James Finster
Subject: Public Events Pricing & Promotion Program

This memo summarizes and expands some of our earlier discussions.

Let me begin by suggesting an operating guideline. As we discussed, Special Events is a deficit operation during the academic year. For example, the total cost of the performances in Lafitte during 73-74 exceeded what the total revenues would have been if every performance had sold out. If the maximum ticket price for Laffite were substantially higher, say $5.50, it would still be necessary to sell in excess of 80 percent of the seating capacity to break even, assuming that the average cost of a performance in Lafitte is about $2,600. *Therefore, as a guideline you should assume that a good promotion program and an optimal pricing policy will continue to result in a net deficit.*

You can think of this overall deficit as an average deficit per performance. In 1973-74 there were 26 performances and a total deficit of about $27,000, or an average deficit of about $1,000 per performance. With 28 performances in 75-76 and assuming a deficit goal of no more than $11,000, *your financial objective would be to reduce the average deficit to about $400 per performance. This objective, I believe, will be difficult to achieve, and the only assistance I can offer comes in the form of suggestions to try out rather than sure-fire remedies.*

PRICING

The previous summary demonstrates in part the value of breakeven analysis. A breakeven analysis determines the point at which costs equal revenues when any of three factors are varied:

1. ticket prices
2. number of tickets sold
3. cost of the performance

The three are interrelated on the basis of what is called "contribution margin," and this relationship is described in detail in the appendix to this memo.

The average contribution margin (average CM) in 1974-75 for ticket sales in Memorial Hall ranges from $3.00 to $3.25 per ticket. For Lafitte the average CM is about $3.50 per ticket sold. Using the formula given in the appendix, you can check the average contribution margin for each performance from the Ticketron printout. The average CM varies as the distribution of sales varies by the price category. If the performance has a low turn out, the proportion of regular ticket sales will probably be significantly lower than average and the average CM will correspondingly be low. For planning purposes, however, I would use the average CM listed previously.

In 1973-74 the average cost of a performance was about $2,700 in Lafitte and $4,000 in Memorial Hall. For breakeven at the present price structure, about 770 tickets or 94 percent of capacity, would have to be sold for each performance in Lafitte; and about 1,230 tickets, or 73 percent of capacity, for each performance in Memorial Hall. A 10 percent reduction in performance cost for Lafitte would reduce the breakeven point also by 10 percent to 694 tickets sold, whereas a 10 percent increase in the average CM would reduce the breakeven point to 701 tickets sold, not a significant difference.

I suggest that the average regular ticket prices be increased by $.75 for all seats in Memorial Hall and by $1.00 for seats in Lafitte for 1975-76. If the distribution of ticket sales by price category remains constant, the average CM will increase by approximately 95 percent of the price increase. The net effect of a price increase depends upon how elastic the demand is for tickets. As a hedge against adverse decreases in demand, I suggest that the price increases be varied in proportion to the popularity of the performance. *The most popular attractions and performance nights should absorb the highest increases in ticket price.* I suggest the following price ranges:

High price and Lafitte:	$4.95-5.95
Medium price:	3.95-4.95
Low price:	2.95-3.95

Series and season ticket specials should all have discounts in the range of 30 percent to encourage commitment to greater numbers of performances.

In 1973-74 the average cost of talent was about 50 percent of the total performance cost for the dance attractions (because of the reimbursement of talent cost) and about 65 percent for all other attractions. You can determine percentages for particular attractions or types of attractions, and then use these percentages to project total performance costs from the contract price of the talent. The total performance cost projection and your estimation of popularity can be used as the basis for determining ticket prices for the performance.

Performance cost can be significantly decreased by having more consecutive performances by an attraction. You mentioned the constraints of this approach, but it does offer the best potential for cost reduction. For popular attractions demand should be sufficient to support multiple performances.

PROMOTION

I can only offer personal suggestions here. You will have to continue to experiment with various promotion strategies on the basis of subjective evaluation. I would advise that you seek to establish an information system to obtain a more objective means of evaluating promotional expenditures. For example:

1. Questionnaire surveys can be conducted through the Mardi Gras Daily or distributed in the lobby during a performance.
2. A short questionnaire can be given to persons who buy tickets at the box office, to be completed on the spot and returned to a box at the box office.
3. A survey can be sent to the names on the mailing lists, either in the University Arts brochure or separately.

Other suggestions:

1. Devise a system to record the names and addresses from checks and the particular performance for which purchased when tickets are purchased from the box office.
2. The "Choose Your Own" season tickets can be promoted as long as there are sufficient remaining performances. Maybe a choose your own half-season ticket can be offered after fall quarter for the remaining performances.
3. The University Arts could be done in a less expensive format and the savings could be used for additional mailings during the year.

CONCLUSION

I believe that the greatest potential for reducing the deficit depends upon reducing the number of performances (for example, about 25 per year), increasing the ratio of number of performances to number of popular attractions, and pricing each performance on the basis of projected demand and breakeven analysis. Improvement of promotional strategy will remain subjective and will occur only gradually as you develop more selective information on who your customer is, why he attends Public Events' performances, and how he can be reached.

Contribution Margin

Definition — Contribution Margin (CM) is the dollar contribution made by a ticket sale to the total cost (talent, allocated promotion, technical, house, and hospitality costs) of a performance. The CM is the sale price of a ticket less any direct ticket sale costs, such as commissions to the Jackson box office (5 percent of the ticket price) and Ticketron charges (10 cents per ticket issued at box office, 25 cents per ticket issued at remote location). For a performance the CM for each price category of tickets must be averaged to produce the average contribution margin per ticket sold (average CM). The average CM will vary as the distribution of ticket sales varies by price category.

Calculation of Average CM

$$\text{Avg. CM} = \frac{\text{Total Ticket Receipts} - \text{Direct Tickets Sales Costs}}{\text{Total Tickets Sold} - \text{Complimentary Tickets}}$$

Direct Ticket Sales Costs:
  .05 (Ticket receipts)   [Jackson]
  .25 (Number remote tickets)   [Ticketron]
  .10 (Number box office tickets) [Ticketron]

Example	Issued	Sold	Receipts
Total sales, box office	532	522	$1,839.85
Total sales, remote	44	44	198.00
Grand Total	576	566	$2,037.85

$$\text{Average CM} = \frac{\$1,839.85 + \$198.00 - .05(\$1,839.85) - .25(44) - .10(532)}{576 - 10^*}$$

$$= \$3.32$$

*Assuming number of complimentary tickets is 10.

Relationship of CM to Breakeven Sales or Costs

CM × Estimated Ticket Sales = Projected Breakeven Performance Costs

Example
$$\text{CM} = \$3.50$$
$$\text{Estimated ticket sales} = 600$$

Therefore, the cost of the performance cannot exceed $3.50 × 600, or $2,100, if a profit or breakeven is desired.

Example

$$CM = \$3.50$$
Projected performance cost = $2500

Therefore, to meet breakeven ticket sales would have to be no less than $2,500 divided by $3.50, or 714.

APPENDIX 2
EXCERPTS FROM REPORT BY MR. SETH GRANGER
Audience Analysis and Recommendations

The goals underlying the initiation of the University Arts Program were presumably two-fold: (1) to service the expressed need for classical entertainment on campus and in the surrounding community (i.e., to satisfy the existing demand), and (2) to foster the development of an appreciation for classical entertainment among those whose prior exposure has been inadequate or nonexistent. This second function in particular serves to differentiate the Mardi Gras Program from other commercial concert series. Missionary work in any field involves a long-term investment in hopes of future returns; to attract new audiences for the performing arts requires a process of exposure and education of indefinite length. . . .

Audience segmentation has been defined as the "process by which a firm partitions its prospective customers (the market) into subgroups or submarkets (segments). The objective of segmentation is to group individual prospects so that their responses to marketing inputs will be similar." I would like to suggest a division of the New Orleans population into groups determined by interest level (current patrons, likely prospects, and unlikely prospects) and by professional status (student and nonstudent). While this initial segmentation is necessarily general, it provides us with a means of selecting promotional messages and media to appeal more directly and effectively to groups whose information channels and promotional needs are quite different. Interest level in the performing arts largely predetermines the promotional needs of the various subgroups. Promotional needs of current patrons are primarily informational; i.e., details regarding time, place and content of scheduled performances, delivered in time to permit a decision and close enough

EXHIBIT 5
Audience Questionnaire

THE ARTS AT MARDI GRAS UNIVERSITY 1972–1973

This survey is being administered for planning purposes by the Mardi Gras Office of Public Events in hopes of better serving you, those who are interested in the performing arts. We would greatly appreciate your assistance by completing the following questionnarie.

Upon completion of the questionnaire, simply place it on the floor under your chair.

1. Age _____ 2. Sex _____ 3. Marital status: single ____ married ____ other _____
4. Profession: _____
5. Are you currently a Mardi Gras . . .(check appropriate) student_____ staff_____
   faculty member _____ alumni _____ no association _____ other _____
6. Is a member of your immediate family currently a Mardi Gras . . . . (check appropriate) student _____ faculty member _____ staff _____ alumni _____
   no association _____ other _____
7. If a member of your immediate family is associated with Mardi Gras, what is their relationship to you? _____
8. Place of residency: Mardi Gras campus _____ other _____
9. How many other arts programs have you attended at Mardi Gras within the past year? 0 _____ 1-3 _____ 4-10 _____ over 10 _____
10. In the space provided, please indicate the number of times you have attended any of the programs by the following groups or at the following locations within the past three months:
    _____ Flint Center   _____ Dollar Opera
    _____ Circle Star Theater   _____ Zellerbach Hall
    _____ Spring Opera   _____ Mardi Gras Music Department
    _____ Tulane Symphony   _____ Mardi Gras Drama Department
    _____ New Orleans Symphony _____ City Opera
11. Did you receive the Arts at Mardi Gras brochure for the 1974-75 season?
    Yes _____ No _____
12. Through which of the following sources did you purchase your ticket for this performance? mail _____ Sears _____ at the door _____ Jackson Ticket Office _____ Maison Blanche _____ Ticketron Box Office _____ Other _____
13. If you did not purchase your ticket on a discount plan, what was the price of your ticket for this performance? _____
14. Did you purchase any of the following ticket plans for the 1974-75 season? (check as many as apply)
    _____ The Theater Series   _____ Early Music Series
    _____ Keyboard Series   _____ Celebrity Series
    _____ Connoisseur Series   _____ Choose Your Own Season Ticket
    _____ Dance Series
15. If you purchased tickets using any of the ticket plans, please estimate the savings per ticket plan that you received over purchasing the tickets separately.

_____

16. Does current advertising provide sufficient information as to the following:
    location   Yes _____   No _____
    time   Yes _____   No _____
    program content   Yes _____   No _____
17. How long ago did you make your decision to attend this performance?
    0-1 week _____ 1-4 weeks _____ 1-3 months _____ over 3 months _____
18. Through which of the following sources did you first become aware of this performance?
    friends _____
    "Arts at Mardi Gras" brochure _____
    news stories (paper?) _____
    radio (station?) _____
    advertising (what paper?) _____
    posters and flyers (where did you see them?) _____
    other (specify) _____
19. Which one of the following sources was most influential in your decision to attend this performance?
    friends _____
    "Arts at Mardi Gras" brochure _____
    news stories (paper?) _____
    radio (station?) _____
    advertising (what paper?) _____
    posters and flyers (where did you see them?) _____
    other (please specify) _____
20. From which of the following sources do you usually seek information about performances of the arts? (check as many as apply)
    newspapers (which ones?) _____
    radio (what stations?) _____
    posters (where?) _____
    friends _____
    other (specify) _____
21. Please indicate your preference as to the days on which performances are given by ranking the following: (1 meaning most preferred, 7 least preferred)
    Sunday _____ Monday _____ Tuesday _____ Wednesday _____ Thursday _____
    Friday _____ Saturday _____
22. Please indicate the time at which you prefer the performances to begin. _____
23. Please give an indication of how you feel about the following statement: "I would enjoy attending an arts performance at each of the following locations:" (please check only those with which you are familiar)

	strongly agree	agree	uncertain	disagree	strongly disagree
Amy Auditorium	_____	_____	_____	_____	_____
Arena Stage	_____	_____	_____	_____	_____
Lafitte Auditorium	_____	_____	_____	_____	_____
Amphitheater	_____	_____	_____	_____	_____
Rittle Theater	_____	_____	_____	_____	_____
Memorial Hall	_____	_____	_____	_____	_____
University Church	_____	_____	_____	_____	_____

to the performance date to inspire action. Likely, though uncommitted, prospects, require somewhat more, in addition to informational details, they also need some exhortation, some indication of the pleasure and excitement which can be derived from an evening of classical entertainment. Unlikely prospects, as might be expected, may not be susceptible to any sort of promotional activity without a prohibitively intense program of education and development; for this reason, this segment, in both its student and nonstudent forms, will not be considered a primary target for the initial program of audience expansion proposed here. . . .

Having established these four segments—current student patrons, likely student prospects, current nonstudent patrons, and likely nonstudent prospects—as primary targets for our audience expansion efforts, I would recommend that efforts be made to acquire information regarding the behavior of each of these groups as regards their responses to various advertising channels, their decision patterns, their alternative entertainment preferences, and their reactions to the Program's content and promotion. A preliminary attempt in this direction was made during this past year, when an audience questionnaire [see Exhibit 5] was designed and distributed to a near-capacity audience at a performance given by the New York Pro Musica in the University Church. Approximately 400 completed questionnaires were returned; from this number a random sample of 50 questionnaires was selected and subjected to examination via the SPSS program at the Mardi Gras University computer facility.

The questionnaire sought to provide information concerning personal

EXHIBIT 6
Occupation of Survey Respondents

Occupation	Number of Respondents
Student	9
Educator	8
Professional	8
Business	14
Housewife	2
Artistic	2
Other	4
No Response	3
Total	50

Source: Audience Survey

characteristics (income, place of residence, profession, etc.), programming and scheduling preferences, and information channels utilized by current patrons. Although time constraints precluded adequate pretesting, resulting in ambiguity in certain questions, and although the small sample size reduced the pure statistical validity of the findings, the survey results proved interesting on a number of points.

The bulk of the respondents (64 percent) were in an age range between 23 and 45 years, 12 percent were below age 23. At least 68 percent of the respondents lived within a three-mile radius, while only 8 percent came from residential areas on the far side of New Orleans. One third of the respondents listed their occupation as student or educator and 28 percent described theirs as business (Exhibit 6). Seventy-six percent of the respondents indicated that they had attended at least one prior performance offered by the Program during the past year, demonstrating the preponderance of what I have termed current patrons, as opposed to likely prospects, in the Program's audiences. No such high prior attendance level was found for any of the other New Orleans cultural events or organizations listed. The effectiveness of promotional material in providing adequate information regarding location, time and content of performances was generally given a high rating, although satisfaction with content information was noticeably lower (58 percent) than with time (72 percent) or location (72 percent). Thirty percent of the respondents decided to attend the performance during the week preceding the performance; another 30 percent made its decision one to four weeks before the performance. Thirty-four percent acted on a decision which they had made over three months before the performance date, while only 6 percent decided to attend during the period from one to three months in advance. In cross-tabulating decision time by brochure receipt, it was found that over 47 percent of those who made a decision to attend more than three months in advance had been recipients of the brochure.

Perhaps most interesting were the ways in which respondents found out about the New York Pro Musica performance in particular, and about cultural events in New Orleans in general. Three sets of questions were posed, dealing with general sources of cultural information, information which made them aware of the Pro Musica concert, and information which was most important to their attending the performance. General information sources most frequently cited by respondents were newspaper advertising (78%) and friends—i.e., word-of-mouth advertising (32%). Information leading to awareness of the performance was derived predominantly from the brochure (34%), newspaper advertising (24%)

and friends (24%). The most important factor leading to the actual decision to attend the performance, according to questionnaire respondents, was the reputation of the New York Pro Musica itself. This factor was cited by roughly 40 percent of the respondents, while the next most important factor—friends—accounted for only 20 percent. Aside from the obvious implication that, in classical as in popular entertainment, the best-known performers and groups are the easiest to sell, these findings suggest an interesting hypothesis. Carrying the preceding truism one step further, it might well be worthwhile to consider varying the intensity of the advertising campaign depending on the relative fame or obscurity of the performer involved. Certain of the performances offered this past year—notably, PDQ Bach, the Harkness Ballet, and the New York Pro Musica—are self-selling to a considerable extent although other individual performers and groups, though possibly possessed of a comparable level of talent or skill, attract smaller audiences. This argument for promotional activity of variable intensity is also supported by an examination of the relative success, measured by attendance levels of the four basic elements of the Program's offerings (see Exhibit 7). While dramatic offerings generally played to average attendance levels of 63 percent of capacity, and vocal and instrumental music both averaged 53 percent capacity, the nine performances of dance offered during the first six months of the 1974-75 season drew only 31 percent of capacity. Excluding the single performance of the Harkness Ballet, this figure drops to 22 percent for the remaining eight performances. Although one could suggest that the dance portion of the Program's "product line" be dropped, classical and modern dance deserve an important place in the Program's efforts to augment academic offerings and to contribute positively to the extracurricular educational experience of students.

EXHIBIT 7
Attendance by Performance Category, First Six Months 1974-75

	Number of Performances	Capacity	Attendance	% of Capacity
Instrumental Music	13	13,437	7,211	53%
Harkness Ballet	1	1,694	1,635	97%
Other Dance	8	13,552	3,092	22%
Drama	3	2,460	1,565	63%
Vocal Music	2	1,640	880	53%

The Second Street Gallery[*]

At the first regular meeting which Lindsay Nolting, newly elected president, chaired and which coincided with the Second Street Gallery's first anniversary, the directors reviewed the gallery's progress to date from its founding on February 11, 1973.

THE ART GALLERY IN SOCIETY:
A SYNOPSIS

The art museums and galleries were caught in the 1960s in the problems of contemporary society. Having slumbered in historical contexts for decades, the museums were now seen as irrelevant and obsolete. Financial sources dried up, costs outstripped income, the possibility of collapse became immediate rather than remote. In the panic, many museums and galleries reassessed their roles in society. New galleries

*This case was prepared by Robert D. Hamilton, III, and John V. O. Kennard under the supervision of Professor Leslie E. Grayson of the University of Virginia. Copyright ©1974, by the Sponsor's of the Colgate Darden Graduate School of Business Administration, University of Virginia.

were founded on principles far different from those of their more famous, now expiring ancestors.

Dr. Eric Larrabee, Provost of Arts and Humanities at New York State University at Buffalo, identified five stages in the history of art galleries:

16th Century	Stage 1:	The Wunderkammer—a cabinet of curiosities for private enjoyment.
17th Century	Stage 2:	Expanded versions of private collections for the public.
18th-19th Century	Stage 3:	The great museum, e.g., Metropolitan, "temples" devoted to the worship of the fine arts.
1940	Stage 4:	The Universities of the common man—state universities in the United States in the 1940s.
1965	Stage 5:	The new, relevant, community-oriented, "with it" art gallery—in tune with an egalitarian society.

There are many, including the directors of the Second Street Gallery, who saw the problems of the contemporary gallery as incentives to a healthy change. They held that "art should be kicking and screaming in the middle of contemporary society, rather than literally and figuratively transferred out of reach and out of touch." A prospective gallery had to know with great precision what kind of gallery it wanted to be, what constituents it needed to attract and whom it hoped to benefit. Marketing was a critical factor to its success.

ESTABLISHMENT OF THE SECOND STREET GALLERY

Eleven resident artists, brought together by the vision and energy of Eugene Markowski, 41, associate professor of art at the University, opened the Second Street Gallery in February 1973. Markowski had been thinking about such a gallery since 1971. The arrival of several newcomers from art circles in other cities was the catalyst for the gallery's foundation. Five months of cooperative planning preceded the opening; the gallery was to function both as an outlet for the exhibition of the artists' works and an opportunity for the area residents to view and buy quality works of modern art.

Discussions of basic organizational questions were necessarily addressed by the original group: How does one form an organization? What types of organizations are possible? Which are better for the founders' purposes? What are realistic revenue expectations? The original members, whose backgrounds were nonorganizational, had some difficulty focusing on these questions.

They looked at the population size, per capita income, education, occupational stratification, the results of earlier area galleries, and intangibles such as the community's cultural environment. A recognized risk was the fact that the Charlottesville-Albemarle, Virginia, area was a traditional, conservative, and slow-paced environment of 80,000 people. The region was a proven market place for antique dealers, purveyors of horse prints, and family portrait artists, but little attempts had been made to sell or show modern art prior to 1973. But, Charlottesville was a growing community. The University of Virginia was located there, as well as a new community college. The trend seemed to be away from a small-town conservative mold into a more exciting University-town community.

As a result of their deliberations, the Second Street Gallery founders concluded that projected sales of art alone would never cover expenses. It was also decided that not all work exhibited would be for sale. Consequently, the decision was made that the gallery would have to "go out" to the community with innovative programs, lectures, and experiments. Their first year's exhibition and lecture schedule is given in Exhibit 1. Establishing the gallery as a nonprofit organization would make contributions tax deductible, usually a good selling point. The founders hoped that the community efforts would attract gifts and donations of both cash and services to help offset the estimated $9,000 annual operating costs.

A location was found in downtown Charlottesville with convenient parking nearby. The exhibition rooms were on the second floor of a local stockbroker's building. Five spacious rooms displayed a variety of contemporary works, well exhibited with natural and spot lighting. A sixth room, used as an office, also displayed art books sold at a discount and small artifacts.

Early in the development of the gallery, managerial assistance came from several sources. John V.O. Kennard, a student in the Graduate School of Business Administration (GSBA) at the University of Virginia and husband of one of the founders, was the business manager for the

EXHIBIT 1

Exhibition and Lecture Schedules for the 1973-74 Season

Exhibitions:
Sunday, Sept. 30–Thursday, Oct. 25
  Peter Fink Photographs
Sunday, Oct. 28–Thursday, Nov. 22
  Henry Stindt One-man Show
  also Prisoner Art Exhibition
Sunday, Nov. 25–Thursday, Dec. 20
  Lindsay Nolting One-woman Show
Sunday, Jan. 6–Thursday, Jan. 31
  Priscilla Rappolt One-woman Show
Sunday, Feb. 3–Thursday, Feb. 28
  George Roland One-man Show
Sunday, Mar. 3–Thursday, Mar. 28
  Paul Martick One-man Show
Sunday, Mar. 31–Thursday, Apr. 25
  Annual Artists Juried Show
Sunday, Apr. 28–Thursday, May 16
  Collectors Show

Lectures:
Sunday, Oct. 14
  "Leonardo da Vinci" by Frederick Hartt
Sunday, Oct. 21
  "Photojournalism" with Murray Weiss and Jim Carpenter
Sunday, Nov. 4
  "Erotic Art Panel Discussion" with Eugene Markowski and
    others
Sunday, Dec. 9
  "Chinese Glass" by Zachary Taylor
Sunday, Jan. 20
  "Electronic Music" by Donald MacInnis
Sunday, Feb. 10
  "Printmaking" by George Roland
Sunday, Mar. 10
  "Stained Glass" by Paul Martick
Sunday, May 12
  "Georgian Architecture" by Pauline King

All lectures are planned for 3:00 p.m.

first six months of the gallery's existence. Opportunity Consultants, Inc. (OCI), a nonprofit service organization of the GSBA, kept the financial records so that donors were assured the books were professionally kept. Another GSBA student, Robert D. Hamilton, decided to write his term paper for the Management of Nonprofit Organizations seminar on the gallery.

ATTRACTING FINANCIAL SUPPORT

Since it was obvious that the member artists could not finance the gallery themselves, community support had to be attracted. Museums and galleries in large cities were having their difficulties in raising funds, and obviously the problems would be compounded in a small community. In its appeal to the 500 potential donors for funding, the Second Street Gallery sent a flyer (Exhibit 2) which stressed participating in a community venture as the motivation for giving. These names were culled from members of a country club, concert and theatre lists, and "outstanding" members of the community, selected for their interest in previous civic enterprises.

The Second Street Gallery members set about attainment of financial backing through the following do's and don'ts:

1. Select the most skillful salesman (or the least unskillful) and send him or her out to canvas prospective donors. Leave the less "outgoing" behind to do the construction and redecorating work. This was a natural, self-selection process.
2. Maximize "in-kind" contributions from businessmen. While many businessmen balk at cash gifts, they somewhat more readily part with their inventories especially since they can count their contributions at retail instead of at cost.
3. Gather a few "outsiders" to lend professional support to the cause by word-of-mouth. A reassuring word from a prominent community member to a prospective donor will ease the donor's anxiety about giving.
4. Never be bashful about explaining the direct benefits to a donor—i.e., public display of name in gallery. Five classifications of potential contributors were identified (see section on Marketing).

The Second Street Gallery was particularly successful in raising "in-kind" contributions. Over $5,000 in carpeting was installed by Charlottesville's two leading rug firms. The same quality was also evident in most other examples, which included lighting, wiring, glass, air condi-

EXHIBIT 2

The Second Street Gallery

The Second Street Gallery, a regional artists cooperative, is a nonprofit association of the area's leading painters, sculptors, print-makers, and photographers. The cooperative has been formed to acquaint people in Central Virginia with emerging expressions of contemporary art and culture. The artists will present their works regularly to the public in a permanent gallery supported by those who wish to foster excellence in and understanding of contemporary art. While all works of art are for sale, it is the educational and innovative aspects of the cooperative and the artists' commitment to enriching their community that make the Second Street Gallery unique in Central Virginia.

Knowing of your interest in art, we ask your assistance. We are eager to open the Second Street Gallery as soon as operating expenses can be met. The members of the cooperative have already made financial commitments to secure a permanent exhibition space. Now contributions are needed to begin operations and to assure the cooperative's success. If you wish to contribute to the Second Street Gallery for the encouragement of excellence in contemporary art, please send your gift to:

The Second Street Gallery
P. O. Box 1095
Charlottesville, Va. 22902

George Roland
President

The Second Street Gallery is located in Charlottesville at
116 2nd Street, N.E.

---

tioners, furniture, plants and refreshments, which were served at the monthly openings of exhibitions. The impact of these "in-kind" contributions in raising both the quality and size of the original investment was significant, as can be seen through the first quarterly receipts and disbursement schedule (Exhibit 3). It was estimated that original investment came to $10,000; $6,213 was "in-kind" and the remainder from artists and contributors.

SECURING COMMITTED ARTIST MEMBERS

Idealistically, a cooperative gallery sounded wonderful. Reality, however, raised its usual problems shortly after conception of the project.

EXHIBIT 3
1st Quarterly Statement of Cash Receipts and Disbursements
January 15 to April 15, 1973

Value of contributions "in-kind"		$6,213.00
Cash receipts:		
Patrons, contributors, and members		$2,090.00
Artists' dues		1,550.00
Sale of art[1]		109.52
Sale of art books		37.85
Total		$3,787.37
Cash Disbursements for Expenses:		
Printing	$172.50	
Advertising	11.70	
Office supplies	125.86	
Insurance	257.00	
License fees	30.50	
Rent	505.40	
Renovation and remodeling	905.00	
Salaries and wages	266.00	
Sales taxes	8.13	
Telephone	82.94	
Postage	234.97	
Total		$2,600.02
Purchase of equipment (assets)		340.58
Cash in bank, April 15, 1973		$ 846.77

[1] Not including sale of 13 works from Printmaker's show.

Minimal standards of participation and commitment evolved, and the work load was spread out as evenly as possible. Since the directors all had full-time jobs elsewhere, evidence of commitment to the gallery was not always obvious. Putting together a show once a month, roughly, was tedious and time consuming. An informal and somewhat amorphous nucleus centered around Messrs. Markowski, Martick, Roland, and Mrs. Kennard, and it provided a locus for decision-making in which new directors became involved as they joined. The original group of artist members came from different geographical areas, generally had a high level of formal art education and training, and as a group provided the public with a variety of art forms. Exhibit 4 is a synopsis of an article describing the artists' styles and interests. A summary of their education is included in Exhibit 5.

From the time the gallery opened until the middle of May, four members, all students at the University, left. Two found the professional expectations and the general quality and quantity of work too demanding. Two others withdrew after a relatively acrimonious discussion. It was their contention that they were getting neither attention nor exhibition space commensurate with their talents. From this low point of only seven member artists remaining, new talent gradually brought membership up to nine. Five of these were affiliated with the University.

During the first Annual Area Artist Juried Show, the work of an artist from nearby Lynchburg was reviewed and accepted by a majority of the members. Shortly after that Linda Kennard resigned from the gallery when her husband accepted a job in New York after his graduation. Two faculty members who had recently joined the Art Department at the University of Virginia (one from Philadelphia and the other from Wisconsin) were asked to join as artist members.

On the average, two applications per month were received by the gallery from those seeking admittance as a full member and/or seeking to show work on consignment. Samples of the artist's work were evaluated and voted upon by all members. While a unanimous vote was not a prerequisite, a large majority was required.

Overall, the centrifugal force of the individualism of the nine artists resulted in varying degrees of seriousness and cooperation from one meeting to the next. The guarantees of tenacity of purpose and good faith were, as could be expected, frail and delicate. Other forces, however, were successful in keeping the organization coherent. Early favorable publicity was found to bring the group together and stir enthusiasm; complimentary local pre-opening press could be an exciting reward for the work hours put in. The artists participated in two radio and one local television program. These media encounters helped produce feelings of group solidarity and, by focusing the attention of the town on their efforts, made failure something that was to be avoided at all costs.

Artist members expressed numerous group and personal objectives for the gallery. It was viewed as a "Service to the community;" "An opportunity to show—to see what the reaction of the public is;" "A chance to get some kind of an art sector going in Charlottesville." From the artists' point of view, during the last decade a three-tier market in modern American art has developed. For collectors of "prestigious" modern American art, "life these days seems to be one profit-making thrill after another," as prices skyrocket. "Prestigious" artists are now pressing to obtain royalties on the resale profits on their work. Some artists are already under contracts which entitle them to about 15 percent of the profit on any resale. Of course, the vast majority of artists are still poor; they are the lower part of the three-tier market. The poor artists are satisfied if they have enough money to pay for their studio, canvas, and paint.

EXHIBIT 4

"Artists' Cooperative Offers Variety"
by Ruth Latter
The Daily Progress

Gene Markowski, an associate professor of art at [sic] who is the catalyst responsible for founding the gallery, has on view a series of his highly distinctive, geometrized and perforated paintings and prints. Markowski has been carefully developing his unique style over a period of several years.

In all of his decoratively structured compositions, delicately shaded or superimposed color areas are balanced with endless rows of tiny punctures. He is certainly one of the most innovative artists in the area.

No less intriguing are the splendidly vibrating color harmonies of George Roland, a new art instructor at UVa. A single redundant biomorphic design weaves in and out of a rainbow of sensous colors in Roland's acrylic paintings and silk screen prints. His brilliantly decorative works are the most eye-catching in the exhibit.

Perhaps, the most original artist in the group is Henry Stindt, an instructor at both the Virginia Art Institute and the UVa. School of Continuing Education. A versatile artist, at home in many media, Stindt has on view a meandering assemblage of hinged two-by-fours and a nautical sculpture of wood and grid-patterned rope.

A more than competent weaver and sculptor, Linda Kinnard [sic] has a heavily looped and colorful woven hanging on view, as well as a rigid assemblage of metal drainpipes of varying lengths.

Unfortunately, once you have seen the works of these four artists, you have seen it all.

Paul Martick, a new art instructor at UVa is an eclectic who combines haphazard brushwork with leaping black lines and arrow. One unusual painting on view resembles fireworks exploding in a flower garden.

*   *   *

One hopes that future exhibitions at the Second Street Gallery will live up to the promises of its founding members. These include offering the community "the best art produced in the Charlottesville area" and "the most experimental art ever seen in the Charlottesville area." Whether these experimental efforts will include such innovations of the last few years as Body Art, Multi Media Environments, Photo Realism and Verist Sculpture remains to be seen.

Nevertheless, we in the community wish them well. A gallery such as this was long overdue.

EXHIBIT 5

The 2nd Street Gallery Directors

Moe Brooker, painter
B.F.A., Pennsylvania Academy of Fine Arts; M.F.A., Temple University. Assistant Professor of Art at the University of Virginia since 1973.

Michael Christopherson, sculptor
B.F.A., University of Wisconsin; M.F.A., Washington University. Assistant Professor of Art at the University of Virginia since 1973.

Letty Roegge Frazier, painter
Studied with Hal McIntosh, Bob Harmon, Ellett Twery. Has won awards in regional shows since 1964. Affiliated with galleries in Lynchburg and Roanoke, Virginia.

Eugene Markowski, painter
B.F.A., Washington University School of Fine Art; M.F.A., University of Pennsylvania School of Fine Art. Assistant Professor of Art at the University of Pennsylvania, Associate Professor of Art at the University of Virginia since 1970.

Paul Martick, painter
Educated at Tufts University and Boston Museum School. Associate Professor of Art at the University of Virginia since 1971.

Lindsay Nolting, painter
Atelier de la rue du Dome, Academie Julian, Paris, France; Art Students' League, New York City, studied with Stamos and Glasier. Affiliated with two artists' cooperatives before the 2nd Street Gallery; Marche d'Art Contemporain, Paris, and the Abingdon Square Painters, New York City.

Priscilla Rappolt, painter
B.F.A., Art Education, Richmond Polytechnic Institute; M.F.A., Painting, Virginia Commonwealth University. Also studied at the Boston Museum School and at the Art Students' League, New York City.

George Roland, painter, printmaker
B.F.A., with honors, Virginia Commonwealth University; M.F.A., painting and printmaking, University of Wisconsin. Associate Professor of Art at the University of Virginia since 1971.

Henry Stindt, painter and sculptor, conceptualizer
B.A., Pennsylvania State University, M.F.A., Pratt Institute, Brooklyn, New York. Also studied at the Slade School of Art, University of London.

MARKETING (OR RAISING FUNDS)

Five classifications of contributors were identified according to the size of the donation:

Artists Dues ($200)
Patrons ($200)
Contributors ($50)
Regular Members ($15)
Student Members ($5)

The present and projected membership profile along with the estimated operating expenses are shown in Exhibit 6.

Contribution entitled the member to attend the openings of shows of member artists and lectures that were given on an average of twice per month. Attendance varied anywhere from 2 to 20 people per day. Total annual attendance was estimated at 2,500 which included a number of repeaters. For the 11 exhibitions, the average number of visitors was between 200-300. Lectures were generally less well attended.

In an effort to increase the number of contributors, pamphlets describing the gallery and soliciting gifts were placed in the lobbies of movie theaters and motels. In the fall of 1973 a mailing list of approximately 1,400 people was compiled from nine different organizations (Exhibit 7). A prominent local woman added her name as Chairperson of a membership drive. A sample of the request for contributions is shown in Exhibit 8.

The gallery appealed to the City Council for support, even if it meant only a token contribution. In this appeal, as in subsequent appeals, the joint notions of "usefulness" and "stability" had to be gotten across. While the group's organizational, financial, and marketing efforts of the first year had met with some success, the directors wondered what decisions could or should be made about setting future objectives and plans and how these plans might be financed. Once the gallery reached its first anniversary, the members' thoughts turned from survival to establishing a firm base. This required all the working members to get together and develop a budget for the coming year, which was easier said than done. While the members had a much better idea as to what they wanted the gallery to be and do than they had had a year earlier, the setting down of these ideas in budget form still posed a problem.

EXHIBIT 6
Estimated Annual Operating Expenses and Membership Status

Rent	$3,000
Wages (attendant)	3,500
Printing & postage (15 openings @ $60)	900
Advertising	50
Telephone	300
Insurance:	
Annual premium	157
Special Collectors Show	150
Office supplies	200
Costs of exhibitions (15 @ $40)	600
Utilities	120
Maintenance & refurbishing	300
Total	$9,277

Sources of Revenue

	Projected	No.	At Present
Patrons (10 estimated)	$2,000	(4)	$ 800
Contributors (10 estimated)	750	(4)	200
Artist's Dues (8 estimated)	1,600	(8)	1,550
Regular Members (300 @ $15)	4,500	(50)	750
Student Members (100 @ $5)	500	(60)	300
Total	$9,350		$3,600

EXHIBIT 7
Sources of Names for Mailing List

1. Friends of the Library
2. Virginia Center for Creative Arts
3. English Speaking Union
4. Wednesday Music Club
5. Albemarle Art Association
6. Virginia Museum, Local Chapter
7. Orange Garden Club
8. Downtown Charlottesville, Inc.
9. New University of Virginia faculty—September 1973
10. Suggestions from 2nd Street Gallery members
11. People who have expressed an interest.

EXHIBIT 8

The 2nd Street Gallery opened its doors on February 11, 1973. The founders, artists, businessmen, teachers and friends, wished to provide an exhibition space for paintings, sculpture, photography, graphics and a place to hold lectures and programs of interest to all who appreciate and enjoy the arts. The quality of the work and potential interest and value of the exhibition for the community are the central considerations in presenting programs. In order to be free to offer variety and flexibility in the kinds of exhibitions presented, the Gallery must free itself of the necessity of selling works of art to survive. While many works are for sale, and the Gallery is glad to sell what it can, it is central to our philosophy that saleability not determine whether something is shown.

Funds for operating the Gallery come from gifts, annual memberships, and sales of art work and books. The Gallery is not a part of, or supported by, any institution or organization. Its sole support and continuance depend on the citizens of the Charlottesville-Albemarle area. The Gallery has received tremendous support from merchants, who have contributed both materials and money to its establishment. The Gallery's artists each contribute $200.00 annually to its support; they hang all the shows, arrange for lectures, provide refreshments at openings and do all cleaning, mailing, etc., without salary. Our lecturers, many of whom are noted scholars in their fields, have freely donated their time to the Gallery and the community, for which we are very grateful.

The family memberships are the financial backbone of the Gallery. Memberships are $15.00 per year for families and $5.00 per year for students. In addition to the satisfaction of supporting this worthwhile effort, members receive the following benefits: free admission to all lectures, invitations to the Sunday afternoon previews of exhibitions, where refreshments will be served, and the artist will be on hand to talk with guests, discounts on Abrams art books and discounts on classes at the Gallery.

The 2nd Street Gallery, in addition to showing the work of individuals has already provided a number of other shows of interest to the community. The Collector's Show, for example, consisted of works of art from local collections. It contained works never before shown in the area, from the Orient and the West, from the third to the twentieth centuries. We hope to repeat this popular show next year with a new group of works.

Our opening show this year will be an exhibition of the work of Peter Fink, an internationally known photographer, represented in the permanent collections of the Bibliotheque Nationale in Paris, the Metropolitan Museum of Art, the Museum of Modern Art and the Chicago Art Institute among others.

While the Gallery is open to everyone, it is our hope that more and more of our neighbors will join us by becoming members, which will help ease the financial burdens, and allow us to expand our offerings. The Gallery has applied to the Federal Govenment for tax-exempt status as a nonprofit educational organization. We wish to thank all who have supported us before this status has been obtained.

A list of our exhibitions and lectures for this season appear on the reverse side.

To become a member, just fill out the form and mail it to the Gallery.

Mrs. William E. Craddock, Membership Chairman

George Roland, President

Eugene Markowski, Vice President

Paul Matrick, Treasurer

Lindsay Nolting, Secretary

Gallery phone: 977-7284

Artists who would like to become members in the Gallery are cordially invited to apply by writing or phoning the Gallery. We are always glad to greet new talent, regardless of the artist's style or age.